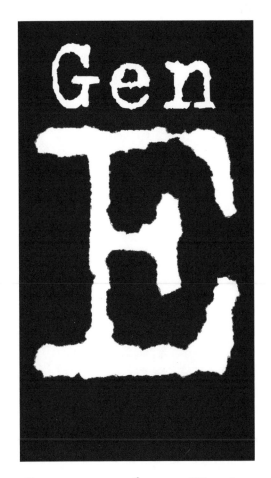

# Gen E

Generation Entrepreneur
Is Rewriting
The Rules Of Busi...
And You Can, To...

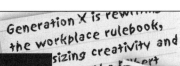

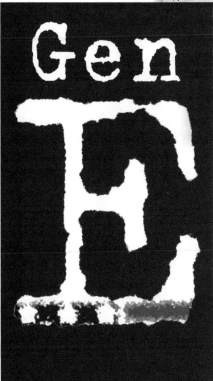

Gen E

Generation X is rewriting the workplace rulebook, ...sizing creativity and ...s over the ...ert ...e's organiz have not only disv...
The young entrep...
...xes and b corporate rigidity,
...-level ma also how they've c...
...rchies + politically and cultu...
...e on w active companies in...
...lun... own image.

Distancing themselv...
...traditional career m...
spiritually failed th...
divorced fathers an...
is at the core of the...
entrepreneur's attit...
about work.

Brian
O'Connell

# Generation Entrepreneur
# Is Rewriting
# The Rules Of Business—
# And You Can, Too!

Entrepreneur
Press

Entrepreneur Press
2392 Morse Ave., Irvine, CA 92614

**Managing Editor:** Marla Markman
**Copy Editor:** Jeff Campbell
**Book Design:** Sylvia H. Lee
**Proofreader:** Marisa Laudadio
**Cover Design:** Mark A. Kozak
**Indexer:** Alta Indexing

BACK COVER PHOTOS
SECTOR 9: PHOTO© AMY CANTRELL
FUBU: PHOTO COURTESY: FUBU THE COLLECTION
BELLY BASICS: PHOTO© JOHN EMERSON

Library of Congress Cataloging-in-Publication Data

O'Connell, Brian, 1959-
    Gen E: Generation Entrepreneur is rewriting the rules of entrepreneurship—and you can, too/by Brian O'Connell.
        p.    cm.
    Includes bibliographical references and index.
    ISBN 1-891984-07-1
    1. New business enterprises. 2. Entrepreneurship. I. Title. II. Title: Generation Entrepreneur is rewriting the rules of entrepreneurship.
HD62.5.028    1999
658.4'21—dc21

                                                          99-33490
                                                          CIP

Printed in Canada

09 08 07 06 05 04 03 02 01 00        10 9 8 7 6 5 4 3 2 1

To my lovely wife, Karen,
who looks after me and still makes me laugh;
to my breathtakingly beautiful children,
Madison, Cooper, and our new baby,
only weeks away, who I can't wait to meet;
and to my father and mother, whose lone demand
for me was to be happy no matter what.
Thanks for tolerating me.
This book is for all of you.

# Acknowledgments

I'm very much in debt to my editor at Entrepreneur Press, Marla Markman. Without Marla's helpful guidance, unlimited patience and genial manner, this book would have been much more difficult to write. Steering stubborn writers to the finish line is a thankless task, but Marla does it better than any editor I've ever blown a deadline for.

# Table Of Contents

# Foreword

I first started working at *Entrepreneur* magazine in 1978—well before most people knew what an entrepreneur was and certainly prior to the time when seemingly everyone harbored entrepreneurial aspirations. The seeds of the entrepreneurial revolution that were sown in the '80s, bloomed in the '90s, thanks in large part to members of my generation, baby boomers who suddenly found themselves thrust out of their comfy corporate niches and into the real world of unemployment. It wasn't so much that the boomers were fueled by entrepreneurial dreams (some were, of course), but rather they were led into business ownership by seeking the answer to the question "What the hell am I going to do now?"

The rest, as they say, is history. Boomer history. So what does that have to do with you? A lot, actually. Sure, the boomers led the way and made the world safe for entrepreneurs, but it is your generation, so-called "Generation X," who embraced the concept. While boomers started out being reluctant, if not accidental entrepreneurs, you are deliberate ones. So consciously have you chosen this workstyle, we at *Entrepreneur* call you Generation Entrepreneur, or Gen E, and we think you have yet to make your full impact on the entrepreneurial world.

Many people of all generations still fear business ownership, erecting a ton of roadblocks in their own paths. But as members of Gen E, you seem to fear less. Maybe it's that "eternal optimism of youth" or maybe it's just that you grew up in the "nothing ventured, nothing gained" 1980s. Certainly you are better prepared to be entrepreneurs, and the world is better prepared for you.

There is no one path to success, no one personality trait or skill set that will take you there. In today's boisterous entrepreneurial environment the old adage "It takes all kinds" has never been more true. It takes all kinds of people and all kinds of ideas. So whether you were born to entrepreneurship or bred for it, there has truly never been a better time to set your entrepreneurial sights. And set them high. If there's one thing we can (and should) leave behind in the 20th century, it's limits. Only you can hold you back. If eBay's Pierre Omidyar can build a multimillion-dollar enterprise around the idea of buying new additions for his wife's Pez collection, then truly, anything is possible.

It is up to you. But you don't have to go it alone. That's what this book is all about. In Gen E, you'll not only find out about how your peers have created thriving businesses, but how to get started building one of your own. But start-up is only the beginning. Many an entrepreneur has crashed attempting the leap from start-up to ongoing enterprise. Don't let this happen to you. Let Gen E tell you how to avoid this fate.

Sure, there are some other similarly targeted books out there. Why do you need this one? Because in addition to being well-written and researched by Brian O'Connell, you hear directly from those Gen E's who've been there and done it. And it is brought to you by the folks at *Entrepreneur*. Remember what I said at the beginning? We've been at this a long time. We know about entrepreneurs. We know what it takes to make it, and we know how to take you there.

So whether the entrepreneurial fire is a raging inferno in your gut or still a small ember in your head, you've come to the right place. Gen E can take you to places you've only dreamed about. Read it and learn. Read it and be inspired. Read it and change your life.

*Rieva Lesonsky*

Rieva Lesonsky
VP/Editorial Director
Entrepreneur Media Inc.

# Introduction

What do you do when you love a job that doesn't love you back? Or worse, what do you do when you hate a job that hates you back? Start your own business, that's what. So say a legion of young revolutionaries who've launched their own wildly successful businesses, shedding the surly bonds of Powersuit Nation to fly free and clear in the rarefied air of entrepreneurial commerce.

In doing so, Generation Entrepreneur is rewriting the workplace rulebook, emphasizing creativity and results over the Dilbert Culture's organizational matrixes and politicized, multilevel management hierarchies, with their meetings about meetings and paperwork dungeons. The baby boomers and their older workplace contemporaries may snicker over the next generation of "slackers," but that generation, which grew up with the computer, is harnessing the power of technology to leave their lower-tech predecessors choking in the dust. In our global economy, Gen E is poised to stake its claim as the workplace voice of the 21st century.

Inside these pages, we'll follow more than 40 up-and-coming and unbelievably successful young entrepreneurs who left behind their overbearing bosses and cynical cubicle-dwelling co-workers to strike out on their own—launching their own businesses on their own terms. We'll take a look at how they formed their ideas, found funding and learned how to market and distribute their products and services in ways that uniquely stamp Gen E as markedly different from their corporate forebears.

This book is a forum for young entrepreneurs to tell their stories and to pass along advice and tips to their generational siblings considering starting their own companies. You'll hear a lot from Gen E business owners who've been there and done that and are more than happy to share their experiences.

In addition, there's quite a bit of how-to information on all aspects of starting a business—like locating money and investors, crafting a marketing plan and hiring employees—as well as plenty of suggestions for where to turn for more information. The book is chock-full of tidbits and resources, and with the names, addresses and Web sites of the organizations and companies that are best suited to getting you and your new business up and running.

But that's not all. What happens when you succeed beyond your wildest dreams? Gen E business owners talk about how they have dealt with their newfound wealth and status. They give you advice on how to grow your business—and when to sell it. I'll also profile 10 hot businesses you might consider starting, and I'll give you the lowdown on 17 cool cities that currently make the best places to stake your tent and set up shop.

While all the advice you'll find here is augmented by commentary from the folks in the trenches, what you won't find are representatives of Generation X. In fact, I don't think Generation X exists, except as a pop-culture stereotype as seen through the refracted prism of the media. Instead, I believe this is a generation of young, independent thinkers who have been scarred by the culture wars of the 1960s, which often left them as latchkey kids in single-parent homes during the 1970s and 1980s. Ironically, left to fend for themselves, with lots of time on their hands and limited parenting, many of the young entrepreneurs I spoke with thrived. They made the most of their situations, developing a sense of self-assurance and honing their computing programming skills on their parents' computers or opening small businesses selling custom-made cosmetics or collectible baseball cards to neighborhood kids. The twentysomething and thirtysomething entrepreneurs you'll meet in these pages scoff at the idea of a Generation X; they dismiss the concept as just another attempt by baby boomers and the media to slap a label on something they don't understand.

So please join me on a tour of the Gen E landscape, which is populated by mature-beyond-their-years young entrepreneurs who have managed to balance their idealism and pragmatism in ways that the corporate culture has yet to give them credit for. With a few notable exceptions, these budding Morgans and Rockefellers may not be on the front pages of the big business magazines or in the lead stories of the network nightly news, but that's perfectly fine with them. Their attitudes, beliefs and ideas are already filtering into the business culture in ways that challenge current corporate tenets.

Make no mistake about it: Gen E is a revolution operating under the radar screen that is already changing the way people run companies. This book is your invitation to join in.

Viva la revolution!

# Chapter

> "All of a sudden we were 'happening.' It takes a lot of hard work and some luck. We had both on our side."

# Hard Work And A Little Luck: Postcards From The Front

# The Birth Of A Company

W ho are the new entrepreneurs who are changing the face of American corporate culture? Here is a look at how three companies got started and the determined, creative young founders who gave them life.

Labor Day 1994: The sidewalk shimmered from the warm morning sun outside Bloomingdale's flagship store on 59th Street in midtown Manhattan. Inside, 29-year-old Jody Kozlow Gardner (right) and her good friend and now business partner, 30-year-old Cherie Serota, exchanged nervous glances. Their store had just opened for business.

PHOTO© JOHN EMERSON

The two women had recently formed their own company, Belly Basics, and 10 feet away in a prime aisle-front location in Bloomingdale's well-trafficked women's clothing area lay the first fruits of their entrepreneurial venture. Seventy white boxes were neatly stacked in rows of four, each stack rising 6 feet off the ground. Stenciled in bold black lettering on each box was the name of their product, The Pregnancy Survival Kit.

Inside each kit was a little black dress, a tunic, leggings and a slim skirt, all in comfortable cotton and Lycra, all fashionably pitch black in color and available for the first time ever to the notoriously choosy maternity shopper. Dangling outside each box was the price tag for the kit—$152. In a display of good taste and crafty public relations, each Pregnancy Survival Kit also included a personal thank you from Gardner and Serota as well as an invitation to comment on the clothes.

After Bloomingdale's had given the duo a green light to test-sell the kits, Gardner and Serota chose Labor Day as their launch date, providing the retail world a glimpse of their savvy marketing style. Both knew, however, that hip marketing could only take you so far. If the product didn't catch the eye of customers, all their hard work to get to this point would be in vain. It was no lock: Bloomingdale's had never carried women's maternity clothing before. Long minutes passed as both women smiled politely, holding hands and nervously chatting quietly with a coterie of family members and friends who had gathered in a mixture of solidarity and curiosity. Everyone waited and watched anxiously to see what would happen.

Slowly, the friends and family members who had come to lend their support found themselves giving way to customers heading for the Belly Basics stand. A shopper took a box, poked around inside, shook it for heft and, smiling, walked away with a kit under her arm looking for a cash register. Two more shoppers, one noticeably pregnant, gasped at the boxes and elbowed each other in delight as they swooped in to pick up another kit. More followed, and the tower of boxes began to shrink to 5 feet and then to 4 feet. The kits were selling like those proverbial hotcakes. Gardner and Serota had founded Belly Basics as a maternity fashions company with an attitude, and it seemed they had struck entrepreneurial gold. "We realized at that time," recalls Gardner, "that this was the birth of something big. Our crazy idea had worked—we were a success."

> "We realized at that time that this was the birth of something big. Our crazy idea had worked—we were a success."

Awash with waves of emotion, the energetic young entrepreneurs stood smiling—unaware that they were about to embark on a journey that would quickly carry them to the top of the maternity fashion world. In a matter of months, their company was featured in *Glamour, Vogue, Self, Fortune, Good Housekeeping, New York Magazine, American Baby* and dozens of other publications. The partners soon expanded their line of maternity wear, adding a small catalog that included a twin set, bootleg pants, T-shirts, swimsuits, bike shorts, unitards, big shirts, a cardigan-and-skirt combination and a sleeveless shift in black matte jersey that delighted moms-to-be as a party dress. They eventually wrote a book, *Pregnancy Chic*, that was published to rave reviews from a maternity fashion-starved press

PHOTO COURTESY: BELLY BASICS

and public. By mid-1998, Belly Basics had sold 100,000 Pregnancy Survival Kits, and by the end of 1998, the company had rung up $5 million in annual sales. "Soon we were selling to England, Canada, Japan and Australia," says Serota. "Our simple idea had become a phenomenon, revolutionizing the way pregnant women thought about style."

# Perfect, To A Tea

Four years ago, in a college classroom in New Haven, Connecticut, Barry Nalebuff, a professor at the Yale School of Management, led a discussion on a case study of Coke vs. Pepsi. Eventually, the talk turned to what products were missing in the beverage market. Everyone agreed that there were plenty of super-sweet drinks—from Coke and Pepsi to Snapple and Fruitopia to diet drinks containing all kinds of artificial sweeteners. At the other end of the spectrum, there were plenty of flavorless drinks, such as bottled waters and seltzers with a flavor aftertaste. But there didn't seem to be any great-tasting drinks that didn't have all the extra stuff, not just the extra calories, but all the artificial ingredients like high fructose corn syrup and sodium benzoate.

For class member Seth Goldman, 34, the discussion really hit home. He had developed a reputation among his friends as a voracious consumer of beverages, and he was now a Snapple refugee: His infatuation with that drink had faded when he could no longer endure another lunch that left a syrupy film on his teeth. After class, Goldman and Nalebuff spoke animatedly about the kinds of beverages that might fill the void between the super-sweet and the tasteless. The discussion lingered in Goldman's mind for a long time.

Photo Courtesy: Honest Tea Inc.

At the end of the semester, Goldman (left) graduated and moved his young family to Bethesda, Maryland, where he worked for the Calvert Group, sponsor of the nation's largest family of socially and environmentally responsible mutual funds. After two years with Calvert, Goldman began thinking about running his own company, one that was both profitable and socially responsible. "While I really enjoyed my time at Calvert—it taught me a great deal about how a business could do well by doing good—I always had it in the back of my mind that I would try to strike out on my own," says Goldman. "And the healthy drink concept was looking more and more viable for me."

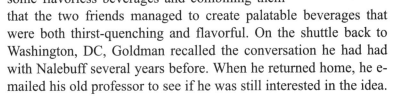

On a balmy day in the fall of 1997, Goldman met a former college track teammate for dinner at a New York City diner. The two had just gone for a run in Central Park and were parched. But when it came time to order drinks, they again encountered the void between the super-sweet and the flavorless. It was only by ordering some sweet and some flavorless beverages and combining them that the two friends managed to create palatable beverages that were both thirst-quenching and flavorful. On the shuttle back to Washington, DC, Goldman recalled the conversation he had had with Nalebuff several years before. When he returned home, he e-mailed his old professor to see if he was still interested in the idea.

The timing of the letter couldn't have been more fortuitous. Nalebuff had just returned from a trip to India, where he had done research for a case study on the tea industry. In addition to nurturing his lifelong appreciation for tea, the trip provided him with an understanding of the tea industry. Perhaps more important, during a visit to a tea auction house in Calcutta, he came up with the name Honest Tea—the perfect moniker for a company that would sell tea that truly tastes like tea.

"It was one of those serendipitous things," Goldman says. "[Professor Nalebuff] convinced me that we could start a business called 'Honest Tea' that was all-natural and does what it says it does on the label. That fall, he and I spent a lot of time brewing up ideas and thinking about what flavors we would use, how we would package it and how I would sell it. We brought people in to taste the recipes, and they were happy with the results."

On February 1, 1998, the duo launched Honest Tea Inc. and got busy writing their business plan. "Barry was right there with me, guiding me along the way," recalls Goldman. "At the end of February, I started making headway in getting my tea brewed."

About the same time, Goldman got his tea into Fresh Fields, a popular Washington, DC, grocery store. "They said they would buy half a truck full. That was difficult because we only use high-quality tea leaves, but we managed to [make the order using] an assembly line, and we learned some lessons about the realities of deadlines and distribution. By the end of summer, we were the bestselling iced tea at Fresh Fields, outselling Snapple and others."

And so Honest Tea began—and began to prosper. The two entrepreneurs sampled a plethora of tea recipes and exchanged hundreds of e-mail notes as they shaped their company. "Though several dozen promising teas were identified, we selected five flagship varieties that would become our initial product line," recalls Goldman. "We spent a great deal of time with our designer, Sloan Wilson, developing a label concept that effectively conveys the authentic, international aspects of our tea while also capturing the elegant simplicity that is often associated with tea rituals. So far, we have been delighted by the results." Indeed, Goldman expects sales of about $3.5 million in 1999.

But Goldman is far from done. "Oh, no way are we satisfied. We still want to do more and help people out in the process," he says. "That's the best part of my job."

> "No way are we satisfied. We still want to do more and help people out in the process. That's the best part of my job."

# Smoothie Operators

Eric Strauss, 30, owner and founder of Crazy Carrot Juice Bars, can remember the day 18 years ago that he opened his first lemonade stand. "I was living in Lake of the Isles, Minnesota. Believe it or not, it gets hot up there in the summer. I took advantage of that," he says. After some early trials and tribulations, Strauss soon had multiple lemonade stands strategically situated around the Minneapolis area serving up thousands of cups of cold lemonade every summer. To staff these multiple locations, Eric tapped his younger siblings and several close friends.

Born with a business sense, Strauss had a history of entrepreneurship even before launching his lemonade empire. "I began

breeding and selling gerbils to local pet stores at age 6," he recalls. "I just had an affinity for organizing and marketing, even then. I used to look forward every day to reading the business section of the local paper, and I was subscribing to *The Wall Street Journal* at the age of 12. I couldn't wait to put what I learned in the business news into practice." It wasn't surprising, then, when Strauss offered his mom stock in the lemonade company in exchange for the requisite lemonade stand supplies—sugar, Kool-Aid mix and cups.

In fact, Strauss still has the penciled ledgers from the business, including sales records, inventory levels, company rules and projected profit margins. "Would you believe that our profit margins are about the same today?" he says. Sales were good—with one lemonade stand capable of bringing in up to $35 a day in revenue—and buying and selling shares in the company wasn't a bad investment, either.

Soon after completing a fourth-grade class on finance (yep, you read that right), Strauss informed his mother that he was interested in making some real-life investments. By the age of 13, a letter he had sent to corporate raider Irwin Jacobs had already been quoted in *Fortune* magazine. At about the same time, Strauss began publishing a computer magazine, *Compuzine*, a bimonthly trade journal focused on personal computer users.

By age 14, Strauss had become serious about investing, and along with two friends, he published the *Rogers, Schalet and*

*Strauss Investment Newsletter*. The newsletter, which recommended eight to 12 stocks per month, had an impressive track record and more than 30 subscribers. Anyone who followed the recommendations would have racked up gains of 55 percent in a year—a high enough return to earn the trio of underage investment advisors billing on the cover of the *Minneapolis Star* and the *Chicago Tribune* business sections.

It wasn't until high school that Strauss really learned how profitable the food business could be. As an ice cream salesman around the Minneapolis Chain of Lakes, he pedaled and pushed his way through thousands of Dove Bars, Bomb Pops and other assorted goodies, eventually becoming the top salesperson three years in a row for the Blue Bell Ice Cream Co. "Nobody could sell more than Eric Strauss," recalls Tom Fischer, vending truck manager for what is now the Big Bell Ice Cream Co. "He's got the knack and energy it takes to be successful."

Strauss opened his first Crazy Carrot Juice Bar in the Macalester-Groveland neighborhood in Saint Paul in January 1998. "I had started planning the business in August 1996," Strauss recalls. "To raise capital, I sold stock to 30 investors and got a [$50,000] loan from the Small Business Administration. I sold $80,000 worth of equity interest and the city of Minneapolis kicked in $35K from a small-business loan program they had."

The Crazy Carrot's ingredients were carefully conceived and orchestrated by members of "Team Carrot," a group of people strategically put together to create a top-flight company. The Crazy Carrot concept—which consists of everything from the distinctive logo to

**Crazy Carrot™ Classics**

Fuzzy Wuzzy Navel
Papango
Raspberry Crave
Raspy Orange Sling
Strawberry Serenade
Very Berry Blast

the one-of-a-kind smoothies to the company's focus on environmental awareness—was more than 18 months in the making.

Beginning in 1996, Strauss and other members of "Team Carrot" began scouring the country, from California to Florida, for juice bars. Strauss himself visited more than 100 juice bars in his quest to perfect the Crazy Carrot concept. Studying every aspect of a juice bar's operation, Strauss soon honed in on the ultimate juice bar prototype. Then he selected a site, signed a lease and began construction.

Demand was strong right off the bat. The company went through more than 3,000 pounds of oranges a week, up to 1,500 pounds of jumbo carrots, and hundreds of pounds of bananas, strawberries, raspberries and other assorted fruits and vegetables.

In September 1998, the second Crazy Carrot Juice Bar opened in Minneapolis' Uptown neighborhood, an area Strauss describes as positively dripping with cachet. A third store opened near the University of Minnesota campus. By spring 1999, two more locations had opened for business. To lure younger juice lovers, Strauss installed personal computers in his stores with free Internet access for customers. His passion for juice drinks and flair for marketing has paid off. Revenues for 1999 are soaring past the $1 million mark.

"I knew we'd hit it big when [actress] Bridget Fonda came in and had one of our wheatgrass juice drinks," says Strauss. "All of a sudden we were 'happening.' I'd like to say that I knew it all along, but I can't. It takes a lot of hard work and some luck, too. We had both on our side."

# Chapter

**2**

More Gen E's believe in UFOs than believe they will collect a dollar of their Social Security benefits.

# What Do You Want To Be When You Grow Up?

If the late 19th century is considered the "Industrial Age," then the turn of the 21st century may go down in history as the "Entrepreneurial Age." Who would argue the point? From the rubble of contemporary corporate life and its rigid hierarchical structures, entrepreneurship has emerged as the single largest business trend since the introduction of the computer.

Even entrenched corporate traditionalists concede that this is true: Eighty percent of business leaders said in a recent Ernst & Young poll that most Americans will engage in entrepreneurial activity "at some point in their lives." Not only that, but 75 percent of business leaders see entrepreneurial activity growing worldwide, even in places that don't emphasize capitalism. Emerging markets such as Africa and the Middle East are the highest growth-sector economies in the world.

What's clear is that, in America at least, this isn't just a business trend; it's a cultural one. Today's corporate managers say that lifestyle issues—like personal and creative fulfillment and the freedom to innovate— are the driving forces behind the Entrepreneurial Age. More to the point, it is increasingly young people who are swelling the ranks of the new entrepreneurs. One recent study notes that a whopping 87 percent of those born between the years 1965 and 1977—a k a Generation X—want to work for themselves rather than for someone else. Call them Generation Entrepreneur, or Gen E—entrepreneurs who don't take kindly to being called "slackers" and are out to prove themselves the hardest-working, most independent-minded generation in American history.

**87%**
want to
work for
themselves

**Gen E:**
born between
1965–1977

The fact that it's the younger members of the global work force who are ditching dependable paychecks and warm corporate cocoons for 20-hour workdays and the adrenaline rush of owning their own business is hardly surprising. In *Rational Exuberance: The Influence of Generation X on the New American Economy* (E.P. Dutton), author Merideth Bagby makes a compelling case as to why so many young Americans are placing their stamps on the domestic commercial landscape. Time and again, the 25-year-old Bagby hammers home two main points. First, with the country's mushrooming Social Security and health-care costs, Bagby and her contemporaries will be the first generation that's poorer than its predecessors, i.e., the dreaded baby boomers. Youth today are told constantly by the media, politicians, friends and family that by the time Gen E bellies up to the bar for their fair share of the country's entitlement programs, the pickings will be slim. No wonder more Gen E's believe in UFOs than believe they will collect a dollar of their Social Security benefits.

Second, Bagby emphasizes that Gen E's have a strong emotional grip, a core self-reliance, as well as technological vision, traits that have personified successful entrepreneurs throughout history. "Many of us were latchkey kids and responsible for not only taking care of ourselves but for making purchases for our family as well," explains Bagby. "We really had to depend on ourselves in large part. As an outgrowth of that, I think you see the entrepreneurism that is so prevalent in our generation."

In addition, younger Americans have been raised with powerful doses of cynicism and skepticism. They've seen firsthand how traditional career modes have spiritually failed their parents, whose own relationships have often ended in divorce. As children, they

## Mamas, Don't Let Your Babies Grow Up To Be Public-School Students

**D**o you ever wonder why America's youth don't place too much stock in government's role in their future?

According to author and social commentator Merideth Bagby, for every $5 spent on government programs for seniors, $1 is spent on education and other programs designed to better the lives of young people.

Shocked? Don't be. Politicians dole out the pork to where the votes are. Young Americans equate voting with a root canal. Older Americans vote with a vengeance; politicians simply act accordingly.

**Government programs for seniors**

**Education and other programs for young people**

witnessed the emotional toll of office politics and corporate down-sizing when Mom and Dad arrived home bitching about the boss, or worse, clutching a pink slip. Above all, the younger generation wants to distance itself from that fate. With those dark visions in their minds, Gen E is determined never to let someone else drive their careers and lives.

The result? A move toward young guns running their own shops. Millions of them. In fact, so many entrepreneurs are launch-ing new businesses, the joke is the U.S. Small Business Administration is considering building a speed-bump in its parking lot to slow down the legions of entrepreneurs looking for licenses, funding and advice. Consider these stats from Small Business Administration (SBA):

● In any given year, small businesses account for anywhere from 66 to more than 100 percent of net job creation (since larger enterprises often shed jobs). And more than half of all workers are employed in smaller businesses.

● The United States is increasingly becoming a nation of entrepre-neurs. From 1980 to 1997, the total number of businesses jumped by 69 percent, from 13.8 million to 23.5 million, while the over-all population increased only 18 percent during the same period.

● U.S. small businesses are active in the international marketplace. Indeed, the U.S. Department of Commerce has found that more than 96 percent of U.S. exporters are small to midsize companies, and the SBA reports that 86 percent of U.S. businesses involved in international trade are wholesalers and other intermediaries, and these businesses are typically small.

The evidence also shows that the younger you are, the more likely you are to launch your own business. According to professor Paul Reynolds of the Boston-based Entrepreneurial Research Consortium (ERC), a business start-up think tank, "Most people starting businesses in the United States are between 25 and 34." In other words, Generation E.

# Baby, It's You

The stampede toward self-employment defies traditional eco-nomic and cultural definitions. Economists are hard-pressed to quantify why so many entrepreneurs are hanging up their own "open for business" signs today. Then again, what do economists know? As humorist P.J. O'Rourke aptly says, "Microeconomics concerns things that economists are specifically wrong about, while macroeconomics concerns things economists are wrong about generally."

One reason for the trend is that it's easier than ever to roll out your own surf shop, Web site, microbrew or whatever. With the advent of cheaper technology like the World Wide Web, lower telecommunication costs and heightened productivity—thanks to new work-force products like high-powered laptop computers and handy-dandy notepads—start-ups can be launched for less than the price of four New York Yankees season tickets (not including Monster Bucket ballgame popcorn).

"There's definitely more willingness for people to go [from college] straight into start-ups," says Edmund Dunn of the Massachusetts Institute of Technology Enterprise Forum. "Young people with very current skills aren't facing the kinds of capital barriers faced in previous generations. You don't need a billion dollars to get a business running, and capital is available."

In fact, young Americans are being encouraged—by society in general and by venture capitalists and government in particular—to

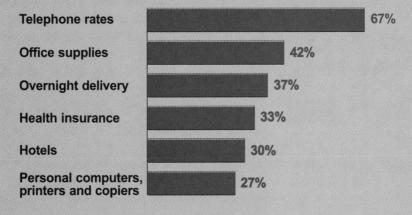

## You Deserve A Break Today

According to Gannett News Service, almost 70 percent of small-business owners say they do not know where to find discounts on products and services they buy frequently. Of the 30 percent that do, here is what they most frequently get breaks on:

| | |
|---|---|
| Telephone rates | 67% |
| Office supplies | 42% |
| Overnight delivery | 37% |
| Health insurance | 33% |
| Hotels | 30% |
| Personal computers, printers and copiers | 27% |

stake their claim in the burgeoning global economy. Traditional barriers to young entrepreneurship, such as lack of capital, limited experience and absence of business contacts, are falling away before a sparkling new set of business advantages for entrepreneurs of all stripes. For instance, corporate outsourcing creates a big demand for customized business services; technological break-throughs like the Internet, e-mail and laptop computers enable busi-ness owners to maintain a lower overhead while staying in touch with staffers anywhere in the world; and there are a wealth of cap-ital funding opportunities favoring emerging businesses. Also in the younger set's favor, they still have their brash, youthful enthusiasm. That optimism serves Gen E's well because they need it to overlook the fact that 40 percent of all small businesses fail.

Traditional business tenets dictate that only seasoned, experi-enced hands should strike out on their own. College graduates should content themselves with learning the ropes of the business world slowly and often painfully by spending several years in a low-paying, 50-hour-a-week job. Better to make mistakes with someone else's money, the wise old-hands say—spend four or five years with Bell Labs as a marketing executive before launching your own cel-lular phone business. But there's a growing school of thought that rolling out a new business in your 20s isn't actually so ill-advised. The 38-year-old entrepreneur has a great deal riding on a potential new business venture: in all likelihood, a young family, a fat mortgage, the safety and security of a regular paycheck, a pension and medical plan and a hefty 401(k). The 22-year-old entrepre-neur likely has few of these lifestyle issues hanging over his or her head. Generally unmar-ried, unmortgaged and healthy (not to mention often eager to reinvent the traditional business model), the younger set has a lot less to lose precisely because they are so young.

> "I was **miserable** in the corporate world. I figured you could let **other** people run your life, **or** you could run it **yourself**."

Of the Gen E's who have tried corporate life, most have decided they don't like it. After too many run-ins with middle-management drones giving them grief for wearing sandals and shorts to work, or after higher-minded disputes over pay, work-ing conditions or a company's social outlook, their dissatisfaction with the traditional workplace has grown until it borders on utter

# 10 questions

**Name:** Sky Dayton
**Age:** 27
**Company:** EarthLink Network, Internet service provider
**Location:** Pasadena, California
**Web Site:** www.earthlink.net
**Year Founded:** 1994
**Start-up Costs:** $100,000
**1998 Sales:** $150 million
**1999 Projections:** $250 million

1. **What was your first entrepreneurial venture?**
   Window washer

2. **At what age did you start it?**
   10

3. **What did you learn from the experience?**
   Window washing isn't a scalable business; it's a physical business.

4. **What age were you when you made your first million?**
   24

5. **What was your first job (as an employee)?**
   Packing tool parts for the family business in New Jersey

6. **Did you go to college?**
   No

7. **What age were you when you started your first "real" full-time venture?**
   18

8. **Who is your role model?**
   Everyone I meet; I learn from everybody

9. **How many businesses have you started?**
   Four

10. **How many were successful, and how many failed?**
    Four succeeded, and none failed.

contempt. Many say to themselves "With so many opportunities elsewhere, why not just leave?"

"I was miserable in the corporate world. I figured you could let other people run your life, or you could run it yourself," recalls Jeff Berman, founder of Shankbone, a clothing manufacturer in Newton, Massachusetts. "Now Shankbone gives me more schedule flexibility, but the big joke is, I can work any 80 hours a week I want."

Berman started Shankbone when he was 30, after a short career as an advertising executive. "For better or worse, I was not cut out to be the person that the advertising agency wanted. They wanted someone predictable, and that wasn't me." He maintains that many Gen E's blanche at the rigidness and conformity of today's corporate culture, even in supposedly "hip" industries like advertising. "There wasn't a lot of room for input outside of the very specific boundaries that the agency had," he recalls. "I'd spend a lot of time getting people to see the value of an idea. But if the idea didn't fit a preconceived framework, the higher-ups didn't even consider the idea. In the end, they wanted good soldiers. I wasn't a good soldier—a good spy maybe, but not a good soldier."

Today, Shankbone is a $1 million company, with clothing lines for men, women and now babies. "Plus, we're selling to nationally recognized stores like Bloomingdale's and Urban Guerrilla," adds Berman. "We've come a long way from talking our way into surf shops."

That same motivation is, as we'll see later, shattering gender lines as well. Twentysomething and thirtysomething women, fed up with the wage disparities and "glass ceilings" of entrenched corporate America, are beginning to show up on chambers of commerce "who's who" lists across the country. A recent survey by the National Foundation for Women Business Owners and Catalyst, a research organization that promotes female business owners, reports that 58 percent of women who've left to start their own shops say they'll "never return" to the corporate world.

# Smells Like School Spirit

Just as the software industry was born in the dusty dorm rooms and luminescent laboratories of college towns like Berkeley,

> **"Never** give up. If you get knocked down, just **get back up** and approach the situation in a **different** way."
> —*Daymond John*

# FUBU, FUBU, Avoiding The Fashion Boo-Boo

Like many young entrepreneurs, Daymond John and his partners were turned down by bank after bank when looking for financial backing for their fledgling apparel company, FUBU (For Us, By Us). "We went to 20 or 30 banks, and no one would give us a contract or a small-business loan," recalls John. "No one believed in us."

**Daymond John, 29**
**J. Alexander Martin, 28**
**Keith Perrin, 28**
**Carl Brown, 28**

*Company:* **FUBU The Collection**
*Location:* **New York City**
*Year Started:* **1992**
*Start-up Costs:* **$100,000**
*1998 Revenues:* **$200 million**
*1999 Projections:* **Lips are sealed**

But the partners believed in themselves and their urban fashions, and they refused to give up. John mortgaged his Queens, New York, home and converted the bottom floor into a factory. Hometown friend and hip-hop artist LL Cool J helped publicize the clothing line by wearing FUBU clothes in his music videos, as did other artists. It was the boost they needed; the company's growth soared.

Today, FUBU fashions are sold in department and specialty apparel stores throughout the country, and the company plans to add loungewear, swimwear, fragrances, eyewear and watches to its already large lines of men's wear, women's wear, boy's clothing and bags. "In anything we did, whether it was trying to get LL to wear a shirt or trying to get funding from a bank," says John, "we never gave up."

California, and Cambridge, Massachusetts, so too were the seeds
for the Entrepreneurial Age sown in university locales.

In the era of the computer chip, it's not as difficult as it might
seem to turn a term paper on online marketing into a fledgling
World Wide Web start-up, or a hotel manage-
ment discourse on five-course menus into a
thriving gourmet catering service. In such
cases, college students aren't even giving the
corporate world a first glance, let alone paying
their dues in cubicle nation for a year or two
before setting out on their own. That's good
news for middle-aged managers who don't
relish the cheaper competition for their jobs
from new waves of college graduates. But it's
bad news for the IBMs and Gaps of the world,
who soon will feel the dearth of good young
management help in their Fortune 500 envi-
rons. Worse, from corporate America's view,
is that not only is the entrepreneurial boom
draining management circles of much-needed younger, fresher
blood, but those same young turks are, in many cases, setting up
shop across the street or on the Internet—as vibrant, eager competitors. In doing so, these fresh-out-of-college upstarts are revamping the corporate landscape at the highest levels of commerce.

> **Who** would have thought a brainy engineer from the University of Illinois would give **mighty** Microsoft a run for its **money**?

Just ask Bill Gates. In 1993, Mark Andreeson, a young
University of Illinois student, developed a World Wide Web interactive search engine that became the foundation of Netscape, which
quickly became Microsoft's nemesis in the Web "browser wars."
By the time it dawned on Gates that Netscape might derail the
mighty Microsoft Express, it was too late. In 1998, Netscape survived a bloody battle with Microsoft to keep its popular World Wide
Web search engine viable. Then the U.S. Justice Department used
the "browser wars" as leverage against Gates, charging his company with unfair monopolization of the Web browser market and argu-
ing persuasively that Microsoft was "out to get" Netscape and force
the company out of business. Some painted this as a David vs.
Goliath story, but it didn't stay that way long. Soon after, Netscape
merged with online titan AOL to form a software supernova, which
is guaranteed to give Microsoft all it can handle for years to come.

These events illustrate just how far entrepreneurship has come.

Twenty years ago, who would have thought that IBM would sit on the sidelines as two companies with less than 25 years of experience between them would fight for control of the global computer market? And five short years ago, who would have thought a brainy engineer from the University of Illinois would give mighty Microsoft a run for its money? Such is the stormy maelstrom that is latter-day entrepreneurship.

But the 26-year-old Andreeson—an entrepreneur's entrepreneur—wasn't through yet. No sooner was the ink dry on AOL's November 1998 deal to buy Netscape for $4 billion than Andreeson invested a portion of his formidable fortune in a small Silicon Valley start-up called Replay Networks Inc. The company is bringing to market a digital TV recording system, called ReplayTV, that's similar to a videocassette recorder. The system will enable viewers to record a complete program that is already in progress, to automatically record programs that meet a predetermined criterion—for example, movies featuring a particular actor—and to intelligently skip commercials. It's simply another feather in the cap of Andreeson, the Michael Jordan of young entrepreneurs, who in five short years restructured the computing landscape, and now is setting his sites on the entertainment industry.

College was also kind to Kyle Bacon, 26, of Columbus, Ohio. As an undergraduate at Ohio Northern University, the electrical engineering and computer sciences major founded Your Connection, a World Wide Web design company in 1994.

## What's Age Got To Do With It?

**Y**ou won't read this factoid in any Fortune 500 annual reports, but Gen E is launching new businesses at a record pace.

According to the Research Consortium at Babson College in Wellesley, Massachusetts, 46 percent of new businesses in 1997 were started by people age 35 and under. That's entrepreneurs born after the death of JFK and before the birth of disco.

New businesses started in 1997

**46%** started by people age 35 and under

After tapping one of his vendors as a partner, Bacon steered the company to the more profitable Internet access market, ultimately founding Fiber Network Solutions in 1996 to sell high-speed commercial Internet access to businesses. By mid-1998, the company had 22 employees and a big office in Columbus. Not only that, Bacon was able to lobby private investors to pony up $1 million in capital funding to push the company to even greater heights.

Despite Bacon's inexperience, clients and partners raved about his maturity. "I think they were impressed that I knew what I was doing," he recalls.

Another Columbus native, 34-year-old Greg Ruf, founded Resume Link after writing a business plan for the company as a student at Bowling Green University. The $4 million company, which employed 32 people through 1998, creates custom-made resumes on hard copy, software or via the Web. The resumes are placed on databases with links to a host of corporate human resources departments, where staffers can pick and choose job candidates as needed. The company recently received a $1 million funding injection from a

## Do The Math

**N**eed further proof that entrepreneurism is sweeping the country, and that Gen E's are leading the wave? Check the numbers:

- Nearly eight out of 10 American adults trying to start their own business are between the ages of 18 and 34.
- One out of four young workers today pursue self-employment.
- More than four in 10 Americans say that owning their own business is something they would like to do, according to Roper Starch Research; this share is highest (63 percent) among those ages 18 to 29.
- One in three high-tech enterprises launched each year are by founders under the age of 30.
- The average business owner today (of any age) has three employees, 1.3 locations and is not a part of a franchise organization.
- The average business owner typically works 50.4 hours a week at a business that generates average revenues of between $150,000 and $200,000 a year.
- More than one-third (37 percent) of Fortune 500 executives say they would own their own company if they could relive their life.

Chicago venture capitalist. "There's no reason you can't run a business in college or even high school," says Ruf.

Colleges are natural breeding grounds for young entrepreneurs not only because smart, savvy young men and women grace their campuses but because academia fosters an ideal environment for entrepreneurial networking. Through 1997, 1,600 college entrepreneurial programs existed nationwide, up from 400 in 1995, according to the Boston-based Young Entrepreneur Network, a national directory of more than 1,000 business owners from teenagers to thirtysomethings. That number is expected to grow by leaps and bounds as demand for business start-up advice swells on U.S. campuses.

Rakesh Gupta, the dean of the Adelphi School of Management and Business on Long Island, New York, agrees. "In the last three or four years, we have strengthened our entrepreneurship program. There's definitely an interest in being your own boss and having your own life in your own hands."

Take stepbrothers Stephen Brody and Anthony Roberts. In 1983 the 24-year-olds co-founded the Southland Bagel Co. while working part time in Brody's father's bagel shop. Both were college students with a curiosity for business. When the duo created a tasty pizza bagel topped with tomato sauce and cheese that proved popular with the shop's customers, they took out a $500 loan from Brody's mother and began peddling their spicy bagels to local catering trucks. Word got around and, soon enough, a whopping order for 24,000 came in from the Los Angeles Unified School District. They filled the order by hand—and became $12,000 richer for their efforts.

"They may as well have said they wanted a billion of them," Brody says now. "It was an unbelievable order. Wow! We were really in business." Brody says their youthful optimism carried them through the early, rough times. "We weren't shy about asking potential customers to help out a couple of young kids," says Brody. "There are people out there who want to do business with you because you show gumption and initiative and innovation."

Good point. To the fresh crop of whiz kids who are focused on building better products and services, failure is not an option. They've seen role models like Dell Computer's Michael Dell, who kick-started a personal computer business in his University of Texas dorm room and today presides over a multibillion-dollar PC empire. Now, it seems, everybody wants to be like Mike.

# It's Just A Piece Of Paper

Then again, there are some young entrepreneurs who aren't even bothering to finish college before starting their businesses. To them, graduating from the school of hard knocks is just as valuable as any Ivy League diploma.

According to a recent study by the Young Entrepreneurs Network, 35 percent of successful Gen E business owners don't have a framed sheepskin from Whattsamattah U. adorning their office wall, and 10 percent never went to college at all. Consider Joe Liemandt, 29, president of Trilogy Development Group in Austin, Texas.

Today, the business software company boasts annual revenues of $120 million and 300 employees. But four years ago, Liemandt's prospects weren't so good. Much to his father's chagrin, he dropped out of Stanford University to pound out a computer program with five classmates in a small office near Stanford's Palo Alto campus. "You're a moron," Liemandt's father told him, fully aware that more businesses fail than not and that a degree from Stanford is, in many circles, a license to print money.

Nonplussed, Liemandt and his crew carried on. Ultimately, his company's revolutionary purchasing software was sold to Hewlett-Packard for $3 million. More big orders followed and soon Liemandt's company had Fortune 500 names like Chrysler, IBM and Boeing shining brightly on its client list.

What do Liemandt and his fellow entrepreneurs have in common besides a desire to call their own shots and a powerful itch to make it big? A sense that their generation is special, much more so than the baby boomers, who many Gen E's feel have squandered their largesse on, as P.J. O'Rourke once scathingly said, "cocaine and Reeboks." The younger set is sick of self-absorbed "elders" in their four-wheel drives, constantly whining about this cause or that. Gen E's want results.

So whatever you do, don't call them "slackers." Generation E is serious about imprinting its stamp on the 21st century. It's a fool's bet wagering against them.

# Chapter

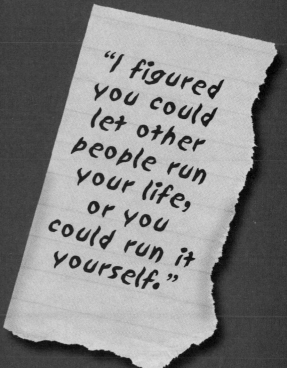

"I figured you could let other people run your life, or you could run it yourself."

# Slacker, Schmacker: How The Great Ones Got Started

One common characteristic of most Gen E business owners is that they don't mind taking risks. On the contrary, they thrive on risk. It's what separates them from the herd. But the successful ones learn not to take just any old risk: They make sure their business idea is solid, and then they do all the research and preparation they can to give it an opportunity to thrive.

Consider John Shriber, 29, the owner of Apartment Source, a 1995 start-up that, for a fee, e-mails customers lists of available apartments in a particular city. In 1995, the Internet had not yet been anointed as a reliable venue for business, but Shriber never doubted that he'd make a bundle using it. He knew firsthand what a chore apartment-hunting was, since he was a real estate agent living in New York City, and he knew how convenient it would be to get new listings at home every day—and not just the same old retreads from the newspaper. So he borrowed $19,000 from his dad to launch his fledgling business using the relatively new technology of the Internet, and he never looked back.

With the luxury of hindsight, Shriber knows that he took the right risks. On the company's first day of business, Apartment Source pulled in $3,000 in revenues. "I wasn't shocked," recalls Shriber. "I knew it was going to work—just not that well."

Today, Apartment Source boasts three locations (New York City, Los Angeles and San Francisco) and well over $2.3 million in annual revenues. Shriber expects Internet commerce (overall, a $32.6 billion business in 1998) to continue to reward risk takers who think outside the box.

# Amazin' Amazon

For every Michael Dell or Bill Gates, there are hundreds, maybe even thousands of smaller entrepreneurs like Shriber. These unheralded businesspeople are the backbone of industry around the world, and the two things they all have in common are a great idea and a burning desire to succeed. Without the requisite fire in the belly, you may find it hard to follow through when debts pile up and your initial efforts are greeted mildly by the public, and without the equally critical market idea, your business will fall flat despite all your gumption and borrowed capital.

Jeffrey Bezos, 33, had both. His Amazon.com online book, music and video store is the hottest thing to hit popular consumer culture since Beanie Babies. But only four short years ago Bezos was a nondescript hedge fund manager.

Bezos' idea was a simple one, and like Shriber, he was one of the first to make a business success out of the convenience of the Internet. He felt consumers eager to buy the latest Tom Wolfe novel

## I'm Mad As Hell, And I'm Not Gonna Take It Anymore!

$\mathbb{S}$ ometimes the drive to run your own business develops not because of all the things you want to do but because of those you don't—like be ordered around by incompetent bosses or have your creative abilities constrained by rigid corporate Politburos. At least the Vatican sends out smoke signals when anointing a new Pope. Try finding out the status of your project from a big company saddled with seven layers of management.

Jack Showalter knows what that's like. The Charlotte, North Carolina, resident started his own Internet access service at age 25, primarily because he grew so frustrated with his corporate job at First Union Bank. "That was interesting for about six months," he recalls. "But I was frustrated with having a lot of good ideas and never seeing them grow to fruition."

> "I was **frustrated** with having a lot of **good ideas** and never seeing them **grow** to fruition."

Like many hot young entrepreneurs, Showalter was able to harness a negative emotion—his frustration toward his employers—and use it in his business. As his enthusiasm grew over the prospect of starting his own venture, Showalter found the perseverance to see it through to the end, from researching the Internet access industry and creating a business plan to successfully urging close friends and family to contribute seed money to the operation.

That's what it takes to thrive in the shark-infested waters of global commerce: good, workable ideas, a ready market, the tenacity to make it on your own, and the ability to adapt and change with consumer tastes.

Of course, $50,000 from Grandma doesn't hurt, either.

or Madonna compact disc would be most happy doing so from the comfort of their own homes, online and 24 hours a day. His challenge was that Americans were still uncomfortable transmitting their credit card numbers and other personal information over the Web. So that became his top priority: putting the best Internet security software in place and then promoting it until consumers got used to the idea of purchasing online. Shopping mall behemoths like Barnes and Noble and Tower Records hadn't pursued this strategy, thinking the technology wasn't up to it yet, and they found out the truth too late—after Amazon.com had leapt to a lengthy head start.

Once consumers felt comfortable, the rest was easy. Bezos simply inventoried as many books, CDs and videos as he could (and if he couldn't fill an order, he'd go get it), then he sat back and watched as Americans triggered more hits on his Web site than Sonny Corleone took at the tollbooth in "The Godfather." Three years into its existence, in 1998, Amazon.com had become the third-largest bookseller in the world, selling a whopping 57,000 books per day on average. It took Wal-Mart 12 years and 78 stores to reach $168 million in sales. Amazon.com did it in just over three years, and business analysts expected the company to reach $460 million in sales in 1999—all without opening a single store. Today, the company is worth well over $4.4 billion.

> Like trailblazers Henry Ford and Sam Walton before him, Bezos had permanently transformed the consumer shopping experience.

To retail industry observers, Bezos' idea was pure gold. Soon Barnes and Noble and others set up their own interactive shopping centers to great success. But to young business owners, Bezos had uncovered the entrepreneurial Holy Grail of the 21st century. Like trailblazers Henry Ford and Sam Walton before him, Bezos had permanently transformed the consumer shopping experience. He changed the competitive landscape, tilting it in his favor, and in the process became the standard-bearer for Internet commerce. Even though his net worth at the end of 1998 was close to $2 billion, his true claim to fame in the eyes of young entrepreneurs the world over was making Internet commerce viable, especially for small companies. To upstart business owners, an idea like that is worth more than a boatload of cash.

Why? Because ideas executed well invariably lead to repeat business—and that's something money can't buy. More than 540,000 people visit Amazon.com every day. That's enough to fill Fenway Park almost 20 times over. Of the customers who shop

## If You Take A Walk, They'll Tax Your Feet

**T**he Beatles understood how onerous taxes were. When George Harrison wrote the song "Taxman," Great Britain was taking about 80 percent of the Fab Four's income in taxes. But that's the price of success. The more money your business makes, the more income tax you will have to pay. And that's just the beginning. You get to be your own boss, but you also become a tax collector yourself, gathering sales tax on your retail products and payroll taxes from your employees' wages.

If you incorporate as either an S or C corporation, or form a partnership or limited liability company (LLC), you must file a separate business income tax return: Form 1120 for a C corporation, Form 1120S for an S corporation, or Form 1065 for either a partnership or an LLC. (LLCs are taxed like partnerships.) If you're a sole proprietorship, you file only a Schedule C as an addendum to your individual tax return.

Many business owners file their own personal tax returns but have accountants complete their corporate taxes, which can grow so complicated, most start-up business owners are afraid they'll do something wrong. Plus, filing your own corporate taxes is not an efficient use of your time.

If you're up for the challenge, however, software is available to help you file corporate and partnership tax returns. If you can't stand the thought of shelling out the dough for a tax professional, here's a compromise: Do your own business taxes, but have your accountant look at the final return. That way, you'll cut costs without sacrificing the safety of having an accountant review your numbers and supporting documents.

Whether you get help or go it alone, be aware that only a C corporation actually pays taxes. All other business structures are "pass-through." In other words, you calculate the income from your business, which then "flows through" to your 1040 and is taxed at your individual rate—just like the income from a sole proprietor's Schedule C.

with Amazon, a staggering 60 percent are repeat customers. On Wall Street, 12 percent repeat business is cause to pop open the Moët Chandon. Hence the love affair young entrepreneurs and financial markets have with Bezos' revolutionary company.

What's next for Amazon? One notion is that Bezos and company will continue to branch out into consumer goods, like toys and TV sets, thereby accelerating the "Wal-Mart-ization" of e-commerce. In fact, Wal-Mart recently sued Amazon for stealing its employees after Bezos hired away Wal-Mart's high-tech guru to head up his own information systems operation. Things are coming full circle for the youthful Bezos and Amazon.com, and Bezos is still pushing the buttons.

# The Entrepreneurial Make-up

So what do you need to succeed? First, a great idea, preferably one that will revolutionize your industry and thereby vault you into the exclusive ranks of thirtysomething billionaires. But if your idea isn't quite that great—and how many are?—a good one will do, one that is well-researched and focused on a defined market. Then you simply need to execute it well. Without good execution, even the most brilliant idea will wither on the vine.

However, a company's execution is only as good as the make-up of the entrepreneur driving the business. Younger Americans who have successfully created their own businesses share traits that separate themselves from their generational peers in cubicle nation. Such traits include an encyclopedia-like knowledge of the market they're entering and an understanding of the sacrifices needed to run a good business, both in terms of time and financial outlay. For instance, when you open your own shop, don't expect an eight-hour day, and forget any visions of nightly pow-wows at the hip pub next door with your fellow associates. More likely you'll spend your p.m. hours alone, crunching numbers, talking to suppliers and wondering what to do about that incompetent marketing director you hired to streamline your business.

The popular conception of young entrepreneurs as hard-charging, take-no-prisoners risk takers isn't that far off the mark. But most young business owners also develop rigid discipline and realistic expectations. You may choose this journey freely, but know that your life is going to change in many ways, and not all of them positive.

In the early years, you must develop an immunity to bad cooking and sleepless nights. Maxing out your credit cards and stringing a good chunk of your financing from family loans will do that to you. The thought of missing a payroll deadline creeps into every young business owner's mind. The specter of continued quarterly income statements recorded in red ink rather than black are a fact of entrepreneurial life.

So take a deep breath and look long at the seemingly healthy creature staring back at you in the bathroom mirror before you commit to going solo. In six months' time, that face may be unrecognizable—a haggard, disheveled shell of your former self who would sell his or her vital organs to medical science if it meant you could make payroll. Then, once you've decided you can live, indeed thrive, in that situation, you need to consider failure. That's right: You need to understand what will happen to you if your business goes belly up within a year or so and you've logged so much debt that the Federal Witness Protection program is starting to look good. Figure out how far you're willing to go, and when you'll jump ship if it doesn't work out.

According to Dun & Bradstreet's report on entrepreneurship, *Starting Your Business*, the two most common reasons that a business doesn't succeed are: 1) The business is poorly managed because the owner lacks the necessary skills, and 2) the owner underestimates how much money it will take to get the business off the ground. If you've decided that you're constitutionally suited to running your own business, then the remaining issues can be broken down

## Act Globally, Think Nimbly

**M**aybe size matters if you are Godzilla, but it can work against you in the global marketplace.

In a recent *Journal of Small Business Management* article on the internationalization of technology firms, professors Necmi Karagozoglu and Martin Lindell claim that small and medium-sized technology firms actually have certain advantages over large businesses in international markets, the clearest ones being "flexibility, speed and advantage-seeking behavior."

In other words, the calling cards of the young entrepreneur.

fairly easily. To determine whether your business will go boom or
bust, ask yourself the following questions:

**1** **Have I blanketed my industry, or does my research consist
pretty much of taking notes during silly TV shows like
"When CEOs Attack"?** The best and perhaps only way to find
out if customers will be banging down your door is through
some sort of demographic research. Researching your market
to recognize and understand your customers' needs, as well as
to find out what your competition is doing, is the first and
biggest step a young entrepreneur must make.

Remember, the stakes are higher when you're a solo voy-
ager. A Coca-Cola can absorb a disastrous idea like New Coke,
replace it with a repackaged Coke Classic, and move on. Not
you and your hot idea. If your gamble on liquid metal widgets
doesn't pan out, there's no "widget classic" to back you up. In
fact, you're likely out of business—and up to your hip in debt
and liquid metal widgets that nobody wants.

So take your great idea to the library, the Internet, industry
trade shows and any other knowledgeable resource and bone up
on what the market for your product or service looks like. Who
are your likely customers? Where are they located? Do they
need to drive to your place of business, or can you easily deliver to them? How much will they fork out for your product or
service, and what will you charge them? Who are your competitors? How will you stand out from them?

Talk to industry experts or indirect competitors; they may
surprise you with their candor. Contact helpful organizations
like the Small Business Administration or your local chamber
of commerce, which can put you in touch with local entrepreneurial organizations. Take a class on marketing and business
at the local community college or university.

The information is out there, and it's up to you to find it.
Market research is how you hone your interesting but rough
idea into a brilliant diamond.

**2** **How much cash do I need to launch my business?** How will
you react when you don't see a paycheck for six weeks? Six
months? Will you roll with the punches, confident that your
idea will pay off over time? Or will you suffer a nervous break-
down, waking up in a padded room, balding and clutching *The*

# 10 questions

*Name:* Michael Serruya
*Age:* 34
*Company:* Yogen Fruz Worldwide
    Inc., frozen yogurt chain
*Location:* Markham, Ontario
*Web Site:* www.yogenfruz.com
*Year Founded:* 1986
*Start-up Costs:* $150,000
*1998 Sales:* $610 million
*1999 Projections:* $850 million

**1. What was your first entrepreneurial venture?**
A newspaper route with my brother Aaron

**2. At what age did you start it?**
19

**3. What did you learn from the experience?**
That if you put your mind to something and if you want it really bad, anything is possible

**4. What age were you when you made your first million?**
24

**5. What was your first job (as an employee)?**
None really; we started Yogen Fruz right out of school.

**6. Did you go to college?**
No

**7. What age were you when you started your current business?**
19

**8. Who is your role model?**
My father. He taught us the meaning of the word "discipline" and showed us the value of hard work and dedication.

**9. How many businesses have you started?**
Five

**10. How many were successful, and how many failed?**
Four succeeded, and one failed.

*New York Times* classified ads in one hand and a frantically assembled resume in the other?

Yep, it's all about the Benjamins. Benjamin Franklins, that is. Estimating how much money you'll need to operate your business and how much you'll need to live on is another crucial exercise for the would-be entrepreneur. Once you've developed a crackerjack business idea, then you have to figure out how much your start-up is going to cost—and only then can you consider where and how to get outside financing.

If you proceed with only vague ideas of how much your start-up will cost, your business will suffer, though it will do wonders for the makers of aspirin and other pain relievers. True, the cost of starting a business is a tad cheaper these days, but even a small venture can demand $25,000 just to get off the Tarmac. Use the work sheet on page 37 to see what you'll need to get your business started.

"Knowing your costs is the key to financial planning," advises one young entrepreneur who owns a string of ice-cream parlors. "My original estimates were that it would take $30,000 to equip my first ice cream shop and another $12,000 to install plumbing, electrical and other improvements. I budgeted another $8,000 for signs and furniture. I cut my $50,000 estimate on shop fixtures down to $12,000 by shopping around and located some used equipment for $7,000."

## When The Big Apple Takes A Bite Out Of You

If you're thinking of launching your brand-new business in New York City, think again. Taxes in the Big Apple, it seems, are as ubiquitous as surly cab drivers and World Series banners in George Steinbrenner's office. A recent study places New York's personal and business tax rate as the "most burdensome" of all U.S. cities with more than 500,000 people. In fact, no other city was even close. New York's $2,474 in individual city taxes was 139 percent higher than the national average of $1,034. The metropolis on the Hudson outpaced the No. 2 worst tax city, San Francisco ($1,296), by 91 percent.

Timing is everything. Thirty-four years ago, New York City didn't even have an income tax. Now it has the highest in the United States!

# Start-up Costs Work Sheet

*The following work sheet will help you to compute your initial cash requirements for your business. It lists the things you need to consider when determining your start-up costs and includes the one-time initial costs needed to open your doors.*

| Start-up Expenses | Amount | Description |
|---|---|---|
| Advertising | | Promotion for opening the business |
| Starting inventory | | The amount of inventory required to open |
| Building construction | | The amount per contractor bid and other costs |
| Cash | | Amount needed for the cash register |
| Decorating | | Estimate based on bid if appropriate |
| Deposits | | Check with utility companies |
| Fixtures and equipment | | Use actual bids |
| Insurance | | Bid from insurance agent |
| Lease payments | | Fee to be paid before opening' |
| Licenses and permits | | Check with city or state offices |
| Miscellaneous | | All other costs |
| Professional fees | | Include CPA, attorney, etc. |
| Remodeling | | Use contractor bids |
| Rent | | Fee to be paid before opening |
| Services | | Cleaning, accounting, etc. |
| Signs | | Use contractor bids |
| Supplies | | Office, cleaning, supplies, etc. |
| Unanticipated expenses | | Include an amount for the unexpected |
| Other | | |
| Other | | |
| Other | | |
| **Total Start-up Costs** | | **Total amount of costs before opening** |

> "**Everyone** told me not to do this and that I was **crazy** to go into the toy business. But we **persevered**. Now, we're the **barbarians** at the gate."
> —*Larry Schwarz*

# Rumpus
## In The Bronx

L arry Schwarz thinks that toy manufacturers have stopped having fun. Lame movie tie-ins, unimaginative products and no real connection with kids have left the industry with a spine like a Slinky and in more disarray than Mr. Potato Head.

Schwarz's company, Rumpus Toys, is out to recapture the magic and wonderment that great toy ideas bring to little kids. A former business magazine editor in New York and a partner in a successful overseas business directory start-up, Schwarz found himself bored. "I liked starting my own business," he says, "but after a while it just became a job. I didn't want that to happen to me."

So he didn't. With a $15,000 nest egg, the self-described "28-year-old kid" rolled up his sleeves and set out to create a different kind of toy company, one that did not rely on warmed-over products and half-baked promotional schemes. His toys tilt toward the unseemly and gross—just the ticket to his core audience of young boys. "Our top seller is Gus Gutz, a doll with a mouth so big that you can reach in and pull out his spleen, gall bladder and intestines," says Schwarz. "Young kids love it."

**Larry Schwarz, 28**

*Company:* **Rumpus Toys**
*Location:* **New York City**
*Year Started:* **1994**
*Start-up Costs:* **$15,000**
*1998 Revenues:* **$1.5 million**
*1999 Projections:* **$5 million plus**

Schwarz can go the softer route, too. His "My Closet" doll is a friendly-looking purple beast that's designed to scare away an imaginative youngster's closet intruders. Making toys with a purpose and not just a marketing gimmick is a point of pride with Schwarz, and all his toys bear his original stamp. "I have a lot of respect for Mattel and Hasbro," says Schwarz. "They gave us the classic toys we grew up with. But what they forget now is that Mr. Potato Head wasn't a movie tie-in. Neither was Barbie or Candyland. I think that's what separates us from those companies. We're about fun—not just profit margins."

Every time Schwarz looks out his downtown Manhattan window, he's reminded of the uphill climb facing him. Right across the street sits Hasbro Inc., with its requisite deep pockets, focus groups and big-time marketing divisions. "We are in a monopoly business, but I think that can change," explains Schwarz. "I think by offering something different we can accelerate that change."

That's a wonderful story—and you can only hope it happens to you—but you'd be prudent to anticipate the opposite: Your tidy $12,000 budget can balloon in an eye-blink to $50,000. Be wary of hidden start-up costs, and overestimate what you will spend. For instance, building a new office or revamping an old one can be fraught with zoning laws and environmental rules. One small manufacturer managed to fund his dream start-up— an economical organic fertilizer company—but was derailed when local officials demanded that he include $150,000 worth of antipollutant protectors in his plan.

**3** **Who will fund my great idea?** Money is the opiate of the entrepreneurial masses. It fosters business owner's dreams and fuels a start-up's heady climb to the top. With it, you're in the game and in control. Without it, you're living in a one-room apartment on the seedy edge of town, living on Top Ramen and warm beer.

Well, maybe that's an exaggeration—the beer doesn't have to be warm—but you get my point. Capital is the most crucial element for the establishment, sustenance and ascendancy of a growing business. It's the lifeblood of your operation. Your strong will can keep you from giving up even in the darkest hours, but lack of money will ensure that the doors to your business will be closed and locked in the morning.

Fortunately, many young entrepreneurs can get away with hitting mom and dad up for a loan to buy some computer equipment or to lease some office space. Ted Waitt, the founder of Gateway 2000 Computers and star of his own TV commercials, started out of a farmhouse (hence the cow spots that grace his computer boxes) with a loan from his grandmother. However, if you do hit up Grandma for a loan, make it a point to pay her back as quickly as you would a banker. Maybe even quicker. Family ties are tight, but money has snapped the strings of many a familial relationship. In the event you do take a loan from a family member, a formal loan arrangement with contracts and lawyers involved is not just a luxury, it's a necessity.

Your other options for seed money are banks and venture capitalists—and whether you need a $30,000 bank loan for a small setup or you're hunting in the $250,000-and-up range, be prepared. Both a bank and a venture capitalist expect to see a detailed business plan, and they will review it with the meticulous eye of an IRS agent combing through a drug lord's tax return. "This is likely true for any venture capital firm or bank," says Bob Crowley, chief investment officer at the Boston-based venture capital firm Massachusetts Technology Development Firm (MTDF). "The business plan is a reflection of how committed someone is to an idea. I could spend all day chatting with an entrepreneur about an idea. But [the business plan] is a tool of self-selection because if someone doesn't want to sit down and hammer out a business plan, I don't want to talk to them. It is a reflection of the entrepreneur's commitment to the project."

What do funding sources like the MTDF look for in a business plan? Primarily, a knowledge of the business and whether there's a market for your product or service (for a more detailed description of how to write a business plan, see Chapter 5). "I really don't care how your product works," says Crowley. "I want to know what problems it solves."

4 **How will I know if I've made it?** No one will arrive to place a crown on your head, but you'll know in lots of little ways. Phone calls to suppliers will get returned—quickly. Phone calls to customers will be taken instead of screened. And phone calls

## Social Security: Safety Net Or Tangled Web?

**I**f Gen E's are starting their own businesses in record numbers, maybe it's because they know they'll never see a penny of their Social Security.

Since Social Security's inception in 1937, the rate that both employees and employers pay has grown faster than the number of long-distance phone company advertisements. In 1937, the Social Security tax was 1 percent of employee and employer wages. In current dollars, that's 1 percent paid on about the first $33,333 of a wage earner's pay. Today, the Social Security behemoth swallows 6.2 percent of employee and employer wages for a combined total of 12.4 percent. Plus, it's applied to the first $68,000 of a wage earner's pay.

The total growth rate for Social Security in the past 60-plus years? An incredible 520 percent—and few people under 30 believe there'll be anything left when they retire.

from the phone company looking for bill payments will stop altogether.

One sure-fire way to know that you've made it as an entrepreneur is when you stop studying the competition, and they start studying—and copying—you. That's what happened to Rick Klotz, 26, a skateboard fanatic disgusted with current board fashions (he found that he couldn't get into clubs with the duds he was skateboarding in). In 1990, he rolled out his own line of hip, streetwise clothes that were loose enough to skate in and cool enough to pass muster with the velvet-rope cognoscenti guarding L.A.'s hottest watering holes.

Klotz knew he'd officially made it when copies of his clothes began popping up in the clothing lines of major manufacturers like Gap and Levi-Strauss. Ironically, some of the fashion chains he used to make fun of were now coming out with their own Klotz-inspired versions of skate 'n' club wear. Achieving that level of success had a surprising result. "When they caught on," Klotz admits ruefully, "it just wasn't as fun anymore."

How do you know when you've really made it? When you're sued by a Fortune 500 company. Consider the saga of nail polish start-up Urban Decay, which opened in Hollywood, California, with 29-year-old Wendy Zomnit at the helm. Soon, Nordstrom and Urban Outfitters were carrying Zomnit's guerrilla nail polish. Of course, colors like Trailer Trash and Jail Bait sold so well that Revlon soon weighed in with its own line of rogue polish like Gun Metal and Blood.

When Urban Decay wrote Revlon a letter alleging trademark infringement, the cosmetic giant fired back with a missive of its own saying it would go to court to get Urban Decay to drop its trademark. What happened? After some huffing and puffing between legal types, the companies wound up settling the case—Revlon paid off Urban Decay to drop its suit, and Urban Decay retained its trademark.

Hey, it doesn't get any uglier than nail polish wars!

# Chapter

Inspirations, dreams and ideas are to the entrepreneur what a blank canvas was to Da Vinci or the hint of a melody to Beethoven.

# My Niche (And Welcome To It)

Gen E is refashioning the business world through entrepreneurship, and it is doing so by tapping its own interests and culture, adapting the fads, trends and pastimes that it loves into some wildly profitable commercial ventures. It's following its own notions of what sells and what doesn't—and more important, what's fun to sell and what isn't.

# The Power Of Ideas

Now that you've decided that you're ready, willing and eager to join the ranks of Gen E business owners, what is your business going to be? Thomas Edison didn't quite get the equation right when he said that success was "1 percent inspiration and 99 percent perspiration." Either the great inventor underestimated the power of ideas or he needed a stronger antiperspirant.

How could the inventor of the light bulb, the record player and hundreds of other gizmos and gadgets discount the power of the idea? Inspirations, dreams and ideas are to the entrepreneur what a blank canvas was to Da Vinci or the hint of a melody to Beethoven. How many times did Michelangelo stroll by the Sistine Chapel

## Polishing Your Image

Got a great idea and not sure how to promote it? Searching for financing and want to look your best? Impress people by dressing up your proposed product or service as stylishly and completely as possible. Presentation is crucial to your product's success. To dazzle people with your idea, try the following suggestions:

● Have an art student or a graphic designer draw your idea in action, especially if you don't have the product to show.

● Pull together some marketing data on your product. Include competing products, target customers, your competitive advantage, the projected retail price and market size on a single, easily scanned sheet.

● Tie in your product or service with a relevant Web site. If you sell car stereos, find a Buick-or Mustang-lover's Web site and cross-promote with them. Web advertising on smaller sites is not as pricey as you might think.

before he got the notion to beautify its legendary ceiling for the ages? How many seagulls and blue jays did Orville and Wilber Wright gaze at before realizing that they, too, could fly?

True, a great idea is nothing without an equally strong work ethic, but without that great idea, all the effort in the world won't create a viable, successful company. And luckily, as a young entrepreneur, you don't have to invent earth-shattering new technologies or unheard-of modes of transportation to start a business. Your task is simpler, if no less daunting: You need to identify a product or service that is needed by someone and that you can provide better than anyone else. In other words, you need to identify a market niche, whether that's capitalizing on an emerging demographic or cultural trend, discovering a new application for or an improved version of an existing product, or providing an important service for an as-yet-unserved population. As the great inventors demonstrate, inspiration is often waiting within the problems and needs of your daily life.

Once an idea creeps up on you—or hits you over the head like an iron skillet—then you have to follow through with the second half of Edison's equation. And if it's not 99 percent of the battle, it will still keep you reaching for the extra-dry roll-on as you struggle to turn your million-dollar idea into a tangible, living, breathing business with staffers, computers, office space—and profits.

## Doomsday Marketing

A good case in point: computer games. In 1991, three computer software developers from Shreveport, Louisiana, had an idea about a "game-play interface" technology that would soon rule the computer gaming industry, and they formed a small company. Their idea, called "first-person, texture-map style," was to create a computer game interface where the player sees the battlefield from a first-person perspective, as if he or she is the superhero fighting crime and bashing mutants in cyberspace. Looking out into a 3-D-rendered world chock-full of realism and depth, game players could become one with their computers, jumping, ducking and shooting at their software adversaries just as if they were on the same turf.

The software developers were John Carmack, 28; his brother, Adrian Carmack, 29; and John Romero, 28. The game they created was Doom. Today, it's one of the single highest-selling computer software games in the world.

In early 1990, Doom was only a germ of an idea as the trio toiled for a Shreveport software company called Softdisk. There, they spent long hours honing new software games called Gamers Edge and Hovertank One, both of which possessed the early 3-D elements of Doom. As they worked, they began discussing the possibility of developing first-person, texture-map-style software.

Word got around the gaming industry, and soon a Texas game developer offered John Carmack a chance to create his own software games using the revolutionary new technology. The developer would fund the venture and Carmack would create and develop the games. Ecstatic over the opportunity, Carmack enlisted his brother, Adrian, and Romero to launch Id Software in February 1991. Soon they were working out of Romero's house, punching code and living on pizza and Pepsi. "The early operations were simple, as everyone had their computers laid out all over the place," recalls John Carmack. Funding was scarce, but that didn't deter the group; they knew all they needed were a few good personal computers and some free time.

"We all worked in the computer industry at the time and everyone had a PC of their own," says Romero. "Just pick 'em up and move them all into the same room, and you're a start-up."

The group was determined to build only the kind of games they themselves wanted to play—intense, graphic fights to the death set in their favorite horror and sci-fi worlds. They soon developed several prototypes, which they critiqued and praised and pulled apart depending on how much fun they were to play. The trio gave their efforts to family and friends for testing, and they used the resulting advice to help fine-tune the game-play. A few months later, the historical predecessor to Doom, Commander Keen: Aliens Ate My Babysitter, rolled out. It was the industry's first 3-D "shooter," and technology-wise, there was no looking back.

But marketing the game was a different story altogether. Id Software decided to try an interesting marketing ploy to sell Commander Keen: The company put a portion of the game on the Internet as shareware and let people download it for free. If people liked the game, they could contact Id Software (using information provided with the sample) to buy the complete version. Id's management team bet that, once players experienced it, they would go bonkers over the new technology, and that the resultant word-of-mouth buzz from Internet users would spill over to the general public and sell the game. Sure enough, Internet chat rooms lit up.

The Id designers followed Commander Keen with Wolfenstein 3-D. As soon as partial, shareware versions of the game hit the Internet, Id Software was inundated with orders. In its first year, more than a million copies of the immensely popular Wolfenstein were distributed through shareware marketing and more than 250,000 copies of the game were purchased by computer game fans.

## Don't Be A Contrarian—Ask A Librarian

When you're starting a new business, you have dozens and dozens of questions that need answers. If you've never had to define a market or determine the growth potential of an industry, such tasks can seem daunting. Luckily, the answers to these and hundreds of other questions are right around the corner . . . at your public library.

Ask to speak with a reference librarian, who can point out resources and show you how to research the information you need. To get the most from your librarian, keep these points in mind:

1 **The more specific the question, the better the answer.** Don't ask for "any information on Japan." That's too general. Instead, do you want "Japanese import data for household gifts and accessories"? Or "help from the government for entrepreneurs wanting to do business in Japan"? Narrowing your questions saves time and yields more useful results.

2 **Get oriented.** Take time to locate the library's business, government and general reference materials.

3 **Learn basic research techniques.** Ask if handouts are available on how to use the library's online catalog. Request a tutoring session (usually free). Learn how to conduct specialized searches of the library's databases and use Internet search engines more efficiently. Some library tours offer this information.

In no time, you'll become a crack researcher, gathering the vital information you need with ease.. The public library is an invaluable resource you'll turn to again and again as your business grows.

"We knew before we launched that we had a good product because we are game players," explains John Carmack. "But never did we realize the monumental success these games would reach. If you had told us that Wolfenstein would be the most-installed software of that period, I would have laughed at you."

On December 10, 1993, Doom finally hit the cybermarket. Id used the same shareware strategy that had proven so successful, and in two short years, 15 million shareware copies of the game had been downloaded and more than 150,000 Doom fanatics were officially registered with company; to date, more than 8 million copies of Doom have been sold. Doom was named "Game of the Year" by a host of industry and national publications, including *PC Magazine* and *Computer Gaming World*. Capitalizing on its newfound success, Id Software launched an 800-number to attract more fans and easier sales. Doom II soon rolled out and was an instant hit, selling more than 1.2 million copies within a year, the second bestselling computer game in history after Mortal Kombat. In 1996, Id unleashed Quake, the most highly anticipated game since Doom. Quake marked a quantum leap in game technology and set a new standard in multiplayer, true 3-D, combat action games.

Today, Romero has left the company, and the two Carmacks remain in Mesquite, Texas, at the helm of Id Software. Named after Freud's term for the instinctual part of the human psyche, Id Software is viewed by many computer game aficionados as the coolest game maker on earth. Their ultraviolent, visceral creations have become a cultural phenomenon, spawning an entire genre of copycat titles—though

## About Face

**T**he face of labor continues to change. According to the *Kiplinger Washington Newsletter*, by 2020 one-third of those joining the U.S. work force will be minorities. Not only that, but the male-female ratio will finally reach 50-50 as more women opt for the career ladder. This means your competition will be more diverse than ever, and thus your business landscape as competitive as ever in a new global economy. Ideas will become commodities, and places to look for ideas will come from many different places. So plug into the Rainbow Workplace and find out what people of all colors and nationalities are tuning into. Who knows? Your next great business idea may just as easily lead you to Bombay as to Boston.

none have surpassed the original. Doom's popularity has led to contracts for books and a "Doom" movie, which is slated to hit theaters in the year 2000, and Id's games have been featured on prime-time TV shows, such as "Friends" and "ER," and in movies like "The Net," "Congo" and "Grosse Pointe Blank."

By 1998, company revenues were soaring north of $200 million, with a plethora of (what the Carmack brothers like to say) "Ferraris, Ferraris, Ferraris" in the company parking lot. Id Software also continued its innovative marketing program with some creative new community outreach programs, such as "Quakecon '99," which was held in May 1998. With this event, the Carmacks took the computer trade show idea and shook it by its Oxford lapels. For Quakecon '99, Id invited hundreds of their dedicated fans to come together and participate in gaming workshops, where players could discuss gaming topics and issues with the Id Software team. It became the largest gathering of gaming fans in the world.

"From game design and programming to the art sketching and Id Software business issues, we offered an open-ended workshop presenting rare opportunities to gain insight into the team behind the phenomenon," says John Carmack.

The Id crew has received a bushel of awards as well. *Computer Gaming World* inducted both Wolfenstein 3-D and Doom into their Hall of Fame, recognizing these titles as among those that set the standard for excellence in the gaming industry. *PC Magazine* listed Id Software as number 30 out of the "100 Most Influential Companies of 1997," and Id was included in *Red Herring* magazine's 1997 list of the "Top 100 Companies in the Digital Universe." High praise indeed for a company born out of a simple idea—that young consumers would go wild over first-person perspective, 3-D-style computer games based on their favorite sci-fi and horror movies.

## Cleaning Up On Dirty Laundry

In the parlance of Hollywood types, computer games are "sexy." But what's wrong with reinventing an everyday product? Some people looking to start their own businesses find inspiration in movie theaters; others head to their local Laundromat.

Take Marc Hodosh, 26. As a college student at Boston University, he couldn't help but notice that nearly every one of his fellow undergraduates had some kind of backpack slung over their shoulders when trudging around town. In 1992, recognizing the "eye appeal" of the ubiquitous backpack, Hodosh extended the idea and designed a similar-looking multipurpose laundry bag. Hodosh founded ChecMarc Inc., and soon Harvard Yard and other Boston-area campus locales were dotted with students toting his new creation, called "Hoosh by Hodosh," over their shoulders.

Hodosh bet that a good, useful product could become a great one by emphasizing style and eye-pleasing design. Once his brainstorm caught on, his new bags could be found at college bookstores all over town. Recently, Hodosh branched out with a hip new soft-sided cooler for the younger crowd, and it, too, has sold well. So well, in fact, that Hodosh recently sold the cooler line to a deep-pocketed investor for big bucks.

# Let Your Fingers Do The Walking

When it comes to getting business ideas—or to investigating the viability of a sudden brainstorm—you are not on your own. There's a wealth of information available to young entrepreneurs looking to research a product, industry or consumer trend. Your local newspaper is a treasure trove of topics on local business issues, from tax climate to real estate opportunities. Publications geared specifically toward young businesses, like *Entrepreneur's Business Start-ups* magazine, can offer you a clearer glimpse of what it's like to develop and run a new business. The Internet is also a great resource for research. Leading newspapers like *The Washington Post*, *The New York Times*, *The Wall Street Journal* and *USA Today* all offer rich databases of articles covering a wide variety of topics from the last 10 years or more. Corporations like Dun & Bradstreet (through its "Power Tools" Web site at www.dun&bradstreet.com) offers access to a vast database of small-business topics targeted to entrepreneurs. And the U.S. government (primarily through the Small Business Administration's Web site at www.sba.com) offers funding tips and business planning ideas for entrepreneurs. You also can't miss with *Entrepreneur* magazine's Web site, Entrepreneurmag.com, and its search engine, Smallbizsearch.com.

While it's important to know where to look for information, you also have to know what to look for. Check for emerging trends,

# 10 questions

*Name:* Paul Frank
*Age:* 31
*Company:* Paul Frank Industries, fashions, furniture and accessories for the "in" crowd
*Location:* New York City
*Year Founded:* 1995
*Start-up Costs:* $7,000
*1998 Sales:* $1.4 million
*1999 Projections:* $3.5 million

**1. What was your first entrepreneurial venture?**
Sewing wallets for friends

**2. At what age did you start it?**
26

**3. What did you learn from the experience?**
That people value unique items in a "cookie cutter" world

**4. What age were you when you made your first million?**
31

**5. What was your first job (as an employee)?**
Graphic designer/silkscreener

**6. Did you get a college degree?**
Yes, in fine arts

**7. What age were you when you started your current business?**
27

**8. Who is your role model?**
[Postwar furniture and houseware designers] Charles and Ray Eames. They showed that good design embraces both style and function and that these things can easily be found in everyday objects.

**9. How many businesses have you started?**
One

**10. How many were successful, and how many failed?**
One succeeded, and none failed.

both commercial and cultural, that will give your new business a competitive edge. For instance, Dun & Bradstreet's Web site encourages young entrepreneurs to examine the "double wage earner" trend. In today's hypercrazy society, many families with both spouses working aren't able to perform all the domestic tasks they could a generation ago. Picking up the laundry, walking the

## School Rules

Learning on the job is great, but learning your way out of one isn't. If you're not sure how to hire and manage employees, keep financial records, write a contract, market and distribute a product or open a franchise, don't assume you'll figure it out on your own in time to keep your business afloat.

One way to prepare for running your own business is to work at it for 50 years. Another is to take some classes on entrepreneurship. Day and night classes at schools, continuing education centers and colleges and universities can help you learn the ropes of learning the ropes.

Class prices range anywhere from $20 for a one-time weekend or evening class to $1,200 for a four-week seminar on starting a business. Interested? Call one (or more) of the entrepreneur training organizations listed below. Or call one of your local colleges or universities for a course catalog.

- **Institute of Entrepreneurship at Muhlenberg College:** For course information from this college in Allentown, Pennsylvania, call (610) 821-3285.
- **Follmer Rudzewicz & Co:** This Detroit-based accounting firm offers an Organizational Development and Training Consulting service. For details, call (810) 254-1040.
- **Premier Fast Trac:** Based in Denver, this company offers classes nationwide. For information, call (800) 689-1740.
- **The Edward Lowe Foundation:** This Cassopolis, Michigan-based organization provides business information and educational seminars across the country. Call (800) 357-LOWE or visit their Web site at www.lowe.org.
- **PricewaterhouseCoopers LLP:** The "Big Five" consulting company offers classes nationwide through its Entrepreneurial Serivices/Middle Market Group. To find a location near you, call (216) 687-4307.

dog, or shopping for groceries are chores that often don't get done until the last minute, if at all. Traditional businesses geared toward these basic needs—like house-cleaning services, day-care providers, and gift purchase and delivery services—no longer provide all the services harried consumers want these days. Many savvy entrepreneurs are poised to fill those gaps.

The "service gap" doesn't exist only on the retail level. Corporations, many of which have pink-slipped countless employees, are farming out jobs that used to be done by in-house staffers to outside vendors, consultants or freelancers. In business terminology, it's called outsourcing. The trick is finding out what specific companies are looking for in terms of outsourcing help and then building a business around filling that need. Some places to start looking are copywriting services, paralegal services, billing and accounting services, graphics design work and public relations. Helpful tip: Many businesses advertise these needs on their Web sites, under the "jobs open" category. Send the company a letter as a business owner who can handle the task at hand and not as a candidate for a full-time job. Chances are, you'll get a chance to talk to a higher-up about what your company can do.

Other potentially overlooked market niches: baby boomers entering their 50s and honing in on their retirements. They will be looking for cool vacations, golf course communities and tools and gadgets to occupy their suddenly open schedules. Businesses offering socially conscious vacations—like trips to the Amazon rain forest or to pristine Alaskan harbors and bays that are fighting commercial development—could take advantage of an aging boomer's wanderlust. And don't forget the boomer's grandkids: After a "baby lull" in the 1980s and early 1990s, the kids of boomers are having kids at significantly higher rates than their moms and dads. That means an expanded market for kiddywear and toys, among other products.

> The **founder** of Federal Express **built** his empire on the **notion** that someone, **somewhere**, wanted a package delivered **overnight**.

Remember, the founder of Federal Express, Fred Smith, built his empire on the notion that someone, somewhere, wanted a package delivered overnight—and he decided to step in to fill the void.

> "People used to **laugh** at the idea of a company that built **skateboards**. Nobody's laughing **now**."
>
> —Steve Lake

Photo © Amy Cantrell

# Chairmen Of The Board Dude

**T**aking the skateboard path less traveled was what propelled Dave Klimkiewicz, Dennis Telfer and Steve Lake—all skateboarders themselves—into the entrepreneurial big time.

**Dave Klimkiewicz, 29**
**Dennis Telfer, 31**
**Steve Lake, 28**

*Company:* **Sector 9 Inc.**
*Location:* **San Diego**
*Year Started:* **1993**
*Start-up Costs:* **$30,000**
*1998 Revenues:* **$4 million**
*1999 Projections:* **$5 million**

"It was something that was really different," says Telfer. "It" was the skateboard they manufactured, which was reminiscent of the longboards of the 1970s and unlike today's shortened boards. Despite being dismissed by other manufacturers and retailers, the trio persevered and created their own demand.

"A lot of companies are jumping on the bandwagon now," says Telfer. "Our style of riding has opened a totally new niche in the industry."

Sector 9 is riding a crest in skateboarding popularity to unbridled success. The sport's evolution dates back to the 1950s. That's when idle surfers discovered they could re-create the sensation of riding a wave if they broke the push bar off a scooter and zigzagged down steep hills. "We're just helping resurrect a great sport," says Lake.

The company is also benefiting from an industry transformation from skateboard parks to more freestyle street skating, which aficionados say benefits from the bigger, wider boards that Sector 9 makes. The new wave is particularly appealing to surfers, Lake says. "Anyone who jumps on one of our boards can feel the relation between surfing and skating. A lot of our boards are sold in surf shops, and we advertise in surf magazines."

Although they may look like visionaries now, the founders of Sector 9 freely admit to humble beginnings, having produced the company's first skateboards in Telfer's backyard. The three entrepreneurs were sustained by a strong belief that there was indeed a market for the less trick-oriented longboards, and now, well, they're on a roll. Sector 9 boards are sold worldwide.

"It's pretty crazy," says Telfer, an ardent skateboarder who oversees board designs. "As stressed as I am, though, I always love it."

SECTOR NINE

Today, FedEx is a multibillion company with enough global brand-name recognition to make a Hollywood publicist green with envy. Now that's filling a gap.

# Giving Your Idea Flight

As any young entrepreneur can attest, developing and researching an idea is one thing. Putting it into play is another.

To create a viable business, you must be able to answer three critical questions about your business concept:

● What consumer need does your product or service fulfill?

● What type of business must you create to best satisfy that need?

● What separates your business from the competition?

Developing your answers to these questions before you start your business is prudent and wise, though it's true that many entrepreneurs prefer to sell first and ask questions later. Either way, it's a "learn as you go" process: You will need to revise your answers and shift strategies regularly as the business and cultural environment changes and as you discover firsthand what works and what doesn't. In business consultant Jan Norman's recent book on entrepreneurship, *What No One Ever Tells You About Starting Your Own Business* (Upstart Publishing), the author offers some lessons on how to take your great idea to the next level.

**1** **Don't sell what you want ... sell what your customers want.** By asking questions of prospective customers, young entrepreneurs can focus directly on what products and services sell well. You may be eager to sell only skateboards, but if your customer base is more interested in skateboard fashions or lessons, you'll be out of luck. One cheap way to find out what your customers are thinking is by offering a toll-free number for customer feedback. From the phone buzz, you should be able to figure out what product or service callers are looking for. Advertise your toll-free number in magazines, newspapers or Web sites geared to your target audience. For example, a company that makes gourmet crockpots would likely advertise its number in the food section of the local Sunday newspaper. Another idea is to invade Internet chat rooms devoted to the product you're trying to sell and see what problems or needs people are expressing (though actually touting your product is considered rude). Ask people whether they see a market for your product, or if they know of an unmet challenge that your product or service could satisfy.

**2** **Get your idea (and your business) down on paper.** Don't try to keep all your vital business data inside your head. Write it down in a business plan or at least keep notes in a computer file or legal pad (and store it in a safe place). Potential investors will want to see a business plan anyway, and by writing out your idea, you will have a clearer and more organized view of your new business. (Turn to Chapter 5 for specifics on how to write a business plan.)

**3** **Focus on what you love to do.** Spreading a new business too thin is often the death knell of a young start-up. If you are in the luxury automobile maintenance and repair business, then you are in the luxury automobile maintenance and repair business. Don't also try to take on every possible make of car as well as repairing yachts and small aircraft. If your business grows to the point where you can branch out, then research those other businesses as diligently as you did your main one.

**4** **Ask a lot of questions.** Many would-be entrepreneurs risk failure by their reluctance to ask questions. Entrepreneurs by nature are independent, especially younger ones, and thus are afraid to expose their potential "ignorance" by querying vendors, suppliers, mentors and friends and family. As Norman writes, it's OK not to know all the answers; just know what questions to ask. One great way to get advice is by developing a relationship with a mentor, that is, someone older and more experienced, who knows your business and the road you'll be traveling. After all, why do things the hard way? Mentors can point out potential obstacles and how you might overcome them. Most people are only too happy to share their insights and experiences.

**5** **Go back to school.** Studies show that when businesses run by young entrepreneurs fail, it is often because the owners didn't know how to bring their product or service to market. Lack of preparation and an inability to deal with unexpected problems are the most frequent causes. Don't let this happen to your great idea. Go to schools, classes, seminars and other training forums to bone up on the financial, marketing, production and employee relations end of running a business. Not only will you receive valuable instruction and get a sense of progress toward your goal, but you will also meet plenty of like-minded people with whom you can network as you launch your business.

When it comes to furthering your education, don't ignore corporate America, either. A growing number of businesses today are creating special classes and training programs aimed at the high-school-and-up crowd. For the businesses, the benefits are twofold: They provide a service to the community, and they also help train their own future work force, hoping that some of the teenagers will return to work for the company with that much more seasoning under their belts. Hartford, Connecticut-based Aetna Corp. has instituted a highly successful mini-MBA program for local high school students that takes place for eight weeks every summer. For the first two weeks, students ages 16 to 18 study *The Wall Street Journal*, take a field trip to the New York Stock Exchange, and learn how to open their own savings and checking accounts. During the rest of the program, students are put to work in small businesses where they use their newfound knowledge. This program, and others like it, gives young achievers a sense of empowerment and plants the seeds of entrepreneurship.

**6** **Live below your means.** When formulating the financial end of your business plan, always assume the worst. Overestimate production and marketing costs, employee salaries and so on, and then underestimate what will be left for your own salary. Without a realistic budget, your fledgling business won't grow at the rate you want—or need. Besides, aiming for and meeting higher earnings goals will give you a greater sense of satisfaction and keep your company in good fiscal shape.

**7** **Remember, cash flow is king.** Wherever you get the money for your initial investment—whether it's a loan from relatives, funding from a venture capitalist or a line of credit from a local bank—you must keep the cash spigot flowing. This is possibly the single most important component of running your enterprise. Vendors may act like your friend, but they'll turn on you like a sand viper if you're slow in paying your bills. And just try to regain the trust of your employees if you miss a single pay day. Some tips: Keep an eye on costs—squeezing a dollar here on travel budgets and five there on advertising will add up and keep more money in house. Also, cut deals whenever possible. With building landlords, reduce lease costs by offering to stay an extra two or three years. Chances are, they'll take the deal if you're a good tenant just to keep their own cash-flow spigot running uninterrupted.

So genuflect at the altar of the almighty dollar and never lose sight of the fact that when cash flows, business grows. And when cash slows, business . . . well, you know.

**8** **Take your product to market, to market.** The bankruptcy courts are full of great ideas that spawned great products but that were marketed ineffectively and so withered on the vine. Who are the people most likely to buy your service or product and where are they? Your answer to this question will tell you whether you need to open a storefront (and where it should be) or whether you should sell by direct marketing or whether you should use a distribution network—or whether you need a combination of channels. A good marketing plan isolates these distribution channels both demographically and geographically and helps pave the way for solid business growth.

**9** **Get the word out.** One key component of marketing is advertising, whether that means slipping fliers under car windshields or taking out a million-dollar ad during the Super Bowl (you can dare to dream). Since most young business owners lack the cash flow to saturate the media with lots of flashy ads, you must make up for it with creativity and ingenuity. Don't blow your entire advertising budget on a month's worth of newspaper ads and then sit back waiting for the business to roll in. Instead, become an active and valued member of your local chamber of commerce; in return, you'll get a lot of free word-of-mouth publicity, and you'll make some great business contacts. Offer to speak as an industry expert to the local press. Make sure reporters have your name in their Rolodexes. Teach a continuing education class on your field or offer to speak in front of civic groups (many of which can be found in your local newspaper). Or join a local small-business association and make yourself visible.

**10** **Don't go it alone.** The business is your baby, but as Hillary Rodham Clinton says, it takes a village to raise a child. Instead of spending all of your time answering phones and filing papers, hire an administrative assistant to do it for you, even if only for a few hours a week. That will free you up to concentrate on the big picture. Starting your own business can be a lonely ordeal, with you acting as CEO, secretary, treasurer, computer guru and marketing director all at once. Face facts: You're going to need a lot of support when you try to launch your own operation. So don't hesitate—delegate.

Above all else, don't fear failure—it happens to most business owners at one time or another. For instance, if you join your local chamber of commerce or a small-business trade group, you will begin to realize that even for the most successful entrepreneurs, the road is rarely smooth or trouble-free. Says Danielle Kennedy, nationally recognized motivational speaker and author of *Seven Figure Selling* (Berkeley Publishing Group), "You'll be amazed how many times business owners have to fail to grow. Sharing those stories gives us courage to continue to try and grow."

# Chapter

**5**

Taking the time to plan a business might mean the difference between a DOA enterprise and one that sails out of the gate.

# Get With The Plan

"**H**ey, I want my company's success dependent on my ability to run it," says Scott Korn, the 35-year-old president and founder of York Paper in Conshohocken, Pennsylvania. "Sure, you want to surround yourself with good people. But in the end, I want to make the decisions."

Korn's "take no prisoners" approach is echoed by many young entrepreneurs, and it has served York Paper—and its work force—well. The firm, which manufactures paper supplies for companies worldwide, made $70 million in 1998 alone, just nine years after opening its doors. How do entrepreneurs like Korn take a great idea and then fund it, produce it, market it and distribute it so successfully?

"Hell, if had an answer for that I'd bottle it myself," says Korn. "But the main thing is I was there every step of the way, making sure the company was run the way I wanted it to be run. That means hiring the right people, making the right decisions and taking some risks. That's the only way to get ahead."

While every business' success story is as individual as its owner, there are in fact some tried-and-true methods for getting off to a good start, though none of them come easy. First you write a business plan, then you dig like a crazed buccaneer for funding, snag office space, hire staff, develop and implement a marketing plan, and, finally, hustle your products to shipping docks and/or store shelves on time and under budget. That's a tall order even for seasoned 50-year-old executives with graduate degrees in management from Harvard University. But it can be done, even by someone half their age and with a fraction of their experience. After all, Scott Korn was only 26 when he parlayed his a germ of an idea into a viable business, which quickly became a powerhouse company with millions in annual revenues.

# Planning For The Future

Perhaps it's human nature. We'd much rather be doing than thinking. And entrepreneurs may be the worst: We're impatient to see the finished product gleaming in our hands—not to mention the gold ducats we've earned from the sale of said item. Thinking and planning is just so, well . . . boring. Never mind that taking the time to plan all the major aspects of a proposed business might mean the difference between a DOA enterprise and one that sails out of the gate: If business plans weren't so necessary for funding, we might never write them at all.

Indeed, a good business plan is an extremely useful financial tool, especially for Gen E business owners. Unfortunately, when young entrepreneurs walk into a bank with their hands out, most bankers brush them off as contemptuously as if they were removing bubble gum from their Bruno Maglis. A solid business plan, presented clearly and confidently, can help turn the tide and get you the money you need to launch and/or grow your business. Show the bank in detail where your business is headed, both in the long and short term, and lenders will feel more confident about giving you financing. In addition, demonstrating to your bank that you have included good, sound accounting practices in your business plan will only help your chances.

Here are the top three reasons why you should go to the trouble of writing a business plan:

1 Preparing a business plan forces you to take an objective, critical, unemotional look at your business concept and whether all the aspects of your idea are working together.

2 The finished product, the plan itself, is an operating tool that, if properly used, will help you manage your business effectively on a daily basis.

3 The completed business plan communicates your ideas to others and provides the basis for your financing proposal.

Don't kid yourself. Going into business is risky—more than half of all new businesses fail within the first three years, and a major reason is lack of planning. The importance of a business plan cannot be overemphasized. A good one helps pinpoint needs you might otherwise overlook, like an unrealistic marketing budget or an insufficient target market. It can help you spot unseen opportunities early so you can take advantage of them right off the bat, or it can identify problems when they're small, allowing you time to solve them before they become big and deadly. And after your business is underway and there's no time to think about anything but the next 10 minutes, an objective, comprehensive business plan allows you to track your progress and identify areas where your company is sagging and where it's robust.

"I'm more of a creative person, but you've got to identify your company's business needs or you're not going anywhere, no matter how much of a creative genius you are," advises Cristina Bornstein, one half of Tony & Tina Vibrational Remedies, a New York City cosmetics company. If you're all thumbs when it comes to the business end of business, the 31-year-old Bornstein recommends getting somebody to help you write your business plan. "Your self-esteem isn't going to suffer—because you can't do everything."

Finally, developing a business plan can help you avoid plunging into a venture that is doomed to fail. If your proposed business is marginal at best, the business plan will show you why and may help you avoid paying the high tuition of a degree in Business Failure. Weigh the cost of a few hours of concentrated thinking against the cost of an ill-fated business venture, and you'll see that a business plan is the cheapest insurance policy against the follies of impatience.

## Anatomy Of A Business Plan

This is what they call the nuts and bolts: for some, not very exciting, but like public television, it's good for you, dammit. A business plan should describe in detail your company's goals, the strategies you'll use to meet them, potential problems and how you'll solve them, the organizational structure of your business and the amount of capital you'll need to finance it. A good business plan should cover the first three to five years of your company's existence, and it should be freely tweaked and modified as you progress. Remember, your business plan is not necessarily etched in stone. If a good market opportunity arises in year three or year five, rewrite your business plan to accommodate funding for your new venture.

Most business plans include seven basic elements:

**1** **Executive summary:** Although this is the last part you should write, the executive summary is the first part the reader sees. Make sure it clearly states the nature of your business and—if you're seeking capital—the type of financing you want.

The executive summary describes your business—its legal structure (sole proprietorship, partnership or corporation), the amount and purpose of the requested loan, repayment schedule, the borrower's equity share, and the debt-to-equity ratio after the loan, security or collateral is offered. You should also list the market value and estimated value or price quotes for any equipment you plan to purchase with the loan proceeds. The summary should be short and businesslike—a half page to a page.

**2** **Business description:** This section gives the reader a more detailed description of your business concept: what and to whom you're selling. Specify your industry. Is it wholesale or retail, food service, manufacturing or service-oriented? Describe your product or service, emphasizing any unique features that set it apart. Explain your target market, how the product or service will be distributed and your support systems— advertising, promotions and customer service strategies.

If you're seeking financing, explain why the money will make your business more profitable. Will you use it to expand, to create a new product or to buy new equipment?

**3** **Marketing strategies:** Define your market's size, structure, growth prospects, trends and sales potential. Document how and from what sources you compiled your information. Then present the strategies you'll use to fulfill your sales objectives:

- **Price:** Explain your pricing strategy and how it will affect the success of your product or service.

- **Distribution:** This includes the complete process of getting your product to the end user.

- **Sales:** Explain elements like sales presentations and lead generation.

**4** **Competitive analysis:** Detail your competitors' strengths and weaknesses, the strategies that give you an advantage and any particular weaknesses in your competition that you can exploit.

**5** **Design and development plans:** If your product is already developed, you can skip this section. But if all you have so far is an idea, or if you plan to improve a product or service, this section is essential. The design portion describes your product's design and materials, and it provides diagrams. The development portion generally covers three areas—product, market and organizational development. If you plan to offer a service, describe only these last two items and don't worry about the design or product.

**6** **Operations and management plans:** Here you explain how your business will function on a daily basis. You describe the responsibilities of the management team, the tasks assigned to each department (if this is applicable) and the capital required. Go over key management personnel and their qualifications and explain what support personnel will be needed.

**7** **Financial factors:** You knew it was coming—this is the math part, where you present your financial statements, including the following:

- An income statement details your business's cash-generation capabilities. It projects things like revenue, expenses, capital (in the form of depreciation) and cost of goods. Develop a monthly income statement for the business's first year, quarterly statements for the second year and annual statements for each year thereafter for the term indicated in your business plan.

- A cash flow statement details the amount of money going into and coming out of your business—monthly for the first year and quarterly for each year thereafter specified in the plan. The result is a profit or loss at the end of each period. Both profits and losses carry over to the next column to show a cumulative amount. If your cash flow statement shows you consistently operating at a loss, you probably need additional cash to meet expenses.

- A balance sheet showing the business's assets, liabilities and equity over the period specified.

# Brother, Can You Spare $100,000?

With your well-written, detailed business plan in hand, you're ready to scour the countryside in search of financing. If you're one of the lucky few who doesn't need outside money, then you can proceed immediately to the next stage: writing a marketing plan. For a one-person shop, you might simply raid your bank account or credit card for $2,500 in start-up money—enough for a new computer, some letterhead and a coffee maker. However, no matter what your current financial situation, there usually comes a time when a business is ready to expand beyond an entrepreneur's ability to fund it, and so you must go calling: to the bank, to family, to venture capitalists and to anybody else with a spare $500,000 burning a hole in their savings account.

There are no hard-and-fast rules. Consider 30-year-old Andrew Ive, co-founder of X-IT Products LLC, a home safety equipment firm in San Francisco. Ive and his fellow founder, Kevin Dodge, 28, developed an idea for an emergency safety ladder, but they decided to bypass the venture capital route to get their company off the ground. Instead they sold 30 percent of the company to individual investors—a group of professors at Harvard University whom Ive knew from his days at Harvard Business School. The professors believed in Ives and his product and encouraged the young founders, with their money, to go into business.

"Having a network is the most important thing in getting a business off the ground, financially," Ive says. "Having gone to business school and joining an alumni group was great, for example. So I talked to a couple of Harvard Business School professors who suggested that we go start a business and they would fund us. I thought they were nuts—it's not everyday that some Harvard professors come up to you and hand you $300,000 and tell you to start a new business."

Before they entered into a financial agreement, however, Ive decided to first demonstrate his emergency safety ladder to retail giants like Kmart and Sears. When they responded favorably, Ive knew he had a viable product—and that he'd need money fast to fill the large orders they had requested.

"So we went back to the professors and told them we'd love to take their money," recalls

## Suggestion Box

A key building block of good marketing is promoting customer feedback. If you really want to know what your customers want, ask them. They'll tell you how to make them more satisfied, and they'll frequently give you good ideas. Turn compliments from your customers into marketing messages by creating testimonials that sing your praises. Encourage customer feedback by giving buyers several ways to reach you: a toll-free phone number, regular mail, e-mail and fax. Rather than just listing your phone number in your marketing materials, include a line that says something like "Call our toll-free number with your comments, concerns and ideas. We love hearing from you." It makes you look warmer, friendlier and more accessible. Those are the things that make people buy.

Ive. "When people offer [to invest in your company], it's very easy to say OK, but the relationship grows more complicated. You're flooded with questions for weeks on end—what do the investors get, what are our objectives, what's the marketing plans, that sort of thing."

PHOTO © WILL JONES

After a while, it became clear to Ive (far left) that the initially supportive professors were getting cold feet. "The questions stretched on for months. There came a point where we said to the investors that time was running out and there would be no more questions—only money. I told them [they needed] to make a decision, one way or the other. If they decided against us and said no, fine. If they said yes, great. If you've never raised financing for your own business before, you think sooner or later they will give you the money. But you really have to jolt them into making that decision. It took me a while to figure that out. They needed to be reassured and that takes time."

The investors finally came through, but the experience left its imprint on Ive. "Don't give investors three months to read a business plan," he advises. "Give them 24 hours, and don't give them too much time to reconsider. I had one investor sign an agreement that made him an investor. Six months later, he asked me what he had signed—he didn't even know. He just trusted me and knew the product was good. I preferred that. He was making decisive decisions based on the individuals involved."

Ive also offers some sage advice on how to use that money: "It's always possible and very easy to spend too much money," he says. "It's like having a bee in your bonnet about having the best computers or the best office furniture. You start to believe that you can't live without these things when you really can. Sooner or later, you take pride in budgeting and saving money. So we streamlined early on, and the first six months taught us to think cheap."

Four years and two rounds of financing later ($250,000 and $350,000, respectively), and X-IT was in business to the tune of $1 million in sales revenues for 1998.

## Advance To "Free Parking"

Where do you find the dough needed to fund your enterprise? The most obvious source is a bank. Banks don't always cotton to lending money to young entrepreneurs (although the wild success of Internet IPOs is starting to raise green-shaded eyebrows). If you don't have a financial track record, you may need a co-signer, like a parent or business mentor. Try smaller community banks before the big boys. They're plugged into the entrepreneurial spirit and will give you more face time to state your case than will the big behemoth bank downtown. Show them your business plan and your budget expectations. Wear a nice suit and be confident. The economy is on your side right now, and banks are looking to give money away. But not to just anybody.

Other sources of start-up cash aren't as hard to get as you might think. Here are a few avenues you can try if your banker takes a pass on your future Fortune 500 company:

**1** **Savings and family and friends:** The hard truth is, most people must tap their own funds to start a business. And if they can't do that, they go to Mom or Dad, their grandparents or even a close friend. According to a recent survey, three-fourths of start-ups got at least some capital from their owners' pockets; banks were the second most common source, but that included second mortgages and home equity credit; third were families. So, in other words, be nice at reunions, weddings and other family functions.

Other ideas for funding close to home include borrowing money from your 401(k) or equity from your own investments (real estate, stocks and bonds or collectibles—if you can bear to part with that mint-condition Batman action figure).

If you decide to go the family and friends route, make sure you pay back the money—if you want to remain friends, anyway. It's also a good idea to put everything in writing and to factor in some profit for whoever is lending you the money.

**2** **Credit cards:** Some entrepreneurs finance their businesses with that little piece of plastic called a credit card. This is fine, but it can cause lots of problems if you max out all your cards and can't manage to pay them back. The bottom line: If you use them, use them wisely.

**3** **Small Business Administration (SBA) loans:** The SBA has several loan programs for small businesses—from Microloans (ranging from less than $100 up to $25,000) to loans targeted to women and minorities. The largest is the 7(a) Loan Guaranty

Program, in which the SBA will guarantee up to $750,000 or 75 percent of the loan amount, whichever is less. The 7(a) program lent almost $9.4 billion to U.S. businesses in 1998.

Two misconceptions about SBA loan programs are that the federal government is the lender and that the lending criteria are more lax than for other commercial loans. In actuality, you are borrowing from a bank, and the SBA is merely guaranteeing a portion of the loan, promising the bank to pay back a certain percentage of the loan if you should default on it. You must still meet the lending institution's requirements for collateral, experience and the like. (Contact your local SBA office for a list of participating lenders in your area, or visit the SBA online at www.sbaonline.gov.)

**4 Business incubators:** Incubators are organizations sponsored by public and private investors that assist start-up and young

## Location, Location, Location

When, by hook or crook, you get the funds to feed and nourish that sugarshack business of yours, make sure you set up shop in the best spot possible. Sure, it's a truism for restaurants, but location can play a decisive role in the success or failure of any business. Always consider your customers: You need to be accessible to them, or they to you, and your office/shop should be attractive and inviting. Even if you launch your business from your garage, polish it up like your mother-in-law's coming to visit.

> Location can play a decisive role in the success or failure of any business.

Don't sell location short. Since opening in mid-1993, the owners of Restaurants on the Run, a food delivery service, have parlayed their initial $10,000 investment into a $6 million business.

You might think for a service business like food delivery, location wouldn't be so important, but co-owner Michael Caito says the key to their company's success was locating in an area with at least 250,000 people within a 15- to 20-minute drive. "Keeping food hot, getting the order complete and delivering on time still is our number-one priority," he says.

companies in their critical early days with a variety of business assistance programs. Incubators provide hands-on management assistance, access to financing, shared office services, access to equipment, flexible leases and more—all under one roof.

The time you can spend in an incubator is limited—typically two years, but it can vary. The idea is to get a fledgling business off the ground, then let it leave "the nest," making room for another start-up company.

"Most incubators offer some kind of financing assistance," says Susie McKinnon, director of member services at the National Business Incubation Association (NBIA). "This can range from hooking [entrepreneurs] up with a network of local investors to making loans from a seed fund that belongs to the incubator."

Incubators generally fall into the following categories: technological, industrial, mixed-use, empowerment and industry-specific. For a list of incubators in your state, visit the NBIA's Web site at www.nbia.org.

**5** **Online matching services:** The Internet has become a popular place for investors and entrepreneurs to hook up. One resource available on the Web is the Angel Capital Electronic Network (ACE-Net) at www.sba.gov/advo. Launched by the SBA, ACE-Net helps accredited investors find entrepreneurs in need of capital.

Investors can access ACE-Net's online listings of companies using a search engine that lets them find out about a business' product or service, financing desired and other criteria. Investors can also place search criteria on the network and get e-mailed whenever a company meeting those criteria appears on the network.

**6** **Speaking of angels:** Angels refer to anyone who invests his or her own money in an entrepreneurial company (unlike institutional venture capitalists, who invest other people's money). Angel investing has soared in recent years as a growing number of individuals seek better returns on their money than they can get from traditional investment avenues.

Angels are not millionaires—most earn between $60,000 and $100,000 a year. What does that mean? That there are likely to be many in your own backyard. Angels can be people you know (affiliated) or don't know (nonaffiliated)—at least not yet, anyway. Start your search for angels by seeking out professionals (your lawyer, doctor, dentist, accountant and so on), suppliers/vendors, customers, employees, indirect competitors and even other entrepreneurs.

If it's an affiliated entrepreneur, simply make an appointment—and make your pitch. If you're after a nonaffiliated angel, you can try advertising, networking or going through an intermediary.

**7** **Private placements:** With a strong business plan, Joe Kunkel attracted 12 private investors who put $570,000 into his business, Oak Park, Illinois-based Wholesome Kidfoods Inc., which makes WOWnies, a healthy snack. "We sent letters to at least 150 people we knew who could invest $25,000," Kunkel says. "We wanted investors who knew what they were doing." Kunkel culled his list of 150 people from a mixed list of venture capitalists, affluent business contacts and rich friends. Professionally prepared documents and Kunkel's consulting background helped sell the deal, he says. "We had to put in our own savings, too; that was part of our pitch. We also agreed not to draw a salary until the company made money."

**8** **Corporate partnering:** A start-up with new technology may be able to find a corporate partner or form a strategic alliance with a large, established company. Large corporations may offer money or access to a distribution network in exchange for licensing rights to new products.

Look for corporate partners that don't directly compete with you but are familiar with your technology. Both companies should have compatible objectives and corporate cultures.

# Marketing Your Way To Millions

Now we come to that other key to success—marketing. As with your business ideas, you need to set your marketing plans in writing. And if you approach your marketing plan with the same dedication and drive as Caryl Felicetta, you should have no trouble marketing your way to millions.

Felicetta used to joke with her friends that someday she'd become a big-time entrepreneur. "I was always a bit of an entrepreneur even in high school," says the 34-year-old owner of Argyle Studios, a creative services and marketing company in Metuchen, New Jersey. "I'd make jewelry and macramé items and sell them. My friends used to get a big kick out of it, but I knew what I was doing."

In 1986, fresh from a few freelance advertising assignments for local ad agencies, Felicetta got the nerve to open her own shop, which does a lot of marketing and promotional work using graphics and visual media. A close friend, Marion Reinson, came along for the ride. In a few short years the company had an admirable stable of clients. With Reinson running the business end and Felicetta driving the creative end, Argyle Studios became a million-dollar company.

But it was the duo's marketing prowess that really shined. In 1991, it became clear the company needed to put some new systems in place to achieve the ultimate growth they desired. They created a marketing plan dubbed The Living and Breathing Document, which Felicetta describes as "nothing a bank would ever want to see"— since it was light on the monetary numbers bean counters usually drool over, and they wouldn't know what to make of the rest of it.

However, it was nothing short of a battlefield blueprint for all the firm's marketing efforts and plans for growth. The Argyle marketing plan included client profiles as well as promotional strategies and tactics. In addition, it archived previous promotions that didn't produce the desired results, analyzed particularly successful programs

## Where Will I Get the Money, Honey?

**A**ccording to a recent survey in *Business Start-ups* magazine, business owners obtained at least a portion of their start-up funds from the following sources:

| Source | Percentage |
| --- | --- |
| Personal savings | 72% |
| Banks | 45% |
| Friends/relatives | 28% |
| Individual investors (not friends or relatives) | 10% |
| Government-guaranteed loans | 7% |
| Venture capital firms | 1% |

and projected future needs, such as training and new equipment.

According to Felicetta, the document's primary goal was to keep the partners focused on their core business values. "The landscape of our business has changed dramatically over the past year or so, as we began offering Web site development," Felicetta explains. "The marketing plan has helped us stay balanced rather than allow one segment or one client to become an overwhelming portion of our business."

> "The marketing **plan** has helped us stay **balanced** rather than allow one segment or one client to **become** an overwhelming portion of our **business**."

The company also aggressively promoted itself, with both women making hundreds of cold calls and setting up a shoestring advertising campaign. "We'd do some print ads and things and then spend most of our time managing the responses we'd get," recalls Felicetta. "That was the hard part."

Felicetta and Reinson review the plan annually—and it's a meeting they actually look forward to. First, they get together in an informal, relaxed setting to discuss the effectiveness of the plan and brainstorm ideas for the coming year. With no phones ringing and no clients demanding immediate attention, they focus on revisiting their goals. Then, in a more structured session a few days later, they rewrite the plan, fitting their analyses and new ideas into the existing document.

Felicetta estimates Argyle's business grew 100 percent the first year they instituted the marketing plan, and it has continued to grow at an astounding rate of 50 percent or more annually since then. The firm now has five employees and a pool of freelance talent.

Felicetta warns budding marketers not to get caught up in making their plans too formal, but rather to make sure the format is easy to use. "After reading about other companies and their plans, I've found the most successful were those that didn't try to be anyone else," says Felicetta. "What they sold was their philosophy, and people bought it. We really found ourselves when we realized that."

She also thinks that working in a bad company is great training for running your own business someday. "In my early days, I'd look at the way some people I worked for did business, and I'd make a mental note to remind myself never to do things that way. I have a long memory."

## Marketing Matchmaking

Before you begin writing your marketing plan, think about how you want to market your business. Most products and services depend on good marketing for their ultimate success. For instance, lighting fixtures are a necessity and, in a way, sell themselves, but why should someone buy yours? That is the crucial step in marketing—getting inside the head of consumers and figuring out what they want, what attracts them. How do you make your product or service seem not just useful or attractive but necessary and vital?

### For the Bookshelf

**T**here are plenty of valuable resources out there to help young entrepreneurs bone up on the facts of marketing and business plans. Here are just a few:

**For sample business plans:**
- *Business Plans Made Easy: It's Not as Hard as You Think* (Entrepreneur Press), by Mark Henricks

**For sample marketing plans:**
- *Knockout Marketing: Powerful Strategies to Punch Up Your Sales* (Entrepreneur Press), by Jack Ferreri

**For sample financial statements:**
- *Industry Norms and Key Business Ratios*, $450 for book or CD-ROM for service or nonservice industries; $135 for report or disk on a single industry. *Understanding Financial Statements*, a free booklet, is also available from Dun & Bradstreet. Contact them at 99 Church St., New York, NY 10007, (800) TRY-1DNB.

**For industry statistics (sales, salaries and other stats for businesses in your industry):**
- RMA Annual Statement Studies, $165 for disk; $119 for book on all industries. Contact: Robert Morris Associates at 1650 Market St., #2300, Philadelphia, PA 19103, (800) 677-7621.

**For budgeting advice:**
- *Budgeting for a Small Business* (Crisp Publications), by Terry Dickey
- *Financial Basics of Small Business Success* (Crisp Publications), by James O' Gill

Marketing your business isn't unlike pursuing a romantic interest and going out on a date. You want to be attractive; you want to
embody all the qualities that the other person desires. You'll put on
flattering clothes and make jokes to display your affection. Does
the other person like movies? What do you know, so do you! Does
he or she like climbing mountains, crossword puzzles, sleeping late
or jazz music? How fast can you get to Tower Records and buy
some John Coltrane?

It's an old refrain, but it's still true: Don't sell what you've got,
sell what they want. Like a young romantic, learn all you can about
your lover's likes, dislikes and expectations, and then do everything you can to embody what he or she most desires.

What does this mean in practice? First, identify the types of people you think will (or already do) make up your customer base; cat-
egorize them by age, sex, income/educational level and residence.
To start out, target only those customers who are most likely to purchase your product or service. In other words, if you're selling surf-
boards, stay out of Minneapolis. As your customer base expands,
you can consider modifying your marketing plan to include other
types of customers.

Here's a quick marketing exercise. Your marketing plan should
answer these questions (and don't peek at the answers because
there aren't any):

● Who are your customers? Define your target market(s).

● Are your markets growing? steady? declining?

● Is your market share growing? steady? declining?

● Are your markets large enough to expand?

● How will you attract, hold, increase your market share?

● What pricing strategy have you devised?

## The Price Is Right: Pricing And Sales

The price you charge for your product or service is actually a
marketing strategy. While you need to determine a base price to
cover your expenses, the final price is more the result of customer
perception and where you want to place yourself in the market relative to other companies. Get a feel for the pricing strategy of competitors in your market area and for the averages in your industry
nationwide. Then figure out how you want to be competitive:

Should you slightly underprice and pull customers with the idea that your product offers savings? Or should you slightly overprice, attracting customers with the claim that you offer higher quality?

# Get Yer Ya-Yas Out: Advertising And Public Relations

Much of your marketing plan comes down to advertising and promotion. How will you get the word out about your fabulous goods and services? Many business owners operate under the mistaken concept that a good business promotes itself, so they channel money that should be used for advertising and promotions to other areas of the business. However, advertising and promotions are the lifeline of a business and should be treated as such. Without them, most people won't know you have a business at all.

For small and emerging businesses, most advertising is of the shoestring variety. A limited budget, however, doesn't mean you have to sacrifice a good promotional campaign. Instead of plowing $10,000 into a TV ad campaign, spend half of that on a good public relations campaign that can get your company's name in industry trade publications. Many entrepreneurs offer their services as speakers at industry and business functions and appear on radio and TV talk shows as "industry experts." Tie your company to a well-known industry Web site and join your local chamber of commerce. All these ideas are either low-cost or no-cost and provide you with the opportunity to get your company's name out there.

If and when you do create a traditional ad campaign, remember one thing: Stay focused. Develop short, descriptive copy that clearly identifies your goods or services and your location and price. Use catchy phrases to arouse the interest of your readers, listeners or viewers. Remember, the more care and attention you devote to your marketing program, the more successful your business will be.

Finally, don't confuse advertising with public relations; they are distinctly different. With advertising, space or time in the mass media must be paid for. With public relations, coverage in the mass media, if any, is not paid for. With advertising, the content of your message and when it appears is determined by you. In public relations, interpretation of the message and the timing is in the hands of the media. Got it?

# Anatomy Of A Marketing Plan

The process of getting the product to the user and all the decisions made to facilitate this movement is called marketing. Simply put, marketing activities and strategies result in making products available that satisfy customers while making profits for the companies that offer those products. "Marketing" is an all-encompassing activity, in which the aim is to focus the various efforts of producing, pricing, promoting and placing the product in  people's hands—that is, those selected groups called target markets. A good marketing plan is comprised of a cornucopia of business outreach ideas, ranging from advertising to sales to public relations. A focus on what the customer wants is essential to successful marketing campaigns. This customer orientation must also be balanced with the company's objective of maintaining a profitable enough sales volume  for the company to continue to do business. There really is no time frame for completing and executing a marketing plan: Marketing is a creative, ever-changing orchestration of all the activities needed to promote your business.

## Who Are You?

Before you map out where you want your marketing plan to take you, analyze where you are now. If you've already started your business, how have you positioned it in the market? Is this how your customers see you? Ask some of them for feedback, either informally, approaching a few that you trust, or use a form customers can fill out themselves. At the top of your marketing plan, write four or five paragraphs that summarize your business, including its philosophy and its strengths and weaknesses. Be as objective as possible.

## Who Are Your Customers?

To market successfully, you need to define who you're selling to. If you say "everyone," you need to rethink your answer. Even the largest companies don't market blindly to every individual. They break their audiences down into distinct profiles, or niche markets, and create messages and vehicles designed to reach each segment.

Define your niche markets as clearly and specifically as possible. If you're reaching out to businesses, describe which type, including the industry, revenue level, location and other important

# The Little Budget That Could

Wait until I tell my friends I'm now dispensing budgeting advice—they'll chuckle while stashing more IOUs in my mailbox. Setting a budget and sticking to it is hard, but doing so is crucial when you're just starting out—and for every day thereafter. When you're just beginning, you need to create two budgets: a start-up and an operating budget. Private funders always appreciate it when you demonstrate your commitment to the bottom line.

**Start-up Budget:**

- personnel (costs prior to opening—mainly salaries and other staffing costs)
- legal/professional fees
- occupancy (rental or lease payments)
- licenses/permits
- equipment
- insurance
- supplies
- advertising/promotions
- accounting
- utilities

The start-up budget outlines all the costs necessary to open your business, and it includes such one-time-only costs as major equipment, utility deposits, down payments and so on. On the left is a list of expenses you should include.

An operating budget is just that—the description of the financial engine that keeps you operating after you open for business. It contains all your ongoing expenses and the income that pays for those expenses. If you're just starting out, your operating budget should include enough money to cover the first three to six months of operation. It should allow for some of the following expenses listed on the right.

**Operating Budget:**

- personnel
- insurance
- rent
- depreciation (on assets like computers and company cars)
- loan payments
- advertising/promotions
- legal/accounting
- miscellaneous expenses
- supplies
- utilities
- dues/subscriptions/fees
- taxes
- repairs/maintenance

characteristics. If you're targeting particular types of consumers, define them using both demographics (physical characteristics) and psychographics (psychological characteristics). Demographics outline such factors as age, sex, marital status, geographic location and education/income level. Psychographics offer insight into trends, buying habits, market segments and so on. If you identify several market segments, rank them in order of priority.

Even if you've done this before, you may need to do some research to get all the information you need. There are a variety of resources, many of them free. For instance, *American Demographics* magazine has a Web site (www.demographics.com) that offers access to articles about various consumer and business market segments.

Trade associations and publications are often great places to start your research, especially if you're reaching out to businesses. Many trade associations have Web sites, and many publications are also available on the Internet. For information about consumer audiences in your region, try your state or county's department of economic development. In addition, the SBA offers limited help with market research. Find out more about its services at www.sba.gov.

The exact kind of information you need will depend on the type of consumer you're targeting. For instance, if you're selling a product to homeowners in Anytown, USA, find out what percentage of people own homes in Anytown. What is the average household income? Do most homeowners have children? Where do homeowners shop? The more specific your profiles, the better.

# I Will Crush You Like A Bug: The Competition Angle

Keeping an eye on your competitors is not just important from a marketing aspect—it's simply good business. It's good to know who your closest competitors are, and even who your indirect competitors are. Are their businesses booming or faltering? What does their advertising look like? Their brochures and Web sites? In your marketing plan, include a section where you describe the strengths and weaknesses of your competitors and how their products differ from yours.

In addition to writing a brief profile of your competition in your marketing plan, keep an ongoing file on each of your competitors.

Keep track of their advertising and promotional materials and their pricing strategies. Review these files periodically, determining when and how often they advertise, sponsor promotions and offer sales. Study their ad and promotions copy and what sales strategy they're using. For example, is their copy short? Do they use "testimonials"? How much do they reduce prices for sales? Studying the competition keeps you abreast of the game, and sometimes it helps keep you from making the same mistakes others have made.

## Setting Your Sights

Now that you have a sense of where you are, you can decide where you want to go. What will you try to accomplish with your marketing plan? Do you want to announce your presence to your target audience? Increase sales in certain markets? Change the perception of your business? Generate more store traffic? Enter a new market where you may not have much experience?

## Help Wanted

**N**eed some help in building your masterful marketing plan? Try turning to these places for low- or no-cost help:

- The SBA sponsors Small Business Development Centers (SBDCs), Women's Business Centers and Business Information Centers nationwide. The SBDC free counseling program, for example, assigns a consultant to meet with you on a regular basis to monitor your progress in almost any area, from marketing to human resources. Call (800) 8-ASK-SBA.

- The SBA's Service Corps of Retired Executives (SCORE) is a group of retired professionals with various areas of expertise. The organization offers free counseling to start-up and established business owners. Call (800) 634-0245 or visit www.score.org

- Propose that a marketing professor at a local or state college make developing your marketing plan a class assignment, or find out whether a marketing or related business club on campus could handle the project.

- Hire an intern. A marketing student may help you write your marketing plan in exchange for the experience or a small stipend. Call the marketing departments of colleges in your area for recommendations.

Outline each of your goals separately, and be specific. While you should be optimistic about what you can accomplish, be realistic and keep expectations limited. Setting a goal to increase sales by 80 percent may be self-defeating since achieving that level of new sales usually takes special circumstances—such as an outstanding new product or a significant competitor's demise. Remember, you need to support each goal with concrete action, and actions take time and money. If you set multiple goals for yourself, be sure to prioritize them so you can spread out your resources in the best possible way.

## Plan Of Action

This is the heart of your game plan. For each goal you've outlined, create a strategy, complete with your key message (kind of like a smaller mission statement) and the steps, or tactics, that will help you accomplish the goal. The good news: You have many tools at your disposal.

Brainstorm about the best ways to reach each of your goals. What are the most cost-effective but efficient vehicles for getting your message out? You have many forms of advertising to choose from: newspapers, radio, television, magazines, outdoor billboards and so on. Then there are direct marketing programs, like postcards, sales letters, fliers, business reply cards, newsletters or toll-free response numbers. Or you could go for a softer sell using public relations efforts, such as publicity, special events, public speaking engagements, sponsorships and opinion polls. Perhaps you can accomplish your objectives and cut costs by teaming up with related, noncompeting businesses for in-store promotions or cross-promotional campaigns. Online promotional opportunities are more abundant than ever, so consider designing a company Web site or uploading your product's information into a newsgroup or special interest forum.

Here's a sample of a how to write a goal, outlining your strategy, key message and tactics:

**Strategy:** Position myself as the market leader in home inspections in my community.

**Key message:** The Home Inspectors is a reputable, trustworthy name in home inspections.

**Tactics:**

● Approach local community colleges about teaching a home-buying class.

# 10 questions

*Name:* Barry Barr
*Age:* 28
*Company:* Kavu Inc., outdoor gear company
*Location:* Seattle
*Web Site:* www.kavu.com
*Year Founded:* 1993
*Start-up Costs:* $5,000
*1998 Sales:* $3.5 million
*1999 Projections:* $5 million

**1. What was your first entrepreneurial venture?**
Selling skimboards to friends

**2. At what age did you start it?**
12

**3. What did you learn from the experience?**
It's all about sales.

**4. What age were you when you made your first million?**
26

**5. What was your first job (as an employee)?**
Making block ice at 11 years old

**6. Did you go to college?**
Yes, majored in pre-law

**7. What age were you when you started your first "real" full-time venture?**
17

**8. Who is your role model?**
Richard Branson [founder of Virgin]

**9. How many businesses have you started?**
Four

**10. How many were successful, and how many failed?**
Three succeeded, and one failed.

- Propose a feature story to a local paper about "10 Things to Look for When Buying a Home," with me as the expert to be quoted.

- Create a brochure titled Secrets of Buying a Home. Offer it free to people who call.

- Issue a press release about the free brochure to local media.

- Send informational brochures to real estate agents and mortgage brokers who refer home buyers to home inspectors.

For each step you plan, keep asking yourself "Why should I do this?" In other words, make sure your tactics match your goals and resources. Don't do a widespread mailing to reach a small segment of customers. Don't do big, splashy promotions if you really can't afford them. Smaller, more frequent communications are much more effective if your budget is limited. For example, a small accounting firm wanted to increase its exposure in local newspapers. The owner made a $10,000 donation to a local charity's annual gala, believing this would make a great news story. While the gesture was greatly appreciated by the charity and its supporters, that money represented the majority of the firm's annual marketing budget. In return, the owner got one brief story in the local paper. If the organization's goal was to become more philanthropic, the donation was an effective gesture. However, if the original goal was to increase publicity (which it was), the money would have been better spent on a diverse program with more components.

Finally, be sure the promotions you've selected project the right image. If your audience is small-town and conservative, urban angst and anorexic models won't sell your appliances. Similarly, if your customers are hip and sophisticated, make sure to project a cutting-edge image with sharp visuals and design.

## Budgeting Basics: Money + Time = Business

One of the most tragic myths in business is that you can skimp on, or entirely do without, a marketing budget. Marketing costs money, sometimes lots of it, but it is not an optional expense. It's a priority, especially in times of slow cash flow. After all, how are you going to attract more business during the slow times if you don't tell customers about your business?

Take a realistic look at how much money you have to spend on marketing. While you shouldn't overextend yourself, it's critical that you allot adequate funds to reach your markets. If you find that you don't have the budget to tackle all your markets, pick the most important and go after them one by one.

For each of your tactics, break down its estimated cost. For example, a brochure includes writing, photography, graphic design, film, printing and delivery—not to mention, in some cases, mailing. To save money, get creative. Maybe you can barter with a printer or write the copy yourself. Just be careful that such strategies don't backfire. If you're selling Jaguars, a cheap-looking ad or brochure will kill you. Again, if you can't afford everything, adjust your plan and accomplish some of the most-important tactics well.

Finally, decide how much time each tactic will take and set deadlines. Some tactics will require multiple steps, and those should be outlined. Get out a calendar and plot all the marketing tasks you've just set for yourself: Can you do it? Can you delegate or hire someone to help you? Again, be realistic about what you can accomplish and trim your goals if you think you're taking on too much. It's better to start with smaller, more achievable goals than to burn yourself out with an overly ambitious program that you'll end up discarding a few months later.

## Don't Stop Now

Congratulations! You now have a well-researched, realistic, detailed marketing plan that will guide your business through the dangerous battlefield of modern commerce. On the way, you've gained knowledge and expertise about your market that will prove invaluable as you adjust and revise your strategy in the months and years ahead.

That's right. It's not over. Don't put your marketing plan on a shelf and forget about it. It should be a living document that grows and changes over time. Review it periodically, at least twice a year. As your business grows, you must evaluate the success of your initial strategies, shifting or increasing the scope of your marketing to adjust to changing market factors or new business horizons. If you find something is not working, change it. Consistency and continuity, delivered with a dash of creativity, give you the formula for successful marketing.

# Keep On Truckin'

At last: The planning is over, the funding's in place, your product or service is ready to go. Now how do you get it to your customers? If you offer a service, you either have an office where customers come (an accountant) or you go to them (house cleaning). If you are opening a retail store, then all you do is open your doors (and pray). If you're selling by catalog or through the Internet, then your products will be flying through the mail to their destination. However, if you're hoping to see your revolutionary product shining on the shelves of Wal-Mart or Bloomingdale's, or in local supermarkets throughout your county, then you have another hurdle before you make your first sale: distribution.

Distribution means getting your product to retailers and convincing them to buy it and carry it in their stores. Generating initial sales is no picnic for young entrepreneurs, who are new, unproven business owners selling new, unproven products, with no track record of business success. When retailers look at an entrepreneur's product, they don't just worry about whether the product will sell; they worry whether the entrepreneur's business will be around in two months.

Entrepreneurs must work extremely hard—and be extremely creative—to generate their first sales to retailers. Most of the time all you can do is cart your samples from store to store hoping for a bite. But you can also try to get picked up by a distributor or a distribution network. These are companies that represent a variety of products (made by a range of manufacturers) that they try to sell to retailers; distributors also handle all the paperwork, physically move the merchandise and take a cut of the profits. For manufacturers who prefer not to sell their products themselves or who want to get into stores that only work with distributors, a distribution network provides an invaluable service.

However, getting a distributor to carry your product is usually much harder than selling directly to retailers or to consumers, who only compare your product to competing products. The distribution network, which can only represent a limited number of items, also compares your product to all the other noncompeting products it could potentially sell. A distributor's goal is simple: to earn the most money for the least effort.

PHOTO © JAY REED

# Hot Stuff

A ndy Husband is willing to break a few eggs to make an omelet. His company is one of the hottest restaurants in Beantown, with hip twentysomethings and thirtysomethings standing in line even on those long Boston winter nights to sample Husband's haute cuisine—as well as to see and be seen.

Husband doesn't look like your average restaurant owner—he rides a motorcycle to work and sports a shiny steel stud that pierces his tongue—but he knows his business. "I know what I want, and I've been able to translate that vision into Tremont 647."

Husband isn't surprised when he strolls out into the foyer, peeks out the door and sees a well-dressed crowd waiting for a table. "I'd call us a bistro, but that sounds almost too cozy," Husband says. "Our diners do enjoy beautifully grilled food that's clever but not too overbearing. We're giving them a nice place to eat and a nice plate of food. It's really not all that complicated.

"I didn't want to serve the same old, same old," says Husband. "We wanted to explore some new territory. Food should be fun, for a guy like me serving it and for a customer coming in to dine," he adds. "That's what we're shooting for."

Like he says, he can cook... and he can run his own business.

---

**Andy Husband, 29**

*Company:* **Tremont 647**
*Location:* **Boston**
*Year Started:* **1996**
*Start-up Costs:* **$350,000**
*1998 Revenues:* **$1.2 million**
*1999 Projections:* **$1.2 million**

Take the case of John Mueller, the 35-year-old owner of The Idea Factory in Menomonee Falls, Wisconsin. Mueller got a fast start selling his product, the Rinse Ace, thanks to home shopping network QVC. In 1995, the network aired a segment showcasing products from Wisconsin inventors—and Mueller's product was chosen as "Best of the Show." But that initial success didn't help him get placed with a distributor. "[Large retailers and distributors] won't talk to any new business until it's been around for a few years," says Mueller.

Why all the attention? The Rinse Ace ain't your father's shower experience. It's a valve that fits onto a shower arm right before the showerhead with a nozzle that attaches to a long hose and sprayer—with it, you can spray the entire shower or any spot you need to reach. Mueller says the product is ideal for television because it offers a powerful demonstration—QVC cued a short video on the product and played it heavily into its product demo rotation.

## Looking For Funds In All The Wrong Places

So you think your business may be a candidate for venture capital. Well, think again, bucko. Make no mistake about it—getting venture capital is about as easy as getting a cab in midtown Manhattan at 2 a.m. or getting a backstage pass to a Beastie Boys concert. You're not likely to get venture capital for your new business unless you're a high-tech company or have a cutting-edge product that will make investors oodles of dough in five years or less. Not only that, but venture capitalists will want you to demonstrate your business acumen by spinning flax into gold and they will grill you with trick questions like: What's worse, spending an extra nickel on a new office chair or holding up nuns on street corners? Oh well, luckily, there are plenty of other fish—or, in this case, funds—in the sea.

"I'd advise young entrepreneurs to try QVC, but it's not easy getting onto the channel," warns Mueller. "They see thousands and thousands of products each day, and they can only pick a few. We got into QVC after they had a 'Quest for America's Best for 1995' media tour. They went state to state to find new products, and we were picked out of 300 products at a local trade show that QVC sponsored in the state of Wisconsin."

Once the Rinse Ace was tapped by QVC, Mueller

knew his product would create a buzz. "Actually, we sold out even before we got on air. The hosts sold our product before we had a chance to pitch it. They sold 2,800 units in a matter of minutes." QVC wound up overselling the product, and Mueller had to scramble to replace inventory. QVC was so happy with the product that they offered Mueller a three-year exclusivity contract that would have made him a wealthy man. But he turned it down. "We said no, but we did wind up giving them a year of exclusivity for a nice chunk of money."

"Getting your product into major retailers is a lot of hard work. You really have to keep plugging away—there's no magic formula for that."

Unfortunately, even though Mueller's product was a hit with the QVC crowd, it still wasn't ready for the majors. Most distributors and major retailers want products that sell based on a package, not a demonstration, so Mueller had trouble getting hardware stores and mass merchants to carry Rinse Ace. Instead, he concentrated on catalogs like *Miles Kimball* and *Damark*. Today, Rinse Ace is in more than 35 catalogs, and Mueller estimates 1998 sales at more than $1 million.

And that was the ticket: Catalog success got Rinse Ace picked up by a few distributors and placed into retailers such as Kmart and Menards, a Midwest home improvement chain, as well as scattered hardware stores nationwide, where it's selling well. Once Mueller had established Rinse Ace's sales potential and generated some momentum, he finally got the widespread distribution he was looking for.

"People often wonder why distributors won't give a new product a chance," says Mueller. "But setting up paperwork and sales training for a new product is a lot of work, and distributors don't want to spend the time unless they're sure the product will sell. Getting your product into major retailers is a lot of hard work. You really have to keep plugging away—there's no magic formula for that."

However, there are some cues to take from entrepreneurs like Mueller. Having an "introductory stage," when you sell to a limited market, allows you to lavish extra attention and promotional efforts on that market. To entice distributors to pick up your product and sell it to their retail customers, promise to give distributors

special promotions, demonstrations, extra-long payment terms, frequent restocking services and any other service you think they
might want. Another good reason to limit your market initially: You
probably can't afford to launch a product in more than one market.

Mueller says you must use every tactic to help your business
succeed. The initial momentum from your first sales, whatever distribution channel you use, is crucial to lining up a larger network.
If you get a distributor to carry your product, don't think your work
is done and you don't have to keep marketing and promoting. Do
everything possible on your own to make sure the distributor's
agents are successful and that your product keeps selling once
placed. Retailers will drop a product if it doesn't produce sales, and
distributors will drop you if retailers start dropping your product.

Consider hiring a demo company—a service that places people
in stores to offer customers free samples. They aren't nearly as
motivated or successful demonstrating your product as you are, but
they'll make a few sales for you. Also try running newspaper ads or
radio promotions, in-store seminars and sponsoring area events.

Don't worry about making money at first. Worry instead about
creating sales momentum. You'll make profits once you have a
wide distribution network. To reach that goal, you need the biggest
promotional budget you can afford and an intense personal sales
effort when you start out. As Mueller realized, young entrepreneurs
can't rely on the product or its packaging to make sales. You must
hustle to get your product off the ground.

Mueller's most recent product, My Own Shower for Children,
was easier for the company to market. "Once you are selling into
some of these [stores] it makes it easier to get new products inside
their doors," he says. "But it's not easy getting your foot in the
door."

# Chapter

It's "gazelles"— fast-growing young upstart firms—that will rule the U.S. economy over the next 20 years.

# Running With The Gazelles

Gen E business owners have become a driving force in the U.S. economy. They started 1.9 million businesses in 1996—that's 43 percent of all start-ups in the country that year. They are part of an ever-growing movement of companies that David Birch, president of Cognetics Inc., a corporate consulting and analytical firm, calls "gazelles." It's these gazelles—fast-growing young upstart firms—that Birch believes will rule the U.S. economy over the next 20 years.

That's all fine and good. But who are these gazelles—how do they operate, and what do they look like? How does a young entrepreneur get to the point where his or her business is going to be around for 20 months, let alone 20 years? In the 1969 movie "The Candidate," Robert Redford plays an ambitious politician whose drive to snare a seat in the U.S. senate borders on the maniacal. Redford's character is so focused on winning his Senate campaign that when he's ultimately elected, he realizes he has no plans for how to govern; he has no agenda, no ideas. In the movie's last scene, a stunned Redford turns to his campaign manager at the election night victory party and asks, "What do we do now?"

Some entrepreneurs interviewed for this book say they understand how Redford felt. "Creating my own business was the culmination of my dreams," says Scott Korn, the 35-year-old CEO and founder of York Paper. "But once you actually get the funding and lease the space to run your business, there's a certain sense of 'Gee, now what do I do?'"

However, once they get over the shock of actually finding themselves in business, most Gen E's know what to do: remake the workplace in their own image, both culturally and in a business sense. Most entrepreneurs want safe, secure, culturally diverse workplaces where like-minded, well-rounded workers can thrive. It becomes an inevitable balancing act between fostering that creative, nurturing environment and dealing with the twists and turns of managing a young business. No matter: Gen E business owners are finding ways to refashion workplace relationships and incorporate new technologies while coping with tough budget issues and the stress of competing in the marketplace. In this chapter, we'll take a look at how some young companies are adapting to the social and political realities of managing a business at the cusp of the millennium.

# Keep It Real, Yo

One thing's for sure: Gen E employers are more down-to-earth and nurturing than perhaps any other generation ever—even more so, ironically, than the boomers, whose rallying cry in the '60s was "make love, not war." Today, the boomer mantra might as well be "make money, not waves." For America's younger generation, this "sell out" goes against everything their natural counterculture beliefs tell them.

"Our management style is a bit more humanitarian," says author Merideth Bagby. "Young entrepreneurs encourage staffers to keep flex hours and make the workplace more homey in terms of allowing pets or plants in the office."

## Ink It

Handshake agreements and verbal OKs are wonderful if you are 15 years old and mowing lawns, but not when you're running your own shop with a partner. Get everything in writing—even, and perhaps especially, if you're best friends—so there's documentation of who is responsible for doing what.

Whether you write up a partnership agreement yourself or hire a lawyer, make sure your agreement includes the following:

● The partnership's name
● When the partnership will begin, and how and why it may be dissolved
● The partnership's initial capital
● Controls on who can withdraw money; agreement that both partners must consent before money is removed
● A specified draw account and a monthly allowable amount for each partner
● How profits are distributed and who handles expenses
● The general rights and responsibilities of each partner

Putting these items on paper shouldn't cause any problems between you and your prospective partner. If anything you include kills the deal, then you'll be better off looking for a more compatible partner.

Most Gen E business owners extend that flexibility because they want it for themselves, since many of them, as employees for other companies, have long yearned for a more cordial, pleasant work environment. Darrel Phillips, the 33-year-old founder and president of Digital Networks Integrated Solutions, a high-tech start-up in Costa Mesa, California, says that unpleasant memories of his former corporate years steeled his resolve to become a better boss. "Some of the people I worked for were the biggest [jerks] in the world," he says. "I didn't want to work for someone who was always treating me badly." These days, Phillips makes it a point to honor his personal life, even at the occasional expense of his business. "I make sure I'm home every day by 4:30 so I can spend time with my son," he says. "If that means leaving a customer site to go home and spend an hour and a half with him—and then burning some midnight oil later—I'll do that. I make time for my personal life."

> Phillips **makes** it a point to **honor** his personal life, **even** at the occasional **expense** of his business.

Titles are another corporate albatross that many young entrepreneurs can do without. At CDuctive, a New York City "music company of the future," co-founders Alan Manuel, 30, John Rigos, 31, and Thomas Ryan, 29, eschew titles. Their custom CD business thrives without presidents and vice presidents, with the trio working 16 hours days spinning heavy metal, acid jazz or any other musical style their customers ask for. Why no titles? "Simple," says Rigos. "Ego."

The company recently added a multimedia Web site to the operation, where customers can dial in and sample whatever fare they like before making a purchase. "Right now, most people buy what the major music labels are promoting because big labels have the most money and basically are going to determine what people are going to listen to," explains Rigos. "Here, the listener has a choice." As Web site traffic rises, company employees put in longer hours to ensure that their clients get the music they want. But that's OK with staffers, who like the fact that disc jockeys come in and rock the house after hours with amped-up indie rock or electronica. During the day, the staff picks its own tunes and plays them just as loud. Try doing that at IBM.

Then there are some Gen E business owners who avoid managing altogether: They've decided to keep the more creative responsibilities to themselves and hire professional businesspeople to handle the daily business of running the company. "Even my schedule is set up so I'm working by myself most of the time," says John Carmack, co-founder and video game developer for Id Software. "I

## Practical Applications

**E**ven if you're a charter member of the Computer Generation, you may not have the techno-savvy of a Jerry Yang or a Sky Dayton. Don't fret. Everybody has to learn sometime. Here are the important questions to ask as you decide what computer gadgets you need to ride to the top.

1 **How do I plan to use my computer?** To work more efficiently? To produce a higher-quality product? To cut costs? You need to answer this question first before you can decide what to buy.

2 **What software applications will I need?** Once you know how you'll use your PC, you'll be able to choose the right software applications.

3 **What operating platform will I use?** While most popular programs work on all platforms, some don't, so choose your applications first, and then select a platform to match.

4 **What are my hardware needs?** First, check all your software applications for their requirements. A program may need a minimum speed or a certain amount of memory. Second, choose peripherals. What type of printer is best for you? Do you need a large monitor?

5 **What can I afford?** Set a budget. At the store, get a price quote for the basic hardware and software. Once you know that cost, add extras if your budget allows.

6 **Where should I buy?** In general, superstores such as CompUSA and Best Buy have the widest selection and better prices, but their salespeople aren't as knowledgeable and their service contracts won't be as good. Smaller stores may not have as many machines in stock and slightly higher prices, but you'll get individual attention to design the computer you need, and you're likely to get better support and customer service. You can also buy computers online or by direct mail (from companies such as Dell) from the comfort of your home.

have a good time working on the challenging technical stuff and leave the office politics to our CEO. Even when we started the business, I knew I didn't want anything to do with the managerial end of things."

Carmack's typical workday is an interesting one. He doesn't arrive at Id's offices until 4 p.m., just as many staffers are tying things up for the day to go home. "That allows me to work through the night on my own without any distractions," he explains.

## Lease Is More

It's a fact of life: Your cutting-edge computer will remain cutting-edge for, oh, the time it takes you to plug it in. It will be outdated within a few months, and virtually obsolete in two years. How do you get out of this trap?

Consider leasing a computer. You not only get state-of-the-art equipment, but when the lease is up, you can trade in your old computer for a new one. Other benefits of leasing include:

- **Capital conservation:** Leasing requires less capital than conventional financing, since you don't have to pay for the PC up front.

- **Improved cash flow planning:** If you lease wholesale, you can get a break on costs. Since payments are fixed for the lease term, they won't change with interest rates, allowing you to plan your budget.

- **Better financing options:** With a lease, you may be able to finance installation expenses and maintenance plans.

Make sure you know from the outset the equipment you'll need. Once you sign the leasing contract, you won't be able to upgrade for a specified time—and you usually can't get out of the lease until it's paid off.

Last note: When do you upgrade your computer? Many technology gurus say that in the age of superfast computer performance and lower prices, maybe never. The thinking is that most computer board or memory upgrades in the PC world can cost up to $1,000—in many cases nearly the cost of a new PC. The wisest advice: Buy ahead of current technology as best you can. If you think you need only 16 MB of memory, buy more. If you think you'll get by with 100 MHz processor capacity, get 200 MHz. It might cost you an extra several hundred dollars, but you won't have to worry about upgrading for a while.

Carmack works until 4 a.m., subsisting on pizza or snack foods while punching away at his PC working on his company's next bestselling video game. "I'll go over some e-mail when I get in and talk with the other managers, but by and large I'm left alone to do my thing. I think concentrating is an underappreciated task for a business owner, especially in our business. I'd rather think about how to develop new product features than get involved in the daily business of the company. I don't care enough about that stuff to make any business-oriented decisions. I'd rather be programming."

> "You can call our little excursions 'testing runs' if you want, but all I know is we have a hell of a trip."

Other Gen E companies blow off stress by dropping everything and taking the entire staff off-site to the beach or camping. "Actually, the off-site retreat is something that companies have been doing for years," says Dave Klimkiewicz, one of the co-founders of Sector 9 Inc., a San Diego skateboard manufacturer. "So we can't take credit for that, although we do go off-site and take whoever wants to go with us." Sector 9 frequently bivouacs to the nearby hills and mountains of Southern California for wild boogie-boarding outings, in part to test out new products and in part to have a good time. "Hey, you gotta use what you sell," says the affable, 28-year-old Klimkiewicz. "So you can call our little excursions 'testing runs' if you want, but all I know is we have a hell of a trip."

Companies that don't have the built-in fun of testing skateboards kick back in other creative ways. Take Olympus Group, a 3-year-old database software design company in suburban Alexandria, Virginia; it was founded by 29-year-old Julie Holdren, who borrowed $5,000 from her 401(k) from her last corporate job to start the company. In the office, Holdren keeps things light by sponsoring push-up competitions and Nintendo extravaganzas, and then she periodically takes the company off-site en masse, where she favors competitive team-building excursions like Laser Tag. Even company lunch hours are unusual: Employees are encouraged to go running together, and ironically, the outdoor exercise frequently proves useful. As they jog and sweat their stress away, coworkers often find themselves bouncing new ideas off one another.

"We've also gone bowling together and plan weird get-togeth-

ers, like a fondue party," says Holdren, who seems to have found a
recipe for success. Holdren says she wants to be "the first woman
to found and run a $1 billion business."

# Hi Ho, Hi Ho ...

Gen E business owners like the ones mentioned above recognize that times have changed and longer work hours are the norm.
Much has been written about the workplace threatening to replace
the family home and neighborhood as the social realm of the 21st
century, which is a fairly recent trend when you think about it.
Staffers are working long hours and weekends, developing close
emotional ties to their co-workers and seeing their loved ones less.

Gen E is taking a page out of the baby boomer handbook in
assuaging rampant workplace guilt by providing employees with
the most comfortable workplace surroundings that they can financially and logistically provide. After all, sooner or later, workers
have to put the SuperSoakers down, hang up the snowboards and
go back to work. When that happens, political and business realities enter the fray, and Gen E business owners are fluidly changing
the office dynamic through their decisions about budgets, technology and each other.

Covering all the fundamental Gen E workplace issues—such as
office politics, telecommuting, flextime, employee/management
relations and corporate hierarchies, titles, day-care issues, maternity leave and vacation time—would require a book all its own, but
there are some common areas that the entrepreneurs interviewed for
this book see as critical for workplaces to thrive in a business sense,
as opposed to some of the recreational freedoms described at the top
of the chapter. For the duration of this chapter, we'll look at forming partnerships, dealing with money and the power of technology.

# I Got You, Babe

Like John Carmack at Id Software, many young entrepreneurs
decide against going solo when they start out. Instead, some business owners bring an experienced hand on board to lend ballast to
an upstart organization.

In many cases, these entrepreneurs start out by working with a

partner, a college buddy or business associate
who shares the same dreams and visions and
who demonstrates the same energy and
wherewithal. After all, where would Batman
be without Robin? Montgomery Burns without Smithers? Ben without Jerry? It's too
ugly to contemplate!

But how do you create and sustain a business partnership? New Yorkers Jody Kozlow
Gardner and Cherie Serota, the co-founders of
Belly Basics (whom we met in Chapter 1), are good examples. Both
women are convinced their operation could never have survived if it
had been a solo venture. "We think the partnership is great for the
business," says Gardner. "We always bounce ideas off each other,
and we're constantly working together to make the company better.
In my opinion, I don't know how people launch companies on their
own. I think that it would be very hard to go solo. I like the fact that
you have someone you can bounce ideas off of."

That doesn't mean that everything is hunky dory all the time.
"Sure, there's some bickering," says Serota. "But hashing things
out just gives us a better product."

The Belly Basics co-founders believe in sharing all the tasks and
not dividing themselves into separate roles. "There's no creative
director or financial director, per se," says Gardner. "We both get
involved with everything and I think that helps us in the long run."

If you think working with a partner is for you, keep these tips in
mind to ensure the right match:

**1** **Take your time.** Partnership disasters arise because people are
in such a rush to get the business started that they don't sit
down and assess if their partnership is really going to work.
Before you commit to working together, talk through the following issues:

● What will each of you be doing in the partnership? Who will
handle bookkeeping? Who's in charge of customer service?
Is one of you taking on a visionary, planning position while
the other handles the nuts and bolts? How will receipts be
handled? "My partner was much better at the marketing end
of the business than I ever was," says Caryl Felicetta, who
runs Argyle Studios, a creative services and marketing com-

pany, with her friend, Marion Reinson. "But I had more of a creative flair. If you can establish a synergistic work environment that capitalizes on both partner's strengths, that's 90 percent of the battle."

● Are your commitment levels and work ethics similar? Do you both believe in finishing a project no matter how long it takes, or do you insist on going home at quitting time? If there's an emergency, are you both willing to drop everything, such as weekend plans, to focus on the business?

It's important to know if the other person is prepared for the long hours and many unseen details that come with owning a business and if he or she is willing to pitch in if necessary. "If not, you'll end up doing the bulk of the work," says Carmack.

● What do each of you want from the business? Are you most concerned about a steady income, or are you willing to take risks and eat cold noodles to grow the company? Is this a long-term investment, or do you want to sell the business within a specified period of time?

● What sort of business do you both envision? Do you want a small, two-person office that hires independent contractors when necessary, or would you like to expand and eventually hire employees? How much time and money are you willing to spend to see your business reach its goal? In other words, do you have a formal or informal cut-off point?

● What stage of life is each of you in, and do those stages mesh? If one of you is just starting a career and wants to expand and the other is winding down, the partnership might not work—unless the idea is for the experienced person to teach the beginner the ropes and then retire.

2 **Make sure each partner is doing something he or she is truly qualified for.** There are no spare slots in an entrepreneurial venture, and the most common mistake in partnerships is that after you've divided up the tasks, one partner is doing a job he or she doesn't know how to handle, most typically accounting. "True, you can always hire an accountant," says Serota of Belly Basics. "But when you're starting a new business, money is tight and you're going to try to do as much as you can on your own." While you can get by learning some office functions in basic terms, Serota advises not get your fin-

gers permanently stuck in a task you don't know how to do. "We waited as long as we could before hiring an accountant, but once we did there was a great sense of relief. Finally, somebody who knows numbers was on the job."

**3** **Don't rely on friendship.** Although starting a business with a friend sounds like a dream come true, it's not so simple. Being good friends is not a precursor to a successful partnership. As a matter of fact, it can add a stressful dimension; the workplace is chock-full of damaged friendships resulting from differences of opinion. Some partnerships may start out as business associates and become friendships in time, but it's no prerequisite for a great business. The same goes for family as well. "You've got to have strong family ties to go into business with a family member," says Michael Caito, co-owner with his brother Anthony (right) and family friend Matthew Martha (left) of Restaurants on the Run, a gourmet food delivery service in Orange County, California. "You're going to have your differences, so you can expect some friction. When that happens, don't take it personally."

**4** **Set limits about the amount of time you'll put into the venture on a weekly basis.** While a 110 percent commitment to your business is admirable and even necessary, doing nothing but working together 24/7 is almost guaranteed to provoke creeping insanity and friction between partners. Set limits to avoid burnout, which will increase your odds for success and make you both happier people.

**5** **Consider values, ethics and integrity.** Forming a partnership is like getting married, and while you don't need to "love" your business partner to form a successful match, you do need to share similar ethics and values. When times get tough, this can be crucial to your business' survival. Discuss together your basic values about how to run a business—and about how to treat people in general, such as vendors, customers, employees and each other. Anticipate conflicts that may arise and try to resolve them before you're fully enmeshed in your venture.

This is especially important when it comes to money. Discuss your financial ethics and habits with each other.

Traditionally, how do each of you pay bills? Are you frugal while your partner is profligate? Are you bothered when your checkbook doesn't balance to the penny while your partner doesn't even keep track? Now that you're putting your livelihood into your partner's hands, differences like these can cause major conflicts. Be honest, and discuss openly how you'll handle such differences. Also, what's the person's credit rating like? Does he or she have a bad history with debt? If your potential partner has a problem with this, the person is not likely to change simply because he or she is in business with you. One last thought on finances: Pay careful attention to isolate your business and your personal assets. Partnerships run an increased danger of exposing both partners' personal assets to the liabilities that a business can generate.

**6** **Trust your intuition.** Don't enter into a partnership without checking your gut feelings. If something doesn't seem right, check it out right away—if there's some skullduggery afoot, you want to nip it in the bud. Perhaps the friendly, well-funded stranger who wants to help you has actually made a habit of cheating past business partners. One red flag: If your partner insists on speaking generally and not specifically on potential hot-button issues, watch out. Don't accept vague reassurances to your specific questions and concerns, especially regarding money. Insist that your partner explain his or her past dealings or present financial status.

**7** **Expand your management team beyond the partnership.** Good empirical evidence suggests that the more key team members a venture has, the better its performance is likely to be. Take the pressure off yourself by delegating responsibility or expanding your partnership to include more people. If the venture is too small to support more than two people, you can achieve much the same result by hiring outside advisors, who can play a limited but real role in supporting your business.

Some entrepreneurs relish the idea of a team-based workplace culture, but they still want to make the decisions themselves. For them, part of the desire to be an entrepreneur is to have that responsibility. Says Scott Korn of York Paper, "Nobody relies on a work team more than I do. We work together to develop ideas, and I'm a great sounding board for advice. But, ultimately, I want to be the one making the decisions."

# Tightening The Budget Belt

Partner or no partner, as your business grows, so does your need for all the capital you can get. Some of that cash can come from implementing some simple budgeting strategies. That doesn't mean settling for a Beachcraft four-seat airplane instead of an eight-seat Cessna (although that could come into play down the line after you've made your first $10 million). No, it's the nickel-and-dime stuff that can spell the difference in the tough years between annual ledgers written in black ink or red.

Consider Lisa Swayne, 29, founder and president of Swayne Literary Agency in New York City. Started in 1997 with a personal nest egg of $3,000, Swayne has grown her business quickly, signing top names like new media author Aliza Sherman and forging financial relationships with heavy hitters like Citibank, which has helped with funding. By the end of 1998 her business was valued at more than $2 million. Swayne not only has an eye for good writing talent, but she also has a precious knack for squeezing everything she can out of her budgeting dollar.

"In the beginning, I was so broke I stole paper clips," she says. "Since I've owned my own business, I've been more frugal than I've ever been in my life." Fortunately for Swayne, becoming a literary agent doesn't take much cash. "In comparison to other businesses, it [requires] very low start-up capital. [All] you really need is a phone or a laptop. If I were opening a coffeehouse, it would be a different story. I had some experience in dealing with writers, editors and publishing houses and was able to bring clients with me. That's very important for cash flow reasons."

> "In the beginning, I was so **broke** I **stole** paper clips. Since I've owned **my own** business, I've been more **frugal** than I've ever been in my **life**."

Still, Swain kept a tight control on her expenses, and in three months, she was out of debt. After 18 months she had cleared her first $2 million in revenues, but she still throws nickels around like manhole covers and is not afraid to admit it. "I recently did one of those informational interviews that college grads like to do with business owners," says Swain. "I told her bluntly that it took a long time for me to receive my first check and I had good experience in the business. The difference was I pinched pennies to survive. It's a hard environment to be in if you don't have that attitude."

Aside from swiping paper clips and keeping head count relatively low, Swain recommends keeping office space overhead low as well. "I work in New York City and I don't have to tell you about real estate prices here," she says. "So I cut back by sharing office space with other businesses, like legal services firms or accounting companies, a move that has really worked out well. I've saved some money and made some new friends and contacts. In publishing, contacts are everything."

# Ladies And Gentlemen, Start Your Search Engines

7:30 a.m.: You're running late. Kicking off your electric blanket, you scamper toward the shower, stopping only to grab a cup of coffee percolating from your preprogrammed java maker.

Twenty minutes later you hop in your new Jeep Cherokee and punch on your preinstalled CD sound system: Instantly, The Offspring are pounding out of your deluxe surround-sound speaker system. Traffic's flowing well for a Monday, but you anticipate problems and call for the latest traffic report on your cellular phone.

The 8 a.m. Express Traffic update informs you that there are tie-ups on the Hammerhead turnpike and a three-car pile up at the Megalopolis toll booths only four miles ahead. You punch a few buttons on your dashboard navigation center and instruct it to seek alternative routes.

Using your hand-free cell phone, you call the office and tell your administrative assistant to begin printing out the PowerPoint presentation for the big lunch meeting today and to cancel your 9 a.m. appointment with your Internet guru and have him fax his proposal about marketing hemp coffee mugs online to your laptop computer via the Cellular Data Network. On her Pentium PC, your assistant prints the report while reconfiguring your desktop scheduling software and then e-mailing the Internet guy at the same time.

Suddenly, your cellular phone's call-waiting feature blips. You're being paged via your phone company's Digital Messenger service,

# A Nickel Here, A Dime There . . .

**C**utting costs is a crucial component of a young entrepreneur's job. To save some dough so your company can grow, try some of these time-tested tips:

- **Cash in your frequent flier coupons.** You can save anywhere from $250 to $750 per flight with these.

- **Dump the coffee service.** Buy your own coffeemaker and grind your own beans. It's a lot cheaper. Buy a coffeemaker that allows you to make only as much as you want each time.

- **Review your list of subscriptions.** Often they get renewed without any thought. Same with dues to associations that may not be providing value for the money.

- **Manage your line of credit closely.** Often banks will transfer in large increments ($10,000 at a time) because you're $300 over. See if they can cut the increment in half, which will save you about half the interest.

- **If you have any kitchen facilities, invest in some nice china and glasses.** Instead of taking clients out to lunch, have it catered in your office by your local deli, and have it served on your china, complete with cloth napkins and so on.

- **Skip the overnight delivery service pickup.** Save a couple dollars and drop off FedEx or UPS packages in local collection bins rather than ordering an office pickup.

- **Monitor your postage meter usage.** With the growth of faxes and courier services, business postage costs are actually dropping. If you're paying more to rent the meter (and scale) than you're spending on postage—don't renew the contract.

- **Buy a telephone system.** Renting from the local phone company is your most expensive, yet probably most convenient option. You're better off buying a system; take advantage of the many used systems on the market.

- **Pay your bills early.** Go to all your vendors and tell them that you will pay all invoices within 15 days if they will reduce each bill by an additional 2 percent.

and the display on your cellular phone reads "Call Mom." You auto-dial your mother, who tells you the family reunion in Walla Walla this weekend has been moved to the following weekend because

> Personal **computers** are a fact of **life**, and they have become the **symbol** of Gen E, which is making its name as the **expert** purveyor of everything **high-tech**.

Uncle Ed has a bad case of shingles and cousin Jarod's been arrested for selling black market pictures of Pamela Anderson Lee on the Web again. You speed dial the airline to cancel your flight, and using voice record on your electronic notebook, you leave yourself a reminder to do a Web search for one of those "price your own" airfare agencies online so you can reschedule the flight to Cleveland.

Seconds later, an alternative route glows on your dashboard navigation system. You cut off at the Pauly Shore Drive exit. Fifteen minutes later, you're at work, where an electronic device within your security badge allows you to enter your building. Five minutes after that, you're at your desk, responding to e-mail and studying the Wall Street Journal Interactive for some news on your company's stock. A quick glance on your screen for David Letterman's Top Ten list from last night, preprogrammed for your convenience by your Web browser, and now your day begins in earnest.

Sound familiar? If it doesn't yet, it will be—computer technology is changing just about every aspect of our lives. In the Gen E workplace, you can't swing a dead typewriter without hitting something with a computer chip embedded in it. Laptops, PCs, palm-sized PC notebooks, scanners, printers and fax machines lead the list of high-tech components. To Gen E business owners, using these machines is second nature, and they are essential elements of any office. No discussion of Gen E businesses is complete without addressing how technology is fueling successful entrepreneurships at the cusp of the 21st century.

As mentioned earlier, Gen E's have grown up with the computer in the same way that baby boomers grew up with television, and the World War II generation grew up with the automobile. Personal computers are a fact of life, no more unusual than the telephone, and they have become the symbol of Gen E, which is making its name as the expert purveyor of everything high-tech."

> "I have **always** had the entrepreneurial **spirit**. My father was an electrical engineer who was downsized at age 55 and **unable** to get a job again. He always told me to be my **own** boss."
>
> —*Ron Stock*

# Take
## Two Twigs And Channel Me In The Morning

**W**hat does a good young pharmacist do when his job leaves him unfulfilled, but he still wants to make a difference in his field. If you're Ron Stock, 33, founder and president of The Herbal Path you start your own "natural" pharmacy that sells natural healing products like vitamins, herbs, minerals and homeopathic treatments.

**Ron Stock, 33**

*Company:* **The Herbal Path**
*Location:* **Dover,**
           **New Hampshire**
*Year Started:* **1997**
*Start-up Costs:* **$110,000**
*1998 Revenues:* **$400,000**
*1999 Projections:* **$500,000 plus**

"The year before I started The Herbal Path I was working part-time as a pharmacist at anywhere from 20 to 40 hours a week," says Stock. "It's not a great job. You have to work all day without a break, and it grew stale quickly. But I had an idea that natural medicines and pharmacies had a future together."

Using $10,000 of his own money, $40,000 borrowed from his family, and $60,000 borrowed from a local bank, Stock launched The Herbal Path in 1997. Spending his days counseling customers about natural remedies is a dream come true for Stock. His business isn't doing badly either, racking up $400,000 in revenues its first year.

"I'm not a millionaire yet, but that's really not important," Stock. "It's just rewarding helping people discover the benefits of natural remedies. Hopefully

# 10 questions

**Name:** Lisa Groppe
**Age:** 35
**Company:** Girl Games Inc., interactive software and Web site for girls
**Location:** Austin, Texas
**Web Site:** www.planetgirl.com
**Year Founded:** 1994
**Start-up Costs:** Under $1 million
**1998 Sales:** Under wraps
**1999 Projections:** Ditto

**1. What was your first entrepreneurial venture?**
Selling tickets to come play in my backyard; we had lots of animals, a pool, a trampoline and a trolley

**2. At what age did you start it?**
10

**3. What did you learn from the experience?**
People will pay for entertainment.

**4. What age were you when you made your first million?**
Still waiting.

**5. What was your first job (as an employee)?**
Office assistant for a stockbroker

**6. Did you get a college degree?**
Yes, in philosophy

**7. What age were you when you started your current business?**
29

**8. Who is your role model?**
My mom and dad—they're perfect.

**9. How many businesses have you started?**
One

**10. How many were successful, and how many failed?**
One succeeded, and none failed.

The Joystick Generation recognized immediately the cultural and, later, the business benefits of the PC. Consequently, many of their businesses have a cyber-edge, no matter what they're selling. Gen E advertises its products and services on the World Wide Web, manages its business data with Windows NT, and creates in-house marketing brochures on Power Macs. In fact, both Gen E and PCs are coming of age together.

"When it comes to technology, the media has done a lot to make someone my age look like the person you look to," says Wil Schroter, 23, president of Next Generation Digital Advertising, which designs internal networks, CD-ROM tools and Web sites for corporate clients. Schroter started the company in 1997 in a small office above the Newport Music Hall in downtown Columbus, a leafy college town that's home to Ohio State University. In 1998, Gerbig, Snell/Weisheimer & Associates Inc., a Columbus advertising and marketing firm, acquired 60 percent of the company for a little more than $1 million—including money earmarked for hiring and equipment.

Technology has changed the dynamic for young entrepreneurs looking for capital to start new businesses. More often than not, a young entrepreneur with a high-tech background will get a longer look from an investor these days. Venture capitalists recognize that when it comes to running a business in the 21st century, the chances of success hinge as much on a company's technological prowess as much as anything else. Many such businesses start out in the high-tech field, like Internet marketing firms or Web design companies.

While many young entrepreneurs are drawn simply by the technology itself, low overhead in many high-tech fields means easy entry for would-be entrepreneurs, according to the Young Entrepreneurs Organization (YEO) in Alexandria, Virginia. Group members are under 40 and own businesses with sales of $1 million or more. Of the group's 1,500 members nationwide, 300 focus on multimedia, computer, telecommunication or online services. These are just the sorts of businesses that can be started out of dorm rooms or apartments with little more than computers.

"We've seen a spurt in [the number of] young entrepreneurs in the past few years," says one YEO member on the organization's Web site. "Clearly that's driven by technology. Just as the software industry was led by baby-faced entrepreneurs in the early '80s, World Wide Web businesses are young businesses. They can handle young managers."

Who are the poster children for the Internet age? People like Jerry Yang, 35, founder and chief "Yahoo" at Yahoo Inc., the Santa Clara, California, Web search engine giant. A one-time Ph.D. candidate in electrical engineering, Yang's stake in the company at the end of 1998 was a staggering $905 million.

Or people like Sky Dayton, the 27-year-old CEO of EarthLink Network, a growing Internet service provider that boasts 6,500 new customers every week. A one-time college dropout, Dayton's stake in the company is worth a reported $115 million. Then there's Halsey Minor, 33, chairman and CEO of Cnet in San Francisco. The Internet media company was recently funded by NBC, making Minor's 17 percent stake in Cnet worth $184 million.

What, besides deep pockets, do all of these young entrepreneurs have in common? An inner drive to call their own shots, a deep commitment to technology and an unrestrained joy in what they do. As one entrepreneur put it, "Who needs IBM?"

# Chapter

The recipe for building a great employee team: Be diverse, rock the culture, choose wisely and build an extended team.

# Deal With It:
# Managing Employees

La Jolla is the Valhalla and Nirvana of Southern California. It's a beautiful slice of pastoral oceanside splendor just north of San Diego—a seaside village where clear, sunny, 75-degree days are the norm. The town hosts thousands of visitors year-round and is home to internationally respected educational and research institutions, Nobel Prize winners, celebrities, artists, authors, designer boutiques and a cosmopolitan shopping district.

It's a great place to work, and that's why it's also home to Columbus Research Inc., a full-service computer and business consulting and programming firm. Columbus is the brainchild of young entrepreneur John Watson, 34, who founded the firm in 1995. Initially, Watson started the business to build customized database applications for businesses. Two years into his new venture, Watson shifted the company's focus to computer training and software development. The change has worked wonders, as the company posted more than $1.1 million in revenues in 1998.

However, Watson didn't move to La Jolla because of its economic opportunities; he set up shop there to keep his 20 employees happy. He could have settled Columbus' offices anywhere he wanted in Southern California, and probably at a cheaper price, but, ultimately, that wasn't most important. "I think you've really got to consider the welfare of your employees," says Watson. "They work hard for you, and you want to give something back. That's one reason we wound up in La Jolla." Columbus' office is near La Jolla Cove, a gorgeous section of beachfront that's popular with tourists and easily qualifies as La Jolla's most visited attraction.

"One of the greatest decisions I ever made was moving to La Jolla, right on the beach," says Watson, who relocated the company in 1998. "We're two blocks to the water and our employees love taking swims in La Jolla Cove. Just going down to such a beautiful spot clears your head and helps you focus better.

## Apples To Apples

Want to get an idea what others in your industry are paying workers? The Bureau of Labor Statistics does Occupational Compensation Surveys (OCS) for most regions of the country. The information is broken down by occupation and by various levels of experience within that occupation. The bureau also has information about benefits. To access the reports, visit www.bls.gov or call the Bureau of Labor Statistics' regional offices.

"We used to be in an office where it was fairly sterile and everybody worked with their doors closed," recalls Watson. "When we moved to the new office in La Jolla, I opened things up and encouraged a more collegial atmosphere, with music and food and plenty of open space for people to banter as they worked. I think our employees appreciate it." A stroll though Columbus Research's offices shows that they do. As programmers pound out code, an eclectic collection of music fills the air, from Gregorian chants to the Barenaked Ladies. The refrigerator is stocked with plenty of Jolt cola as well as both health food and junk snacks for staffers.

Watson, like many young entrepreneurs, is turning the tables on traditional workplace environments, where employees often feel underappreciated, ill-served and sometimes even taken advantage of by company policies. Watson (above) spent some time in the corporate world and knows what it can be like. He decided that when he ran his own business, he would provide his staff with a nice work environment; he felt it would result not only in more creative and satisfied workers, but in a healthier bottom line.

"You're not going to go too far in business if you don't have good, solid, talented people working for you," says Watson. "And making them happy is part of your job."

## They Shoot Goof-offs, Don't They?

Getting good people and keeping them happy sounds simple right? It ain't so.

Great employees can help a young company overcome many barriers. Mediocre employees, on the other hand, can derail even an established business boasting a great product. However, good employees are hard to come by (and if you're not getting them, that's a big red flag, but we'll get to that in a moment), and good teams take time and effort to build. According to Christine Comaford, managing director and general partner at Artemis Ventures, a Sausalito, California, consulting firm that specializes in helping young businesses get off the ground, the recipe for building a great employee team is as follows: Be diverse, rock the culture, choose wisely and build an extended team.

# You Can't Win With Just Pitching

"A successful team must be composed of diverse players," says Comaford. "You'll need visionaries, leaders, implementers and infrastructure builders/supporters." Just like in baseball, a company won't run well unless it has skilled people at every important position; stock your team with nothing but fastball pitchers, and you'll lose more games than you win.

However, Comaford's terms refer more to the types of people you need rather than to specific jobs or positions. Visionaries can and should appear at all levels of a company, but they are crucial as part of your executive management team. "These are the people who will 'see' the future of the products or services of your company as well as new markets you should enter," Comaford explains. Leaders, on the other hand, are skilled at guiding that vision into reality—they see what the vision requires—and implementers make things happen. They build the product or provide the service; they do the marketing and the selling. The infrastructure builders/supporters create the foundation for the company; they develop and run the processes and procedures that keep your employees working smoothly together.

In a larger company, these four functions are roughly equivalent to the CEO, the upper management, the employees and the human resources department. In a small start-up, you simply want to make sure your team, whatever its size or structure, possesses all these talents, and that everyone is working on jobs that complement his or her skills.

"The visionaries need the leaders to check and disseminate their vision, the leaders need the implementers to execute their orders, and everyone needs the infrastructure builders/supporters to support the company's operations." If you are missing one of these roles in your young business, warns Comaford, fill it soon. If you can't afford a full-time staffer, Comaford advises, "hire a temp executive or outsource the work—a rent-a-controller is better than no controller."

# Rock The Culture

The best way to build, support and retain a great team, says Comaford, is to encourage a hip culture in your business—one that has young, savvy, enthusiastic workers pressing their noses up against your front window panting to get in. Create friendly work environments, take a personal interest in employees and encourage their involvement by giving them a stake in the success of your business. To get the word out on your new operation, take the "Garfield" route and paste your company's logo on everything that isn't nailed down, like coffee cups, baseball caps and T-shirts. Your logo should personify, or better yet, amplify your corporate philosophy. At Artemis Ventures, Comaford urges her employees to add massive value, take ownership, make and keep commitments, respect one another and be positive. "I've seen solid, enduring and humane work environments created by endorsing values—and I've seen crumbling, oppressive ones without them," she explains. "Encourage the following virtues, too: humility, communication, empowerment, generosity, focus, fiscal responsibility, innovation and patience. Remember: Hiring grade 'A' people creates grade 'A' teams."

## Pop Goes The Question

At a loss for words when it comes to forming interview questions? Here are some to get you started:

- If you could design the perfect job for yourself, what would you do? Why?
- What kind of supervisor gets the best work out of you?
- How would you describe your current supervisor?
- How do you structure your time?
- What are three things you like about your current job?
- What were your three biggest accomplishments in your last job? In your career?
- What can you do for our company that no one else can?
- What are your biggest strengths/weaknesses?
- How far do you think you can go in this company? Why?
- What do you expect to be doing in five years?
- What interests you most about this company? This position?
- Describe three situations where your work was criticized.
- Have you hired people before? If so, what did you look for?

One more tip: To help team members envision their next promotion or two, let them know where you're leading them and what you expect of them. "I once had a start-up client where I told the senior execs that I expected them to start their own companies in a few years," she adds. She wanted them to consider this their "next promotion"—and she offered an unusual incentive. "I told them to learn all they could, then when the time came, I'd help finance their new ventures. Talk about building loyalty!"

## Bozos Make Great Clowns, Lousy Employees

When you begin your campaign to mine the best talent you can find, keep in mind the following desirable qualities:

- **Smarts:** Hire the smartest people you can find, not necessarily the most charming. It's not that smart people won't make mistakes or create messes, but they'll find their way out of the majority of them.

- **Pedigree:** According to Comaford, an MBA doesn't impress her as much as a GSD—that is, a person who "Gets Stuff Done." "Someone who has results, results, results all over their past has a pedigree every bit as powerful as an Ivy League degree," she advises.

- **Commitment:** Commitment to your company is something you can encourage, but not the innate drive to succeed. You want the fire-in-the-belly go-getter who will eagerly follow you into battle. "When the grenades are flying, the committed person doesn't go AWOL," says Comaford. "There is nothing more powerful than emotional equity. No amount of stock options even comes close."

- **Plays well with others:** In fact, many entrepreneurs became business owners because they didn't always get along with others (such as their old co-workers or bosses). Now that you run your own business, remember how hard communication can be. Hire others who are equally enlightened—those who know when to be flexible and when to speak up.

Another tip from Comaford: The best way to find your team is by schmoozing. Go to every industry event you can and tell everyone about your great company and the kind of people you are looking to hire.

# 10 questions

*Name:* Jack A. Martinez
*Age:* 34
*Company:* Black Flys, retail store chain selling everything from Black Flys-brand sunglasses and clothing to music CDs
*Location:* Costa Mesa, California
*Web Site:* www.flys.com
*Year Founded:* 1991
*Start-up Costs:* $14,000
*1998 Sales:* $10 million
*1999 Projections:* $14 million

1. **What was your first entrepreneurial venture?**
   A streetside flower stand

2. **At what age did you start it?**
   9

3. **What did you learn from the experience?**
   Plenty; the police came and demanded a business license.

4. **What age were you when you made your first million?**
   28

5. **What was your first job as an employee?**
   Selling bon-bons at Anaheim Stadium [now Edison Field]

6. **Did you go to college?**
   Yes, majored in architecture

7. **What age were you when you started your first "real" full-time venture?**
   18

8. **Who is your role model?**
   Andy Warhol and Walt Disney

9. **How many businesses have you started?**
   Six

10. **How many were successful, and how many failed?**
    Four succeeded, and two failed.

# Build An Extended Team

Scott Korn, the founder of York Paper, says that the most important thing he did as a young entrepreneur was grabbing the best
help he could find, pay them well and then work hard to mesh them
as a unit. "That not only means the employees you hire directly but
anyone else you can draw lessons from," says Korn. "I've talked to
consultants, other paper manufacturers, family members, anyone I
thought could give us an edge."

Your business's extended team is like a gathering of your
friends, cousins and neighbors: They're all there for you and want
to see you happy. Your extended team will be made up of your
investors (if you have any), a board of advisors (which may include
a knowledgeable parent, business colleagues, previous business
mentors, members of industry organizations, even indirect competitors) and family members. These are the people that—whether
for love or money—give you the advice you need to understand
and grow your business. If you're just starting out and have little or
no knowledge of your industry (both a brave and foolish act),
relentlessly cull your new industry for sources to add to your
extended network.

"I didn't know anyone in my industry when I just started out,"
recalls Matthew Glitzer, founder of FeMail Inc., women's pharmaceutical mail order supply company in Washington, DC. "I did
have the advantage of a supportive family—I couldn't have survived financially without them—but I also aggressively sought
people I thought could help
me learn more about women's
health products and how to
build a mail order distribution
system. There's a lot of foot-
work involved when you don't
know the industry, but gathering help can be done."

Many young entrepreneurs
consider it vital to add seasoned voices of reason to the
mix in the form of a board of
advisors. A board of advisors
should consist of entrepre-

## How Do You Rate?

**A**s a boss, are you a saint...or a
Scrooge? Read Jim Miller's *Best
Boss, Worst Boss* (Fireside) to get an
idea about how you rate. Miller collected real-life stories (like the tight-
wad boss who charges employees 30
cents per personal call). Good bosses, by contrast, are generous, com-
passionate and empowering. Result?
Happier, more productive and loyal
employees.

neurs who've already run successful companies or high-ranking corporate executives who've traveled the same road your young company is setting out on. Keep five to seven slots open on your board of advisors and choose advisors with the following profiles: deep experience, deeper pockets, good connections and an affinity for a specific area, like marketing or sales. "Make sure that each advisory board member plays a specific role, such as helping with strategic alliances, or working with the sales, marketing or technical teams," says Comaford. "This keeps them focused." Also keep your extended team committed and passionate with monthly e-mail updates. Above all, take your time. It's more important to find the right board members than it is to build an advisory team quickly. Be choosy and don't worry about openings you can't fill. If you're picky, you'll fill your board seats eventually and with better people, too.

# Before You Hire, Determine Your Needs

Hiring the right employees rates near the top of any young entrepreneur's "critical" list. "I can't imagine how I got by without an assistant," recalls Lisa Swayne, founder of Swayne Literary Agency. "I struggled early to do everything on my own. It really took me 18 months to get going, and it wasn't until I got to that point that I could hire an assistant, who turned out to be great. I only wished I'd done it sooner."

Eventually, Swain hired three more employees and formed an excellent work team, which allowed her to cut back on her own rigorous seven-day schedule. But before you can hire the right people, you have to figure out what tasks need to be done and how many hands it will take to accomplish them. You may know you need an accountant, but do you have enough work to employ one full time? Do you need a single marketing person to handle all the promotion, or do you need a marketer, a publicist and a copywriter? If you're not sure what you need, it may be better to hire slowly until you do know. After all, the last thing you want is to hire people who aren't really necessary and then have to fire them or restructure their jobs six months later.

Finally, before you begin interviewing, think about your company policies as well: Be prepared for any question a prospective employee might ask about your company before he or she is sitting in front of you, waiting while you make something up.

# How To Create And Advertise Your New Job

- **As you determine your need to hire a new employee, consider the following questions:** Are you properly using your current employees' skills and talents? Do you know what needs to be done? Can your business growth support a new employee? How will the new employee fit into the current office structure? How might the job you're creating now grow or change in the years to come?

- **Conduct a thorough job analysis to determine what kind of personality, experience and education are needed for the new position.** The job analysis should cover the following areas: the physical and mental tasks involved, how the job will be done (the methods and equipment used), the reasons the job exists and the qualifications needed.

- **Write both a job description and a job specification for the position based on the job analysis.** The job description is basically an outline of how the job fits into your company. It should point out in broad terms the job's goals, responsibilities and duties, as well as how the job relates to other positions in the company.

  The job specification describes the personal requirements you expect from the employee. Like the job description, it also includes the job title, whom the person reports to and a summary of the position. However, it also lists any educational requirements, desired experience and specialized skills or knowledge required. Include salary range and benefits. Finish by listing any physical or other special requirements associated with the job, as well as any occupational hazards.

- **Determine the salary for the position, based on internal and external equity.** Is the salary comparable and proportional with the salaries and responsibilities of other positions inside your company as well as with similar positions in the marketplace?

- **Write your recruitment materials, such as newspaper or Internet advertisements, based on the job description and specification.**

● **Finally, decide where and how to find qualified applicants.**
What are the recruitment techniques to be used? What is the time
frame for conducting your search? Remember, advertising in the
help-wanted section of your local newspaper or through an
industry-specific job-search Web site are not the only, or necessarily the best, ways to recruit. You can also tap into your personal and professional network, contact school placement
offices, use an employment agency, advertise in industry publications or list your position with an appropriate job bank.

# Conducting A Successful Interview

Once you have collected and reviewed a fair amount of applications and resumes, select only the most qualified candidates for
further consideration. Whittle the pile down to the people you really want to talk to, and eliminate the job candidates whose work
history or lack of expertise clearly disqualify them from the position.

Then, conduct your interviews, call the employee references
and hire the best person for the job!

It's simple, really, but it's also one of the most stressful and anx-
iety-producing tasks in any business, especially for new entrepreneurs. Here are some tips on how to prepare for and conduct a job
interview.

**Do your homework:**

● Know what you want in a candidate and know the job and its
responsibilities before you start the interview. Review the
job description and specifications.

● Prepare a list of standard questions concerning the candidate's skills, abilities and past work performance that you
want him or her to answer.

● Prepare a list of prioritized and measurable criteria, either in
the form of a work sheet or other method, for analyzing and
comparing candidates. However, be prepared to justify the
use of any employment test. Typically, the most legally
defensible tests are those that involve a potential employee's
direct job responsibilities, although tests of all stripes are
employed in the business world. Microsoft is famed for

using "personality tests" that allegedly tell managers whether a candidate can solve problems in an "out of the box" fashion, which the company prefers. On Wall Street, basic investment test questions like "What's an initial public offering?" or "What's a call option?" are mixed with more character-flavored queries like "What would you do if the trader next to you was engaged in insider trading and you knew about it?"

For the most part, tailor your tests to the job in question and leave the generic stuff alone. For example, if you are interviewing a potential controller or accountant, keep the queries related to budgetary issues and financial acumen. In other words, no Barbara Walters-esque questions like "If you were a houseplant, which houseplant would you be?" While I would choose tiger lily, it really doesn't help you decide if your controller can be counted on at tax time.

- Review the candidate's resume prior to the interview.

- Set appointment times and reasonable time limits for the interview. If possible, have at least one other person meet and/or interview candidates who are finalists, and establish how the process will be run. A good rule of thumb is no more than a half hour per staffer or manager.

**Break out the magnifying glass:**

- Since past behavior predicts future behavior, look for the candidate's behavior "patterns" as you collect information. For example, has the candidate enjoyed "big picture" work or detailed analysis more? Is he or she more of a generalist or more of a specialist? Oftentimes, by listening to how the candidate responds to your questions about previous jobs, you will be able to get a very good idea of what his or her behavior will be like in the future.

- Try not to offer too much detailed information about what you're looking for up front since this can prompt a candidate to formulate answers that merely echo the job description you've written. Don't put the right words in his or her mouth. Remember, the candidate (hopefully) wants the job and will be looking to say the right thing to impress you.

- Ask questions that focus on the candidate's past performances. For example, if the job you're hiring for, such as an office manager, demands an individual who is well organized and handles paperwork easily, you may want to ask, "How did you keep track of your schedule and desk work in your previous positions?"

● Ask specific, structured questions in regards to problems that the job holder may face. Focus on past behavior and the results of the candidate's actions in a particular situation. For example: "As the customer service representative, you may encounter a few unhappy campers who will yell and scream at you over the telephone or in person. Have you had any experience dealing with difficult customers? Who was the most difficult customer you had to deal with? What was the situation? How did you resolve the problem?"

## Manual Labor

**S**ooner or later, every entrepreneur needs to write a manual. An employee policy manual, a procedures manual or a safety manual are just a few of the more important ones.

Even if you only have one employee, it's not too soon to start putting policies in writing. Doing so now—before your staff grows—can prevent bickering, confusion and, worse, lawsuits later when Steve finds out you gave Joe five sick days and he only got four.

How to start? As with everything, begin by planning. Write a detailed outline of what you want to include.

As you write, focus on making sure the manual is easy to read and understand. Think of the simplest, shortest way to convey information. Use bullet points and numbered lists, where possible, for easier reading.

A lawyer or human resources consultant can be invaluable throughout the process. At the very least, you'll want your attorney to review the finished product for loopholes.

Finally, ensure all new employees receive a copy of the manual and read it. Include a page that employees must sign, date and return to you stating they have read and understood all the information in the manual and agree to abide by your company's policies. Maintain this in their personnel file.

- Notice how well the candidate listens and responds to the questions asked.

- Note the candidate's choice of words and nonverbal behavior. Is he or she answering your questions clearly? Does the job candidate become evasive around certain issues. Does he or she become restless, looking anywhere but at you?

- Listen to the questions the candidate asks. Clarify the reasons why these questions are being asked. Notice which questions he or she asks first, as they may indicate the person's primary concerns.

- Write down any information pertaining to the set criteria that will help in the evaluation of candidates.

- Organize and analyze the information immediately after the interview when your memory is fresh. Don't try to remember everything; it's impossible. One idea is to "rate" each candidate on each of the criteria immediately following the interview.

**R-E-S-P-E-C-T:**

- Dress appropriately.

- Begin the interview on schedule.

- Set a businesslike atmosphere. Structure the interview and inform the candidate of the structure. Let the candidate know you will be focusing on past results and that you will be taking a lot of notes.

- Provide information on the company and the job to each candidate. Either send the applicant a company package or point him or her toward your Web site. The latter places the initiative on candidates' shoulders, which provides insight into how much drive they possess.

- Show a genuine interest in every candidate you interview; don't appear bored or fatigued.

- Conduct the interview in a private place away from distractions. If possible, don't take calls and avoid interruptions.

- Appreciate the candidate's accomplishments.

- Do not patronize the candidate.

- Do not argue with the candidate.

- Thank the candidate for his or her time and interest.

**Query fairly:**

- A job interview is inherently stressful. Immediately attempt to establish a rapport with the candidate and lessen this anxiety; for example, break the ice by asking about his or her experiences in a particular industry or geographic location (refer to his or her resume).

- Promote a relaxed environment with free-flowing conversation.

- Do not dominate the discussion by talking too much. Many experts use an 80/20 rule—you talk 20 percent of the time and the candidate talks 80 percent of the time.

- Use your list of standard questions during each interview so that you treat the applicants the same and so that you can compare apples to apples.

- Refer to your criteria for analyzing candidates. Ask questions in regards to the job criteria.

- Keep all questions job-related.

- Avoid too many yes-or-no questions. Ask open-ended or structured questions that require multilevel answers. These will provide insight into the candidate's values and traits as well as into how they think and approach problems.

- Listen carefully to the candidate's answers. If the person does not provide a specific-enough response to a query, politely probe until he or she does.

- If you have candidates interview with other people in the company, make sure each person rates the candidates using the same criteria; ultimately, all interviewers should compare their ratings and discuss any discrepancies. Having more than one interviewer helps control personal biases.

## Test-Drive

**I**f relevant, ask employees to send samples of their work with their resumes or to bring them to the interview. Another technique: Ask them to complete a project similar to the actual work they'd be doing (and pay them for it). This gives you a strong indication of how they'd perform on the job...and gives them a clear picture of what you expect from them.

- Explain the selection process to the candidate. Offer a realistic time frame for when you will make a final decision, and stick to your word!

## The Cringe Factor: Interview Gaffes To Avoid

We're all human, and we all make mistakes. But some mistakes have larger ramifications than others—especially in delicate situations like job interviews. You probably already know what it's like sitting on the job prospect side of the desk; that is, you worried about talking too little or too much, forgetting to mention the great job you did for Company X on Project Y, or, heaven forbid, failing to remove that piece of broccoli from between your teeth after lunch. Now that you're on the other side of the desk as the interviewer, some of these same worries still apply—along with a few new rules. Some job interview gaffes are minor, while some—like comments about race, sex or a physical disability—can inspire charges of bias or discrimination and can get you into more trouble than you want to know. Bias or discrimination complaints against a company's hiring practices can be dealt with severely, with fines and tons of bad publicity for the company in question—newspapers love that kind of stuff.

So in an interview, or on an employment application, do not ask questions . . .

- concerning the candidate's age. Be careful using the phrase "over-qualified" with older candidates, as it could become ammunition in a discrimination suit.

- about the candidate's arrest record (this is different from convictions—in most states, it is permissible to ask if the candidate has ever been convicted of a crime).

- concerning the candidate's citizenship in the United States prior to hiring (it is permissible to ask "Will you be able to provide proof of eligibility to work in the United States if hired?").

- concerning the candidate's ancestry, birthplace or native language (it is permissible to ask about their ability to speak English or a foreign language if it is required for the job).

- about religion or religious customs or holidays.

- concerning the candidate's height and weight if it does not affect their ability to perform the job.

- concerning the names and addresses of relatives (it is permissible to ask after only those relatives employed by the organization).

- about whether or not the candidate owns or rents his or her home and who lives with the person (it is permissible to ask for addresses for future contact.).

- concerning the candidate's credit history or financial situation (in some cases, such as for a bank teller or financial advisor, credit history may be considered job-related, but proceed with extreme caution).

- concerning education or training that is not required to perform the job.

- concerning pregnancy or medical history (attendance records at a previous employer may be discussed in most situations as long as you don't refer to illness or disability).

- concerning the candidate's family or marital status or child-care arrangements (it is permissible to ask if the candidate will be able to work the required hours for the job).

- concerning the candidate's membership in a nonprofessional organization or club that is not related to the job.

- concerning physical or mental disabilities (it is permissible to ask whether the candidate can perform the essential job duties. The Americans With Disabilities Act allows you to ask the applicant to describe or demonstrate how he or she would perform any essential functions when certain specific conditions are met. Check the law or consult with an attorney before moving forward).

A good rule of thumb: When in doubt about whether a question is offensive or not, play it safe and zip your lip. You can also check with the federal government's Equal Employment Opportunity Commission or your state attorney general's office to find out more about which questions are off-limits.

## Double Agent

Whenever possible, look for employees you can cross-train into different job responsibilities. A welder with college courses in engineering and a secretary with human resources experience are workers one small business has successfully cross-trained. Cross-trained employees can fill in when others are absent, helping keep costs down.

# It Takes More Than Starbucks To Perk Up An Office

Now that you've hired your tight group of talented, smart, energetic employees, you need to do all you can to keep them. You can start by offering a competitive wage, but that isn't always enough. Just ask Eric Strauss (below, center), the founder of Crazy Carrot Juice Bars (whom we met in Chapter 1).

When the 30-year-old Strauss set his sights on the $500 million-plus smoothie market in the mid-1990s, he didn't count on having to do so much to keep employees happy. In 1996, Strauss opened his first juice bar in Minneapolis to rave reviews. Two more followed, as did a partnership with two friends, Liem Nguyen (below, left), 25, and Tony Barranco, 25, to grow the business. Helped by the booming economy, Crazy Carrot Juice Bars became a $1-million-plus chain, but at the same time, the surging economy had created a seller's market for employees, many of whom could choose where, when and for how much cash and perks they would work for.

"One of the first challenges we faced was keeping good people," explains Strauss. "I brought people on board like Liem and Tony and hired some full-time workers shortly after. I hired the managers, who do all the training, hiring and computers. We put a lot of work into getting good people and found it frustrating that we always couldn't hang on to them."

Strauss had already deployed some savvy strategies to keep customers coming back, like offering juice tipplers free Internet access inside his store; now he needed to do the same with his employees. Ultimately, Strauss sweetened the pot. "We began offering health benefits and a souped-up retirement account package with 3 percent company matching for employees. We gave them better discounts on food and merchandise and things got better. But in a good economy, keeping good employees is tough."

Like Strauss, when you own a small business, it's not always easy to offer expensive perks to your employees to thank them for a job

PHOTO COURTESY: CRAZY CARROT JUICE BAR

well done. At the same time, fierce competition for top employees is causing compensation costs to soar as small companies compete with large corporations with deeper pockets. A Coopers & Lybrand study released in 1997 reported that more and more companies of all sizes are relying on stock incentive programs and customized benefit plans to attract new professionals and to hold on to their best talent. Smaller companies, however, may need to be even more creative about what perks and benefits they offer to motivate and keep employees.

"In a **good** economy, **keeping** good employees is **tough**."

It's no secret that fringe benefits such as medical, dental, vision, disability, life insurance and retirement benefits are huge expenses for all businesses. The Coopers & Lybrand survey found that employee benefits added approximately 9 percent to the typical respondent's direct labor costs, and they added 19 percent to the labor costs of the largest corporations. While small companies with revenues of less than $250,000 spent slightly less (7 percent) in relation to labor costs, that number represents a much larger chunk of their overall financial picture.

Small businesses can help make up the difference by offering a few well-selected, thoughtful perks to staffers. In Strauss' opinion, basic benefits like medical insurance and retirement programs are must-haves for full-time staff, but you can also develop a variable reward system, with some of the perks distributed companywide and some singled out for individuals who have done a great job. For example, you may consider giving a gift certificate for a $50 dinner at a local restaurant to workers who put in extra hours to complete a project. Or you could offer a coupon for a free movie as a small token of appreciation for those who give above-average service to customers. While small rewards like this are a relatively light financial outlay, they can be just as rewarding as big expensive programs if handled correctly.

Another great idea is to offer a 'free' day or half day off—one that doesn't count against allotted vacation time—to show your appreciation to exceptional workers. These days should be dispensed sparingly because they will lose impact over time if given too freely, and they can leave you temporarily short-handed.

When considering which perks are best suited for your employees, never underestimate the power of good, old-fashioned cash.

Bonuses are the most conventional reward method, but they are proven motivators and are always appreciated by workers, especially those who don't earn large salaries.

"Research shows that a key concern of employers is finding and keeping good employees," says Don Bagin, publisher of *Communications Briefings*, a business communications newsletter in Atlanta. "Too many bosses feel that giving employees a paycheck is reward enough—it's not. Research also shows that employees rate being appreciated as a top job concern. Managers, however, rate being appreciated among the lowest concerns they thought their employees would have."

To reward properly, Bagin suggests the following:

**1** Reward initiative and creativity. Organizations thrive on people who can come up with ideas and carry them out

**2** Keep in mind that the sooner you reward a person's good work, the stronger the reinforcement.

**3** Be specific when giving accolades. Don't just send out general notes congratulating someone on a job well done. Explain what made it well done.

**4** Understand what's important to the people getting the rewards. Give them something they'll appreciate.

**5** Reward people for setting and meeting goals that are consistent with those of the organization.

**6** Don't send a message that mediocrity—or worse—will be rewarded. Spend time and effort improving employees with poor work habits, but let them go if they fail to improve.

## Baby, Please Don't Leave Me

There is an old sales adage that says keeping current customers is more important than finding new ones. The same goes for your work force. In fact, there is really no excuse for not being able to keep good employees. Are you fostering a professional work environment or one that leaves employees wondering if they have been conscripted to Hitler's bunker? Unhappy employees can eventually kill your business, so don't be complacent with this issue—check out these tips on attracting and keeping good workers:

**1** **Sell job applicants on working for you.** Desirable job applicants usually get multiple job offers. Up your chances of winning the best workers by using the interview to sell them on your company. You'll hire more of the applicants you want if you take time to tell them why your company is right for them.

**2** **Know your mission.** The more dramatically you state your business' mission—whether it's to make the world's best bagel or to outperform Wal-Mart—the easier it will be to hire and retain good employees. Employees want to know why they are working so hard. The mission tells them.

**3** **Get your name in the local newspaper.** People want to work for businesses they have heard about, so getting local publicity can be a big plus in recruiting staff. Even a little ink can win you visibility and enhance your credibility with prospective employees.

**4** **Offer benefits.** Many small businesses scrimp on benefits. Big mistake. You won't attract quality workers if you offer nothing but a salary. You don't have to match what big corporations offer, but cover the basics. Health insurance and paid vacations are mandatory.

**5** **Give employees the right tools.** Without the proper equipment, employees can't perform to their or your expectations. Don't pinch pennies on computers, photocopiers, phones and the like. The money you save on equipment will be spent replacing lost workers.

**6** **Give regular feedback.** Employees want to hear how they are doing, and they really value pats on the back. Research is emphatic that one of the best—and cheapest—motivators is sincere, specific praise for a job well done. So when workers perform, tell them!

**7** **Train for success.** A terrific way to reward workers—and benefit the company—is to invest in them by paying for training. Training pays off by boosting loyalty and job performance.

**8** **Match the worker with the job.** Whenever possible, put workers on tasks they want to do and are good at. The payoff is a happier worker—and better work.

**9** **Let workers design the work.** Whenever workers can choose how to do a job, let them. It substantially raises satisfaction.

**10** **Give bonuses.** Money talks when it comes to keeping high-performing employees, and the best way to reward them is with bonuses. It lets employees know that when they perform at high levels, they'll prosper—and so will your business.

> "We were very **young** when we started our business; about **14** and **18**, respectively. But we've come a **long** way in a **short** time."
>
> —*Sarah Levinson*

# Tougher Than Nails

**N**ext time you see Demi Moore or Jennifer Aniston on-screen, check out their fingernails. They shouldn't be hard to notice. Chances are they're wearing the bodacious nail polish from Ripe, one of the hottest cosmetics outfits this side of Revlon. Sisters Anna and Sarah Levinson started the company, which features 70 shades of polish and 50 lipstick colors, after spending their early years mixing and matching nail polish and lipstick colors that were glam before the term was in vogue.

The duo started out selling their homemade nail polish at small stores on trendy Melrose Avenue in their hometown of Los Angeles, selling bottles of polish for about $7 each, compared to $10 and up for other models. Then they would reinvest the profits for more supplies, from empty bottles and colors to mix-and-match sticker labels. "We had our colors and our ideas together in January 1995," explains Anna, who had just turned 20 at the time. "But we didn't have the capital, so even though it may seem as though we're a step behind competitors like Hard Candy, we really weren't. It just took us a while to get a manufacturer."

**Anna Levinson, 23**
**Sarah Levinson, 20**

*Company:* **Ripe**
*Location:* **Los Angeles**
*Year Started:* **1995**
*Start-up Costs:* **$7,000**
*1998 Revenues:* **$500,000**
*1999 Projections:* **$700,000**

Celebrity intervention helped. TV viewers nationwide couldn't help but notice Danny DeVito wearing some of Ripe's nail polish ("Nannah" if you want to know) on his left pinkie at the 1997 Emmy Awards. Actress Tori Spelling regularly wore Ripe polishes like Cumulus and Crystal Palace on "Beverly Hills, 90210," a fashion trendsetter for the younger set. And both Courtney Love and Alicia Silverstone have been spotted at the Oscar's wearing Ripe nail polish and lipstick. "We knew we were going to be a hit," says Sarah.

The money didn't flow in overnight, but the Levinsons weren't worried. "We knew we were going to be OK because the colors we offer are better than the competition and any girl can buy the stuff from her allowance," Anna says. "We think nails are the perfect way to express yourself."

Ripe offers plenty of colors that won't meet with Mom's seal of approval, like Firecracker over Plasma and Crystal Palace over Lotus. That's part of Ripe's appeal. But when your product is carried by brand-name retailers like Nordstrom and Urban Outfitters, you know even Moms are getting into the act.

# When The Water Reaches The Bridge

Some entrepreneurs are so busy scanning the horizon, they never see it coming: a vital distributor who has become fed up with chronically late shipments, a dishonest treasurer who's manipulating the accounting ledgers, a change in consumer attitudes toward your product. While external economic factors are often to blame for a company's demise, internal factors are equally devastating—and they are fixable. Even the most well-intentioned and determined entrepreneurs may find themselves floundering on a sinking ship, but fortunately, there are plenty of warning signs that can alert you if your young business is about to go under.

- **"I Quit"**: If key employees are jumping ship each quarter, you've got a problem, matey. Fortunately, it's also an easily quantifiable one. Make sure to find out why people are leaving, and fix the problem.

- **Difficulty in hiring talent:** If you can't get good job candidates to sign on, that's another sign of trouble. Smart workers avoid problem companies more than they do Pauly Shore movies. Believe me, they know when something's not right—whether it's a rumor about a belligerent management culture, a newspaper article questioning the long-term viability of your business, or simply bad vibes. If the best people always tell you no, waste no time in getting to the root of the problem, even if it means calling those people who turned you down and asking why.

- **A lonely office after 5 p.m.:** If your workplace reminds you of Death Valley five minutes after closing time, and your footsteps echo down empty hallways, it's time to reevaluate. No indication of a troubled company is more accurate than an empty parking lot at 5:15.

- **Divided we fall:** Is there tension between management and staffers? If a communications gap or worse exists between managers and workers, a serious problem may be brewing. Seamless units stay together. Frayed ones eventually fall apart.

- **"Dilberts" show up on your desk:** If one of Scott Adams's "Dilbert" strips is anonymously pushed under your door, it's nothing to fret about. Get heaps of them, and it's no longer a laughing matter. In other words, when you become the target of caustic cartoons, you're in trouble with your employees.

- **Falling customer satisfaction:** Are complaints increasing? Are customers leaving you for competitors? If so, don't blame the fickle public. Most likely, the underlying reason for customer dissatisfaction is a drop in quality. And when workers no longer put out top effort, it's proof they have stopped caring about the company's future.

- **Low attendance at company events:** Have workers stopped showing up for company get-togethers? Or if they go, do they merely nod and grunt at you as they make their way toward the bar? When attendance at off-hour events falls, it's a sign that people are doing only what they have to do to get by.

- **Lack of honest communication:** When employees begin lying to you, their co-workers and customers, you'd better address the problem—fast.

If your company exhibits only a few of these warning signs, it's probably not too late. A first step is to get back to basics. Call a companywide meeting—off-site at a nice restaurant or hotel if you can—and reaffirm your company's goals and mission. Open the lines of dialogue with your staffers and find out why there's discord. Most won't talk, but the brave ones—or the ones who've already lined up other jobs—will. Listen to what they have to say and admit you don't know all the answers. That's one reason you hired them.

The healing process from a bruised business culture won't happen overnight. Treated effectively and promptly, your business can eventually regain its health and viability—but only if you continue to listen to what your employees have to say.

# Chapter

Many younger entrepreneurs are willing and able to risk failure rather than compromise their ideals.

# The Righteous Stuff: Gen E And Social Responsibility

By nature, young entrepreneurs are idealists. Most are college-educated (some, like Bill Gates, nongraduates), and most are driven by political and social issues that influence the way they run their businesses. Some young entrepreneurs, for example, refuse to do business with tobacco companies or with companies that have ties to countries with notorious human rights records, like Haiti or China. Others encourage employees to contribute money to favored political candidates or to actively participate in favorite causes, like Earth Day or AIDS awareness events. In short, these companies take on the personalities of their founders—for good or for bad. After all, people whose closets are larded with mink coats may not be too excited about writing a check to People for the Ethical Treatment of Animals.

By disavowing corporate conservatism and rigidity and crafting politically and culturally active companies in their own image, many young entrepreneurs are, on the one hand, merely expressing their individuality and rebelliousness, but there's also growing evidence that it can be good for business. Establishing ethical codes of conduct and acting in a socially conscious manner—both within a company and between the company and the community at large—brings tangible rewards, above and beyond profits and time invested. Like-minded employees are more productive and will likely stick with a company that shares their particular brand of politics and social awareness. That's a big bonus in a tight labor market. According to a recent Walker Information survey of 1,694 employees, 86 percent of respondents shared a favorable view of their company's social outreach efforts. Seventy-three percent said they work in organizations that have written standards of ethical business conduct. Nearly four in 10 worked for organizations that provide ethics-related training, and 31 percent said their companies had either an ethics office or an ombudsman.

> Employees are **more** productive and will likely **stick** with a company that **shares** their particular brand of **politics** and social **awareness**.

"I think more and more companies are recognizing that there are greater demands placed on them by stakeholders," says Marjorie Chorlins, executive vice president of Business for Social Responsibility (BSR).

"Investors and employees in a tight labor market are taking into account socially responsible practices before they invest in, or go to work for, a company. Everyone is paying closer attention, and good companies realize that."

The same sense of loyalty is bred in customers, who are drawn to businesses that share their political and cultural views. In a recent Walker Information poll of consumer trends, 47 percent of the 1,036 polled said that given a level playing field, they would base their final buying decisions on which company was more politically correct. Seventy percent said they would not—at any

## Do The Right Thing

S ome resources for the socially conscious business owner:

- **Business For Social Responsibility:** Regards social responsibility and profitability as compatible goals. Offers conferences, educational programs for the public and consulting for members. Call (415) 537-0888 or visit www.bsr.org.

- **Co-Op America:** This national nonprofit group helps businesses and individuals solve social and environmental problems. Their Web site features the Green Pages, a searchable directory of products and services from environmentally and socially conscious businesses. Call (800) 58-GREEN or visit www.coopamerica.org.

- **Social Venture Network:** A 400-member group of business leaders and entrepreneurs. Their Web site has information on the group's special initiatives, such as a program to involve businesses in urban areas. Call (415) 561-6501 or visit www.svn.org.

- *Beyond the Bottom Line: Putting Social Responsibility to Work for Your Business and the World* (Touchstone Books), by Joel Makower: Gives a history of Business for Social Responsibility as well as advice on making your business socially conscious.

- *75 Best Business Practices for Socially Responsible Companies* (JP Tarcher), by Alan Reder: Offers practical case studies on how raised social responsibility can increase profitability.

- *Companies with a Conscience: Intimate Portraits of Twelve Firms That Make a Difference* (Citadel Press), by Mary Scott: Profiles of 12 profitable U.S. companies that demonstrate social responsibility.

price—buy products from a company that was not socially responsible. In other words, a company earns some points for doing good
deeds, but it gets hammered if it indulges in unethical business
practices. All things being equal between two otherwise similar
businesses, the one that matches a customer's social philosophy
will invariably walk away with the business.

Of course, it's impossible to quantify just how many young
entrepreneurs are running their businesses in socially conscious
ways, but the fact that more youthful companies are thinking green
or supporting other political causes by itself is hardly surprising.
Young people are frequently more idealistic and socially conscious—or at least more vocally so—than their established elders.
Many younger entrepreneurs aren't married, have no children and
have never held a corporate job, a fact that makes them willing and
able to risk failure rather than compromise their ideals. Gen E's
bring a singular political point of view that's unique to the younger
set. Of the 40 or so Gen E business owners interviewed for this
book, about a third said that "doing well by doing good deeds" was
a top priority.

# A Little Tea And Sympathy

Take Seth Goldman, 34, owner and co-founder (along with Yale
economics professor Barry Nalebuff) of Bethesda, Maryland's
Honest Tea. "We provide better tasting, healthier teas, iced and otherwise, the way nature and their cultures of origin intended them to
be—tea that truly tastes like tea," explains Goldman, who takes
great pains to brew his tea and conduct his business in a socially
aware fashion. "We also strive for relationships with our customers,
employees, suppliers and stakeholders which are as healthy and
honest as the tea we brew."

The company's brand is based on authenticity, integrity and
purity. Unlike most tea-flavored beverages—which are made with
powder, tea concentrate or tea waste—Honest Tea is brewed with
select tea leaves from around the world. The company's production
process is quite similar to the way tea is made in the kitchen, except
on a much larger scale. "As a result," says Goldman, "a drink of
Honest Tea becomes a cultural experience, from the genuine tastes
to the distinctive international art and quotations on the labels."

Goldman's company features flavors like Assam, Black Forest Berry, Kasmiri Chai and Gold Rush.

Social responsibility is also central to Honest Tea's identity and purpose, and the management team is committed to those values as well. "We will never claim to be a perfect company, but we will address difficult issues and strive to be honest about our ability or inability to resolve them," says Goldman. "We will strive to work with our suppliers to promote higher standards. We value diversity in the workplace and intend to become a visible presence in the communities where our products are sold. When presented with a purchasing decision between two financially comparable alternatives, we will attempt to choose the option that better addresses the needs of economically disadvantaged communities."

Shortly after launching the business, Goldman got a big chance to test his company's commitment to social responsibility. He was intrigued by a recipe for peppermint herbal tea that had been sent to him by I'tchik Herb, a women-owned company on the Crow reservation (where unemployment is 40 percent). "The Crow Indians believed that rivers represent the bloodlines of the Earth," explains Goldman. "Drinking the peppermint tea they got from the leaves that grew near the Big Horn River represented a way for the Crow to bring themselves into harmony with the Earth, thus renewing the bloodlines in their body. Crow sundancers drink peppermint tea before and after their four-day fast to align their spirit, body and mind.

"Because the ingredients were fairly simple, we could have easily copied the recipe, called it something like 'Sundance' tea and brought it to market ourselves," says Goldman. "In many ways that seemed like our best option, since I'tchik was hesitant to enter into a relationship with yet another company that was

## Get Online And Get Green

The Web site Green Pages Online shows you where to find everything from energy efficient light bulbs and children's clothes made from pesticide-free cotton to socially responsible financial planners. To check out the site, go to www.greenpages.org. If you don't have Internet access but want more information about ordering the Green Pages, call Co-Op America at (800) 58-GREEN. The cost is $7.95 per copy, including shipping and handling.

interested in commercializing Native American culture."

Instead, I'tchik and Gold-man entered into a lengthy bout of negotiations. I'tchik wanted to bring the peppermint-flavored tea onto the market in a way that would make the Crows full partners in the product. It was an unusual situation, but the two parties eventually came to an agreement: I'tchik would be the sole supplier for the organic peppermint tea leaves, and the Crow nation would be full-time marketing partners in the promotion and distribution of the new tea. Under the arrangement, I'tchik would be paid, based on sales of the tea, a royalty. Seventy-five percent of that royalty would go to the tribe and 25 percent to the Pretty Shield Foundation, a nonprofit organization that addresses the ample needs of foster and homeless Native American children.

On January 1, 1999, Honest Tea, working closely with the Crow Indians, finally launched First Nation Organic Peppermint Herbal Tea. The new brand realized the company's commitment to doing business in socially responsible ways, specifically meeting the mission to work with economically disadvantaged communities. Says Goldman, "It's a win-win situation for everybody." Indeed, Honest Tea earned $500,000 in 1998—its second year in business.

# Politically Juiced

Goldman stands tall among entrepreneurs who go out of their way to emphasize their commitment to political and social causes. Other Gen E business owners who engage in similar practices seek more of a middle-ground approach, balancing profits and political awareness so that a business's need for cash and cachet are equally satisfied. Eric  Strauss, 30, owner and founder of Crazy Carrot Juice Bars in Minneapolis, is one such entrepreneur. Strauss learned the ropes more than 15 years ago when he ran a successful chain of lemonade stands in suburban Minneapolis. Some of the lessons he learned—waste nothing, recycle (that is, wash your plastic cups), and leave the land, or your temporary neighborhood "storefront," the way you found it—have stayed with him over the years.

Today, being a good corporate citizen and an environmentally aware company are important tenets of the Crazy Carrot concept. The company's efforts begin with reducing the amount of waste accumulated making smoothies. Of the waste that is generated, more than 90 percent is recycled. Every month, Crazy Carrot sends more than 2,000 gallons of fruit and vegetable waste to a food recycler to be turned into livestock feed, with all remaining food waste composted by the nonprofit Youth Farms project, a program designed to teach urban children gardening and farming skills.

"The company invests heavily in a waste reduction and recycling program," adds Strauss. "It's a three-tiered program that includes reducing the amount of waste generated by the company, providing frequent customers with reusable plastic mugs at a nominal cost, and recycling all food waste into compost and livestock feed."

Crazy Carrot's commitment to the environment goes beyond the storefront and into the neighborhoods. Recently, the company joined the Clean Rivers Team through the Minnesota Department of Natural Resources (DNR) and is now responsible for keeping a portion of the Mississippi River in tip-top shape. Crazy Carrot was also a proud sponsor of the 1998 Great Mississippi Riverboat River Cleanup, another project of the Minnesota DNR.

## The Color Of Money

If you think that socially responsible businesses don't pay off, think again. Consider the Domini 400 Social Index (DSI) that was launched in May 1990 by Kinder, Lydenberg and Domini, an investment tracking firm. This blueprint for an investment portfolio, not a real fund, tracked 400 companies that passed multiple social screens (green-speak for passing an environmentally correct litmus test):

- From May 1990 through April 1998, the DSI demonstrated the long-term profitability of socially responsible investments (SRI) by returning 364.0 percent compared with 316.4 percent for the S&P 500 and 318.8 percent for the Russell 1000 Small Company Index.

- For all eight years, the DSI has out-performed the overall market. The eight-year annualized return figures are 21.2 percent for the DSI and 19.5 percent for the S&P 500.

For more information about the DSI, call (617) 547-7479 or visit www.kld.com.

"We take a lot of pride in the fact that we try to be socially responsible citizens," says Strauss. "It's as important as anything we do. I can't speak for other young entrepreneurs, but acting in a socially conscience manner is something we're seeing a lot more of these days."

# Bagel Benefactors And Cosmetically Correct Businesses

Charitable giving is another big endeavor of Gen E businesses. At Bagel Works in Keene, New Hampshire, staffers gather each December to sift through a list of local charities in need of help, then vote on the ones that need help most desperately. After a secret ballot among the 140 employees at all nine chain stores, a charity is selected that wins not only significant financial help (the company is too polite to reveal the actual amount given) but also promotional space for its cause in store windows and countertops—and last but not least, mounds of free bagels.

Bagel Works co-owners Richard French, 34, and Jennifer Pearl, 31, maintain that the charitable work provides an aura of goodwill among employees and helps workers understand that the bottom line isn't just about money. The $5 million company has donated 10 percent (or more) of its pretax profits to noble causes like homeless shelters and battered children's organizations. "Some could argue that we may be able to make more money," concedes French. "But if we weren't doing some of those things, we might have a lesser quality of employee or more turnover."

However, Bagel Works has also learned that it's possible to go overboard—that your zealous promotion of social causes can get in the way of the company's main business. One afternoon the staffers were promoting AIDS awareness, complete with pink and red ribbons and condoms for the taking, but this didn't sit well with some of the folks in conservative New Hampshire. "Some mothers came up to us and said they were here to buy bagels and not receive a lecture on sexual freedoms. We apologized, and since then, we've tried to tone our idealism down when necessary," says Pearl.

Other companies are just as ardent politically and socially, but they are less willing to wear it on their shirtsleeves. "We try to do

# 10 questions

Name: Tish and Snooky
Age: 30+
Company: Manic Panic NYC
Location: New York City
Web Site: www.manicpanic.com
Year Founded: 1997
Start-up Costs: $400
1998 Sales: $3 million
1999 Projections: $6 million

**1. What was your first entrepreneurial venture?**
A Kool-Aid stand using tiny glass bottles to show off the colors

**2. At what age did you start it?**
5 and 7, respectively

**3. What did you learn from the experience?**
Presentation, packaging and cool colors bring in the bucks—and pennies.

**4. What age were you when you made your first million?**
Both thirty-something

**5. What was your first job as an employee?**
Snooky: salesperson in a department store; Tish: temp in JC Penney art department

**6. Did you get a college degree?**
Only Snooky, in English

**7. What age were you when you started your first "real" full-time venture?**
Both twenty-something

**8. Who is your role model?**
Our mother, Estelle, and our friend Cleo Rose. Both are strong, determined and never take no for an answer.

**9. How many businesses have you started?**
One

**10. How many were successful, and how many failed?**
One succeeded, and none failed.

what we can," says Sarah Levinson of Ripe cosmetics in Los Angeles. "Our collection has never been tested on animals, and we don't use harmful products, like formaldehyde, in our products. But being socially responsible has to be weighed against running a successful business. If you pay too much attention to that stuff, you may not have a business to promote your special causes."

# A Goodwill Hunting Checklist

As most young entrepreneurs discover, cultivating socially responsible business practices can make good business sense. It is possible to follow your moral compass and create an ethical business framework. Think about it. If beefing up your company's moral fiber seems like a lot of work, consider the alternative. Imagine your up-and-coming, but ethically undisciplined outfit derailed by disgruntled clients, renegade employees, hapless decision-making and a corporate reputation that makes Jerry Springer look like Walter Cronkite. Under these conditions, it's difficult for any company to thrive.

However, it's not easy for young entrepreneurs to juggle the demands of social responsibility with those of growing a fledgling company. And being "socially responsible" can become quite complicated itself. According to the Green Journal, an Internet-based socially responsible business organization, business owners have much to account for when crafting politically correct commerce practices: They must consider their company, employees, customers, shareholders, the community, business partners/suppliers, global business and the environment.

## Cause And Effect

"Cause-related marketing" refers to donations to nonprofit organizations that are triggered by the purchase of a product or service, and it epitomizes enlightened marketing. Of all the media in the marketing mix, cause-related marketing is the only one that concurrently benefits consumers, society and businesses.

Cause-related marketing is the means by which American Express raised more than $22 million for Share Our Strength, a national anti-hunger group. It's what Wal-Mart used to generate more than $104 million for the Children's Miracle Network. And it helped 7UP raise more than $18 million for the Muscular Dystrophy Association.

"Start by looking at resource centers on the Web, like ours, that have databases of information on corporate citizenship issues and have examples of leadership company practices," advocates Chorlins at BSR. "When you're doing your research, make sure you keep a reasonable [monetary and time] limit; focus on the ones you can realistically handle. You are already going to have a lot on your hands by opening a new business."

> "Being socially responsible has to be weighed against running a successful business."

Chorlins adds that BSR has a package that can help young entrepreneurs get going fast. "New companies can use our Social Responsibility Starter Kit, which is an introduction to corporate responsibility and identifies ways that companies can reflect their own values," she says. "For example, you can look in the environment section at energy efficiency and pollution levels. Community involvement is also big. There are lots of creative ways of pitching in without cash donations, like providing the use of your company's facility for a community gathering."

Here's a checklist of questions you should ask yourself about your company. They cover the range of issues you should think about as you shape a socially responsible course of action. It may be impossible (and perhaps isn't even advisable) for any one company to follow through on all of them, all of the time, but by thinking about them, you can get a better feel for how you might approach your corporate relationship with your community and the world at large, and for how you might best contribute to your favorite cause or causes.

- How does your company handle its corporate openness, citizenship and accountability?
- Where does your company advertise (radio/television/publications), and what events do they sponsor?
- Does your company have a corporate code of ethics or principles, a mission statement?
- How does your company react to shareholder resolutions?
- What is your total compensation package? How are your board members (if any) compensated?

- Is your company a member of responsible business organizations?

- Does your company manufacture alcohol, tobacco or weapons?

The way companies treat their employees is also important. The following questions address management's role in creating a diverse, ethical workplace:

- Does your company have responsible workplace policies and practices including nondiscriminatory employment practices and positive labor relations?

- Does your company have women and minorities in senior management and on the board of directors?

- Does your company have comprehensive health-care and benefits packages for employees, domestic partners and their families?

- Does your company have on-site day care, an employer-supported child-care center or elder care?

- Does your company offer profit-sharing or gain-sharing programs, a stock purchasing plan or an ESOP—an employee stock option program?

- Does your company have flexible scheduling, flex-time, telecommuting and job-sharing available?

- Does your company offer continuing education and training programs for employees?

- Does your company have a socially and environmentally responsible 401(k) investment plan?

Global consciousness is a big buzzword in the early 21st century. Here are some questions to ask yourself as you ponder how your business should relate to the world around it:

- Do your responsibilities extend beyond your immediate community, town or city?

- Does your company have a global code of conduct on working conditions and labor sourcing as well as human rights?

- Does your company have business activities in countries known for their oppressive governments or human rights abuses, such as Burma, Nigeria or China?

- Does your company have effective policies and practices addressing child labor, wages, worker health and safety?

Vendors, suppliers and other business partners must be factored in as well. Like Honest Tea, if one of the things you're selling is your company's social responsibility, then you need to do business with other companies that also uphold those standards. It's an imperfect world, so while it might do no harm to be linked with a company that serves veal cutlets at its company picnic, you probably want to avoid a supplier who gets all their goods from sweatshops in Southeast Asia. Such connections only undermine your credibility as a socially responsible corporate citizen. Here are some questions to ask:

- Does your company have a code of conduct, standards and guidelines for all their suppliers, vendors and subcontractors worldwide?
- Does your company, its vendors or subcontractors use child labor or forced or prison labor?
- Does your company have supplier standards for products, materials and workers?
- Is your company purchasing socially and environmentally responsible products?
- Is your company using women-owned, minority and responsible vendors?

## Welcome To My Neighborhood

Planet Neighborhood is a multimedia environmental project that highlights grass-roots movements to help all of us live better, cleaner and cheaper lives. Produced by WETA-TV in Washington, DC, Planet Neighborhood was hosted by world-renowned "Green" architect William McDonough in September 1997. The program aims to raise public awareness about the environmental and economic benefits of recently developed green technologies for protecting the environment.

With new technologies, environmental preservation is now being integrated into the design, manufacturing and distribution of goods, and the use of recycled products is growing. The program looks at water, green consumer issues, recycling, energy efficiency, green workplaces and sustainable communities. For more information about purchasing videocassettes of the three one-hour programs, visit their Web site at www.pbs.org/weta/planet.

# Don't Go Overboard

Creating a socially conscious company is a noble, heartfelt goal for any entrepreneur, young or old. It's a good business practice, and it's the "right" thing to do. However, don't become so relentless about promoting causes and policing your vendors that you drive business away or get caught not practicing everything you preach. Give some thought as to how much of a good-faith effort you want to make to go green and be socially responsible because customers will hold you to the standard you set for yourself. Fall from that standard, sometimes even just a little bit, and they will not hesitate to criticize you and take their business elsewhere. Decide what you can reasonably accomplish and don't overreach because it can backfire.

In addition, most employees have limits on how many lectures they can sit through from management on the impact of discarded pencil shavings on global deforestation or the importance of wearing animal-testing-free cosmetics to the big sales pitch in Chicago. Getting socially like-minded staffers on board is great, but don't force everyone to think the same. Again, set standards and practices that are important to you, but don't make them so rigid or difficult to achieve that you wind up creating internal conflict. Even the most socially responsible companies must make compromises and operate within the limits of the society around them.

Just ask Ben & Jerry's, perhaps one of the most high-profile and successful companies to make its name by touting its ethical business practices and its corporate donor program. A few years ago they

decided to give away gallons of extra, diluted ice cream to local pig farmers instead of washing it down the drain, as most ice cream companies do. Here was seemingly the feel-good corporate story of the year: Ben & Jerry's solves a minor environmental problem while local pigs get to chow down on Rainforest Crunch, Cherry Garcia and other tasty ice cream delights. Or so everyone thought.

Unfortunately, their act of benevolence turned unexpectedly ugly and fatal. Piglets that happily slurped Ben & Jerry's homemade sugar water never made it to 600-pound adulthood. They suddenly began expiring at

# So What Are You Waiting For?

There's no end of good causes that can use a helping hand. Here are just a few ideas:

- Food for the elderly or homeless: Help financially or by serving meals.
- Audio books for the blind: Audiotape producers are always looking for readers and funding.
- American Red Cross blood drive at your place of business.
- Help with fund-raising for any number of good social causes.
- Let a spokesperson for Big Brothers or Big Sisters speak at your workplace.
- If you're in the food business, donate excess food to homeless shelters.
- If you're in the music business, arrange for small free concerts at homes for the elderly.
- If you're a financial person, offer to give some counseling at a neighborhood center on budgeting or debt management.
- Promote adopt-a-pet programs from your local Humane Society.
- Have employees contribute old clothing to give to the needy.
- Work with a local environmental group to clean up a neglected nearby natural area.
- Print up some T-shirts and do some construction work for Habitat for Humanity.
- Consider sports sponsorships, especially for teams from disadvantaged neighborhoods.
- Promote literacy programs in connection with schools or community organizations.
- Young people these days need mentors, adults who can teach them about life. Look into existing mentoring programs.
- Talk to your local social service people. They can steer you to hundreds of additional worthwhile opportunities.

Limit your involvement to a few ventures. It's far better to work with two or three causes where you can make a difference than to spread yourself so thin that your money or your effort have little impact.

> "**We** wanted a business that **emphasized** our personal **philosophy** and tastes, and we didn't want to be **pigeonholed** into one type of product."
> —*Greg Zedlar*

# Sorry
### About That Haircut, Bub

**M**any cyber-hip people are big on sending e-mail or facsimile greeting cards for a friend or loved one's special occasion. Sorry, way not cool.

At least, it's passé according to Greg Zedlar, president of Cardstar. com, a company that makes business-to-business greeting cards. Zedlar believes that everyday life events warrant their own greeting cards just as much as birthdays and wedding anniversaries do. His cards hallmark more mundane events like bad haircuts and surly bosses. He got the idea while working for American Express where, as a financial advisor, he had to find creative ways to market his services to clients.

"I tried everything," he recalls. "I came to the conclusion that if I used greeting cards I would reach more people. So I went with the idea, tracked the results and found my cards were a hit."

Designing the cards at home and selling them directly to customers via the Internet, telemarketing and mass mailings, things clicked in a hurry. With his wife, Lisa (pictured), and six employees, Cardstar.com earned $1 million in revenues its first year. "I'm having the time of my life doing what I want to do," he says. "I couldn't have written a better script." Or, as it turns out, greeting card.

---

**Greg Zedlar, 33**

*Company:* **Cardstar.com**
*Location:* **Burbank, California**
*Year Started:* **1997**
*Start-up Costs:* **$15,000**
*1998 Revenues:* **$1 million**
*1999 Projections:* **$1 million**

200 pounds, victims of oddly humanlike arteriosclerosis. And, according to local pig farmers, the slaughtered pigs yielded a fattier pork. Unfortunately, neither Ben & Jerry's nor the farmers had explored the implications of feeding pigs premium ice cream, and the experiment was quickly dropped.

For another lesson in how a company's politically correct reach can exceed its grasp, there's The Body Shop, the omnipresent health, mind and body store. This suburban mall fixture made headlines for its socially conscious practices, and its ad campaigns were full of high-minded lectures and smug political correctness. Baby boomer devotees stood impatiently in line, waiting for a crack at bottles of cruelty-free Brazil Nut Shampoo and Conditioner so they could boast to their friends how "sensitive" they were.

Media reports eventually exposed the idealistic company as corporate hypocrites. Among the revelations: The Body Shop sold expensive, mediocre products filled with petrochemicals, according to recent articles in *Consumer Reports* and *Utne Reader* magazines; had a history of miserly charitable contributions (nothing at all in the company's first nine years); and fought constantly with troubled employee and franchisee relationships across the world, spawning numerous lawsuits and a Federal Trade Commission (FTC) fraud investigation. While the FTC didn't find The Body Shop guilty of fraud, the company continues to be besieged by lawsuits. There are currently two in court with the company in America, and litigation is underway in Canada, France, Spain and Britain.

As you can see from the setbacks suffered by Ben & Jerry's and The Body Shop, idealism isn't always easily translated into a marketing or business strategy. Once you've decided to make your new business a socially responsible one, you've got to walk the walk. Make sure you understand the cultural terrain you're about to navigate.

One last point: It's all well and good to toot your own horn, to clear your throat and point at yourself at cocktail parties (or in glossy advertisements) when the talk turns to socially responsible businesses. But don't get too caught up in yourself. If your green image is seen as nothing more than a marketing ploy, it won't work with customers. Also, corporate responsibility may be newly fashionable, but it's not new: Corporations have been engaged in socially conscious activity for years as a way to burnish their image and to return some good to the society that nourishes them.

That said, there's no reason why you can't merge your social views with your business views as your venture grows. If anything, knowing that your business is making a difference culturally as well as commercially is quite an achievement for a young entrepreneur. Definitely something to tell your grandchildren about.

# Chapter

The gung-ho '90s may have ushered in an era of affluence and oppulence, but you wouldn't know it by talking to Gen E.

# The Millionaire Wears Tennis Shoes

According to the Associated Press, five of the 100 top Internet companies are run by entrepreneurs younger than 35. One of those five, Yahoo co-founder David Filo, has an estimated net worth of $1 billion. That's a lot of Pringles and Pepsi—and it's just the tip of the iceberg when it comes to the burgeoning numbers of Gen E millionaires, some of whom we've already met in this book.

How does the rising tide of entrepreneurial wealth impact the lives of young CEOs? Some maintain that they're so busy they don't have time to spend their newfound wealth. Others don't want wealth to change their lives at all, and they are busy establishing philanthropic endeavors to share their profits with favorite causes and charities. Either way, it's an issue that many Gen E business owners are unprepared for and that changes their lives in unexpected ways: success and the wealth and responsibilities it brings.

# Today's Slimmer, Trimmer Millionaire

No hard numbers exist that quantify how many Gen E millionaires exist today. All we know is that the number of U.S. millionaires has roughly doubled every two years since 1994, leaving us with about 4 million millionaires in the United States. But a million bucks ain't what it used to be—not by a wide margin. It may sound like a lot of money, but it's equal to only $150,000 in 1948 money. Conversely, if you'd had $1 million in 1948, you'd have had the equivalent of $6 million today.

Depreciation isn't the only factor to consider when figuring your relative worth as a Gen E millionaire. Many entrepreneurs say they're only paper millionaires, with not enough access to their money as you might think. Stock options and shares of company stock may amount to $1 million today, but they are subject to the whims and vagaries of the financial markets—something a wealthy business owner is quick to emphasize. Take Bill Gates: He lost almost $2 billion in four days during the bear stock market of August 1998.

So becoming a 26-year-old millionaire isn't quite what it used to be. Overall, the Gen E business owners interviewed for this book are an unassuming lot—nobody's boasting about their $2,600 Austrian crystal violin-shaped evening bags or $4,000 custom-made Alfred Dunhill suits. The cigar-smoking, martini-sloshing, gung-ho '90s may have ushered in an era of affluence and opulence—with $500,000 McMansions dotting newly bulldozed suburban tractlands and $60,000 Humvees rolling onto pebbled driveways—but you really wouldn't know it by talking to Gen E.

Most young millionaires, like the rest of us, tend to hold personal finances close to the vest. Co-authors Thomas Stanley and

## Learn It, Love It, Live It

The thing rich people have figured out that the rest of us haven't is that it's better to have money work for you than you work for it. That's not always readily apparent to young Gen E millionaires, but it should be. For a peek into the mind-set of how the affluent view wealth creation and money, allow me to share the following observations. They're culled from my years as a bond trader on Wall Street, where wealth abounds (though it bounded right by me).

1 Most people want to become wealthy, but they lack the discipline to control their spending.

2 The fundamental rule of wealth-building? Whatever your income, always live below your means.

3 A key to becoming wealthy: Make financial independence a priority over high social status and peer acceptance.

4 It's much easier in America to earn a lot than it is to accumulate wealth. Interest and taxes are two of the biggest roadblocks to wealth accumulation. Learn how to legally minimize both.

5 It's easier to accumulate wealth if you don't live in a high-status neighborhood or don't have to finance the purchase of a high-status car.

6 According to the IRS, many people worth $3 million have total realized annual household incomes of less than $80,000.

7 Why are so few Americans affluent? They believe in spending tomorrow's cash today.

8 If you're not yet wealthy but want to be some day, never purchase a home that requires a mortgage that is more than twice your household's total annual income.

9 Self-employed people are four times more likely to be millionaires than those who work for others.

William D. Danko of *The Millionaire Next Door* (Pocket Books) say that the "typical" millionaire acts pretty much the same whether they're 35 or 55. On average, they are self-employed, probably in a humdrum business, like accounting software development, building contracting or nursing home care. They're homeowners, their homes have an average property value of $320,000, and they make an average of $247,000 per year.

The typical millionaire also lives below his or her means, wears inexpensive suits and drives an American-made car. He or she works between 45 and 55 hours per week and invests about 20 percent of taxable income each year. The typical millionaire has a net worth of about $3.7 million.

However, Gen E millionaires differ from their older contemporaries in all the usual areas—in terms of culture, family life and philanthropy. Many young millionaires work grueling hours, worry at night about losing it all and pay unique emotional prices for their

## Do The Right Thing

When it comes to philanthropy, many Gen E millionaires are wary of being publicly identified as wealthy, fearing they will be badgered for money. As business executives who have built careers on attention to detail, they worry about being bamboozled by half-baked appeals to save the Belgian blowfish or to support "humanitarian" relief efforts in which funds are funneled directly to corrupt dictators. They have a strong social conscience and desire to help, especially with new or trendy causes such as expanding the national parks program or treating sudden infant death syndrome, but they have little or no time to research the organizations involved. In the murky underworld of charity abuse, unscrupulous predators often hide behind the most heartrending causes.

Most Gen E millionaires are more likely to join together and give communally, seeking safety in numbers, and a growing number want to be actively involved in overseeing how their money is spent rather than just firing off a check. A lot of Gen E philanthropists would like to run their charity-giving the way they run their successful businesses—by setting precise goals, targeting their resources and being eager for results. Unfortunately, they usually run up against the same roadblock: Most just don't have the time.

success. They shudder at the suggestion that it must be fun to boss older people around, and they agree heartily when asked if they miss the days when survival depended on loose change under the sofa and a box of macaroni and cheese. For Gen E, success means working and worrying more, not less. Gen E has become a bit frazzled trying to juggle the demands of business with their almost nonexistent personal life.

Many got into business while they were still single, and now they haven't time to date, let alone begin starting families and developing long-lasting relationships. Some speak of an inability to find true love. For them, "dating" consists of wrapping up the latest board of directors meeting in time to make the blind date that a best friend arranged. Generation E could also be called Generation D—for divorce. The products of a million broken marriages, younger entrepreneurs understand perhaps better than any generation before them how cruel it is to have to choose whose parents house to go to for Christmas or Thanksgiving and how emotionally roiling it is to be a bargaining chip in a divorce settlement. This will never happen to their children, they tell themselves time and time again, if only they could find the time to meet someone, get married and have those children.

Lack of time is a familiar refrain. While baby boomers talk about how they want to balance their personal and professional lives, their younger brothers and sisters talk about needing to develop any kind of personal life at all to balance with their professional lives. That kind of imbalance can happen when you're routinely awake for 26 hours and have meetings planned for 12 of them. The toll taken by flying 600,000 air miles annually, speaking at industry organization breakfasts, lunches and dinners, and subsisting on doughnut holes and Starbucks Special Peruvian Blend adds up.

# Babies Vs. Boardrooms

Take Kristin Knight, 31, founder and president of Creative Assets, a $9 million creative services staffing company in Seattle that places graphic artists, marketing copywriters and Web designers, among others, in West Coast companies. A world-weariness seems to envelope Knight as she discusses her weekly schedule, a cacophony of meetings, conference calls, business dinners and enough red-eye flights to wear out Charles Lindbergh.

"I'm running all the time," says Knight. "I feel like I'm missing out on other things in life sometimes. But, when you're wearing my shoes, that's something you have to resign yourself to."

> "I figured that even if I failed I could always come back and get a job. I think at a young age you can take such risks."

Like many young entrepreneurs, Knight says she misses the early days, surviving on tins of tuna fish and tomato soup as she fought to get her company off the ground. "Those were great times," she says. "I always wanted to work in some creative industry. I was one of those early Macintosh adopters, and I thought that while I could not succeed as an artist, I could make a big splash on the business side of things.

"When I got out of the University of Washington in 1992, I thought I'd move to New York and work in advertising. But the job sector was changing—people were downsizing and I grew a bit afraid that I wouldn't get a job. So I wound up taking a contract job at Microsoft and worked there a year before getting hired full time."

Her primary task at Microsoft was to find good graphic designers to help on the company's myriad marketing and product development projects. "I found that I really liked doing it. I didn't have the temporary agency mentality. I had always viewed temporary agencies as a bit embarrassing or demeaning," Knight says. "So I thought, What if I could create a cool agency for artists and be a clearinghouse for creative workers who traditionally worked freelance?"

In 1993, after a stint at HandyMac, a Seattle employment agency, Knight decided to buy out the agency's owners. The 24-year-old Knight set out to fulfill her vision of a creative staffing agency, using her experience at Microsoft and HandyMac as a springboard and $16,000 she had amassed to cover her start-up costs.

"I figured that even if I failed I could always come back and get a job," she says. "I think at a young age you can take such risks. All your peers are in entry-level jobs and scraping by, just as I was. Ten years later, you might have family responsibilities and be drawing a higher salary you might not want to risk losing."

Setting up shop in quaint digs in Seattle, Knight's idea took flight. Business was slow at first, but steady, and before long she was able to establish a branch operation in Portland, Oregon. "Looking back I was flying by the seat of my pants," she says. "I had no accounting background and little help. I was blissfully ignorant, which helped."

In 1994, Knight received aid from an investor who took a 10 percent interest in the company. The partner helped Knight install a much-needed accounting software system and, more important, helped her realize that Creative Assets could be big. Really big. "We were already quite profitable and I was already very comfortable financially," she recalls. "I was already battling the decision over whether to expand the business or not. Don't get me wrong. I really loved what I was doing but it was already taking a toll on my personal life." Making the decision to expand the business was

## I'd Love To, But I'm Down To My Last $10 Million

Americans may be getting richer, but they're not getting any more charitable. Aside from the celebrated international gifts of CNN's Ted Turner and financier George Soros, most of America's 4 million millionaires—and most notably the 170 billionaires among them—have been slow to make significant gifts, and slower still to use their wealth to try to reshape society, according to scholars who study philanthropy.

The run-up in the stock market alone has increased the nation's wealth by about $1.4 trillion in 1998, with roughly half of it going to families with annual incomes of $200,000 or more. Yet their rate of giving hasn't nearly kept pace with their increased capacity to do so. According to a study by Treasury Department analyst Gerald E. Auten, the rich are not donating the same proportion of their wealth to charity as did equally wealthy people back in 1979.

U.S. fund-raisers say that one reason why America's rich aren't giving more is because they can't get to the money—the wealth of most of these newly minted millionaires is on paper in the form of stock holdings and options rather than in the more tangible steel mills and oil wells of turn-of-the-century philanthropists. As for young millionaires, fund-raisers say their time will come. Older Americans typically give more money away because they're already settled and aren't as afraid of losing their businesses.

made easier by the fact that the company was beginning to gain traction in the marketplace. Assets grew from $3.5 million at the end of 1997 to $5.5 million in the middle of 1998. Her client list boasted high-powered names like Microsoft, Boeing, Nike and Starbucks. More offices opened in San Francisco and Los Angeles, and revenues were expected to surpass $10 million in 1999.

But just as business was peaking and her professional goals were being wildly exceeded, Knight (below) began questioning her personal life—or lack of one. "The stage was set for us to do something even bigger," she says. "Plans were underway to open another office in Denver and after that we were already thinking about Chicago and New York City, which would take a lot work and eat up a lot of my time. There are a variety of ways of going national: either merging with an existing firm that has an East Coast presence or do it yourself from the ground up and go out and get your own location. The latter would take more time but be less expensive.

"At the same time I was wrestling with the fact that I turned 30 in 1998, something I was really excited about beforehand. Finally, I would be old enough for my position. Before, I would lie about my age so I would not lose credibility with my older customers, or so I thought. The crazy thing was that I had already reached my professional goals at an early age. Financially I could stop and be OK for a long time. But as business grew and things went a lot faster, I started thinking about the personal costs to my life if I continued running the business.

"I mean, let's face it. If I continued running the show, we would be in about five more cities in the next few years. I'd be on airplanes traveling all the time, something that has always taken a toll on me physically and mentally. Then there are the costs of my personal relationships: Here I was turning 30. I had this great company with lots of potential, a company that could be a national company in three to five years. I wanted to have children, and that's obviously a different issue for women than it is for men. Wanting to have a family and wanting to keep the business was really tearing me apart. At some point you have to ask yourself, 'How much is enough?' "

It's a question Knight continues to ask, and she has yet to find an answer. She looks back fondly to the days when she was just starting out, when there was less pressure, and nobody expected her to make much of a splash commercially. "When you are building the company and nobody is paying attention, it's a heck of a lot more fun," she adds wistfully. "Today, Creative Assets has more press, and people ask to interview me or have me come speak at events all the time. I'm spending more time wondering why people would want to talk to me. That's always been a big change to me—people treat you differently even though I'm the same person inside. It's like everyone is pointing at you and saying 'There goes the expert!' and all you want to do is tell them that you're the same person you've always been who just happens to be doing her own thing."

Knight is still running Creative Assets with no immediate plans to leave. "It's still unresolved. Time will tell, I guess."

# You're Gonna Make It After All

Young entrepreneurs like Knight who want to stop and smell the roses can take heart—they're not necessarily doomed to Mary Tyler Moore-land, successful career gals and guys who never seem to find that special someone, get hitched and start a family. It can be done. It's possible to balance work and family, and you don't even need magic powers or a pact with the devil to do so.

Take Katrina Garnett, 35, founder and owner of the wondrously successful Crossroads Software Inc. in San Francisco. The $100 million software application developer is one of a handful of players in the booming market for providing software that links a company's existing hodgepodge of packaged programs, custom-written software and database applications into a seamless business tool. Crossroads' corporate investors include Compaq Computer, among other heavy hitters, and its software applications, at an average price of $930,000, are strictly for huge corporations.

In 1986, when she was 22 years old, the Australian native arrived in San Francisco with an MBA in international business looking to make a name for herself in the male-dominated world of high-tech. "Like most entrepreneurs, I guess, I knew when I wanted to run my own company." After graduating from college and spending a few years learning the software business, she became the manager of Unix platforms at software giant Oracle. From there, she moved on to database software rival Sybase, where she oversaw a $150 million division.

"I started at Oracle at 1986 and left in 1990," says Garnett. "That was a fun period to be there: The company went from $400 to $1 billion in revenues and everyone was excited to go to work in the morning. It was sponge mode for me, soaking up as much information as I could. I'm very goal-oriented, so I deliberately exposed myself to a lot of different issues. I moved around a lot, networked a lot and went to a lot of lunches. In 1990, I was lured to Sybase, which liked the experience I had at Oracle. There was a bit of cultural arrogance at Oracle at the time—if you hadn't gone to MIT, you wouldn't survive. Sybase was different. A woman could grow at Sybase if she worked hard and got results, no matter what her background. That taught me a lot about how a company could be run."

Within a year or so of her hire, Garnett established a new division with 300 engineers whose job was to design the company's next generation of database, networking and messaging software. One of the products her group developed brought in $50 million in revenue its first year, thanks in large part to Garnett's talent for understanding and nurturing technical types. Eventually, Garnett supervised a design team whose products generated $150 million in revenue the first year. Her career trajectory at Sybase was skyrocketing, but again she got the itch to move on.

"At 32, I left to go on sabbatical, partly to spend more time with my 1-year-old daughter and partly to consider what I wanted to do with my professional life," says Garnett. "I had a lot of time to think about running my own business. I was really bored and felt like I had technically stagnated. This was when the Internet was getting really hot. There was no conscious envy factor, but I thought [Sybase] was moving slowly and the Internet was moving so fast. I liked that."

When the day came to go back to work, Garnett realized what she wanted to do. "It was funny. I came back and told my boss I wanted to leave," she adds. "She gave me a big guilt trip and wound up leaving herself two months later." Cashing in $1 million worth of stock options, Garnett started her own business in April 1997.

"I think you have to get to that point in your life and reach closure and say 'I've accomplished what I need to here,' which is what I did

# 10 questions

Name: Stephen Kahn
Age: 33
Company: dELiA*s, mail order catalog for the teen set that sells clothing, shoes and accessories
Location: New York City
Web Site: www.delias.com
Year Founded: 1993
Start-up Costs: $200,000
1998 Sales: $160 million
1999 Projections: $250 million

1. **What was your first entrepreneurial venture?**
   dELiA*s

2. **At what age did you start it?**
   28

3. **What did you learn from the experience?**
   If you visualize it, you can create it.

4. **What age were you when you made your first million?**
   31

5. **What was your first job (as an employee)?**
   Management associate at Paine Weber

6. **Did you get a college degree?**
   Yes, in classical civilization

7. **What age were you when you started your first "real" full-time venture?**
   28

8. **Who is your role model and why?**
   None; I try to look forward.

9. **How many businesses have you started?**
   One

10. **How many were successful, and how many failed?**
    One succeeded, and none failed.

at Sybase," says Garnett. "You want to leave when you're on top, so I left when things were in good shape, but my work there was done." Taking two key staffers from Sybase with her, Garnett set up shop inside her house and set about creating new "middleware" software that would save companies barrels of money by linking disparate computer applications. She saw a treasure trove of prospects for her middleware—manufacturers, retailers, hospitals, law and accounting firms: Any business with multiple computer applications and more than a few employees would be potential customers.

> "Starting a company is the best stage of a start-up. There's the creative aspect. You also have to articulate your idea. There's a million things going on."

"Starting a company is the best stage of a start-up," Garnett says. "There's the creative aspect of a start-up. You also have to articulate your idea again and again, and you have to raise money and hire employees. There's a million things going on."

With a staff of 10 rolling up its sleeves and working hard, Crossroads shipped its first product in November 1997. "We wound up doing $23 million our first year with about 32 customers," she says. Garnett raised more than $50 million in private financing and plugged $20 million into research and development. "A lot of our funding is from corporate investors—you try to surround yourself with people who will add value. If I go to Whirlpool Co. for a potential sale, it helps that I have a business relationship with SAP, for example, which handles a lot of Whirlpool's systems needs." Profits have soared, and the company projected revenues of more than $100 million for 1999.

## Balancing Act

Garnett has not only been able to launch a $100 million company that has captured the attention of media mavens like *The Wall Street Journal*, *Fortune* and *Entrepreneur* magazine, but she also is happily married and the mother of three children. She enjoys tweaking the noses of the staid corporate software industry, which is mostly male-dominated. Garnett is a mega-celebrity in Silicon Valley, not just for her management savvy but for her suggestive magazine ads that appear in a cross-stream of publications, from the avant-garde *Vogue* to the bits-and-bytes, bulls-and-bears *Forbes* magazine.

# When It Gets To $100, Sell!

**W**ith wealth comes responsibility. Specifically, the responsibility to yourself not to squander your newly gained fortune. Unless you're knowledgeable about finances, that means hiring a professional.

Money management is critical for a fledgling business. Many new businesses are often underfinanced and don't realize it until it's too late. A qualified financial advisor can help design a business plan and a realistic budget to avoid surprises. Once your business is underway, a financial advisor can also help you improve cash flow, increase profits—and maybe even enjoy early retirement.

It's important to choose someone with a broad range of experience. CPAs might know about taxes and financial statements, but they generally aren't familiar with investment securities, business plans, debt management, insurance and retirement planning.

To find a good advisor, get referrals from friends, business associates and professionals (such as your attorney or accountant), or call the International Association for Financial Planning (888-806-PLAN). Fees generally range from $100 to $300 an hour; there usually is no charge for the initial meeting. Before making an appointment, interview several advisors by phone. Ask these questions:

- Do you specialize in small businesses? (Get references.)
- Do you have working relationships with other professionals? (Get names and numbers.)
- How long have you been practicing? Do you have a degree in financial planning?
- What designations do you hold?

Someone designated as a certified financial planner (CFP) or chartered financial consultant (ChFC) usually has expansive knowledge of financial planning. Chartered life underwriters (CLUs) are insurance experts, and most CPAs have extensive experience in tax issues.

To verify an advisor's designation:

- As a CFP, call the Board of Standards at (303) 830-7543.
- As a ChFC or CLU, call American College at (800) 368-4684.
- As a CPA, call the American Institute of CPAs at (212) 596-6200.
- To determine Securities and Exchange registry, call (800) 732-0330.

The Crossroads ad campaign features an Armani-clad Garnett staring back suggestively at readers. As one breathless media writer declared, "She stares confidently from the magazine page, her lips shaping a wisp of a smile, her body sheathed in a low-cut black dress. She could be advertising liquor or cigarettes, perfume or cosmetics. But she's not a model; she's the president, chief executive and founder of the company—a woman who works hard to burnish her reputation as a technologist and a feminist."

The ad copy reads like a *People* magazine profile. It states her age: "Younger than Bill Gates, older than Michael Dell." It coyly lists Garnett's birthplace: "Australia's Gold Coast." Her favorite charity: "Started Garnett Foundation to encourage girls to pursue technical careers." Crossroads' investors: "Raised $45 million from Intel, Compaq, SAP, Manugistics, JD Edwards, Ernst & Young," and "Big-time backers: Dave Duffield, Michael Dell, Andy Ludwick."

> "Customers aren't **just** buying our **software**, they're **buying** a relationship."

"Customers aren't just buying our software; they're buying a relationship," Garnett says. "They want to know who is behind Crossroads. I put a face on the company."

Garnett relishes her role as the software siren of the computer industry, secure in the knowledge that the real Katrina Garnett enjoys her family, is financially secure and is committed to her growing company. "I have three kids now and it does get hard to put things on hold," she says. "But I really wouldn't have it any other way. I appreciate the fact that there are not any other women running middleware application companies, and I like being the rebel. While that reduces the luxury of networking with other women—I really enjoy talking about my children, but men don't talk about their families as mothers do—I've never experienced any discrimination. People don't care if you're a man or women, as long as you can deliver."

The key to her personal balance and well-being, says Garnett, is taking all the responsibility in stride. She encourages women in business to have children if they want to. "I get a lot of letters from women asking me how I could possibly run a business and have kids simultaneously," she says. "I tell them to go ahead and have their families and enjoy them. Just don't make a big issue out of it, and nobody else will. I have a nanny and I manage her like I would any other employee, only more closely considering the responsibil-

> "**York** Paper is a **hell** of a **success** story."
>
> —*Scott Korn*

# The Paper
# Chase

**S**ome Gen E business owners fit the mass-cultural stereotype of laid-back Generation Xers who sprinkle words like "whatever" and "chill out" in every other sentence they utter. But not many.

Certainly not Scott Korn, the hell-for-leather leader and founder of York Paper. Unsatisfied with the slow direction his career was taking him, Korn left his job as a manager for a paper recycling plant and started a paper brokerage business out of his home. Working 15-hour days, York paper racked up almost $1 million in sales his first year.

Now, 10 years later, Korn is at the wheel of a $60 million company with 75 employees and a printing operation that supplies high-grade paper to publishers and printers throughout North America. "Sometimes I can't believe how fast York Paper has grown myself," admits the gung-ho, rah-rah Korn, who sounds more like the coach of nearby Penn State's football team than the president of a paper company. "I'm constantly challenging my 'team,' as I call them, to reach greater heights. And they always answer the call. I'm not about to stop until we make York Paper the best in the industry."

Then he acknowledges, "Even then, we wouldn't stop anyway."

**Scott Korn, 35**

*Company:* **York Paper Co.**
*Location:* **Conshocken, Pennsylvania**
*Year Started:* **1989**
*Start-up Costs:* **$17,000**
*1998 Revenues:* **$70 million**
*1999 Projections:* **$74 million**

ity I've given her. I trust her and spend as much time with my children as I can. Just try to be sensitive to their needs and your business' needs, and get as much good support as you can."

Garnett walks the walk when it comes to reaching out to other women who want to balance work and family. "I think the work culture is very important to a company," she says. "I like to hire employees with families; it's something I really enjoy doing. You know, I still interview everybody we hire, and I think good job candidates who happen to be parents are almost relieved to hear I've got three children of my own whom I enjoy doting over."

Garnett has also spent $500,000 to establish the Garnett Foundation, a nonprofit organization that encourages young girls to pursue careers in math and science. During the summer of 1998 she sent 50 teens to a women-in-technology conference in San Jose to meet some of the powerhouse females in high tech. Naturally, Garnett was there to greet them.

# Lifestyles Of The Rich And Not-So-Anxious

For many Gen E business owners, it's not the person with the most money who wins—it's who has the most fun. While it would be foolish to argue that fame and fortune aren't important to millions and millions of Americans, many young entrepreneurs are satisfied to run a business that simply makes them a comfortable living and then to live comfortably while running it. There's no need for fancy homes or fat, seven-digit bank accounts. Just a nice income, a chance to do what they love to do, and some friends and family to do it with—and they're as happy as a 14-year-old seeing the latest "Star Wars" movie for the 20th time.

Such is the case with Gregg Levin, 30, president and founder of Perfect Curve Inc. in Boston. Levin and his father, Barry, an attorney and businessman, founded the company in 1994. Gregg, a former sales and marketing executive, was inspired to develop their signature product, the Cap Curver, when he grew frustrated with the rubber-band contraption he used to curve the brim of his caps. He vowed to find an easier way and sculpted a prototype out of Play-Doh.

To entice investors, Levin (below) took pictures of thousands of cap-wearing Red Sox fans at nearby Fenway Park to demonstrate the widespread need for his product. In the summer of 1995, Levin found a capital investor in real estate developer Roy S. MacDowell Jr., who liked the idea, admired Levin's moxie and agreed to fund the Perfect Curve project. Since 1995, the company has doubled its growth every year. The original Cap Curver has been joined by a highly successful Cap Cleaner & Deodorizer and more recently by the CapRack System, which stacks caps on doors and closets so they are neat and easily accessible. Currently, Perfect Curve products are sold in more than 2,500 stores nationwide and in Canada, Japan and Western Europe. Their products are available at major chains such as Champs Sports, Lids, Olympia Sports, Hat World, The Sports Authority, Pro Image and many more.

"We've experienced phenomenal growth," says Levin. "It's not often that a small start-up can launch a revolutionary new product. I consider myself very lucky—so few products make it to market and are successful."

"That said, I am not a millionaire, or anything like that," Levin offers. "If you take my ownership in the company, I am close, I guess, but it's not something I dwell on or worry about. I'm not living the high life and may never live the high life. I don't care. I'm more concerned with running a young, growing company and having fun in the process. I think there is a difference between affluent and wealthy, and I'm not even sure I care. I still save for a rainy day, still live in the same apartment with the same three roommates, and still drive a Honda that I've leased for five years.

"I am only 30 years old and I have set the bar at a high level. But I'm realistic, too. Am I going to pass this company down to my kids? I doubt it. Am I going to retire at 37? No. What is my market value? Who knows? All my friends are getting great jobs, but I am the unknown, the X-factor, and I like that. Hell, maybe I am underpaying myself, but that is not a big concern to me."

The same goes for Kenneth Felberbaum, 28, president and founder of Viam Communications, a New York City magazine publisher. The company was formed in 1993 to publish information regarding Vietnam and Southeast Asia. Print publications include *The Vietnam Business Journal* and the *Vietnam Business Yellow*

*Pages.* The company also produces and sponsors conferences and seminars on Asian business issues and provides consulting services to companies seeking to do business in Vietnam.

"I've always wanted my own business since I was 12 or 13," explains Felberbaum. "I used to sell antique watches and trade new high-end watches. When I was in prep school, we sold food out of our room; everything from Twinkies to tuna fish. We used to take special orders. If someone wanted sardines, you'd get them, no questions asked. In prep schools, you get access to grocery stores once a week, so we took full advantage of that.

"At the University of Pennsylvania, I started a business where we sold canisters with a Mace-like substance attached to key chains to sororities and fraternities. When I graduated from school, I immediately started Viam. I had spent a semester in Japan and traveled quite a bit through Asia, which I really loved. I got an airplane ticket when I got out of college, and the last place I got to was Vietnam. I saw an opportunity for doing business there. That was the birth of my company, quite simply."

Overcoming some early financial and cultural difficulties, Viam was able to establish a publishing beachhead in Manhattan with two magazines about Vietnam. "We went from a 16-page newsletter to a 68-page color magazine in five years, which isn't bad," Felberbaum says. "We had zero advertising in the first year and grew to one or two ad pages per issue. Now we have about 35 advertisements in every issue.

"I think my life has changed in two respects. I used to stay in the office twice a week and work straight through the night hand-stuffing thousands of envelopes. I don't have to do that anymore, but I did for a long time. For a long time, I didn't have a personal life— my business was my life—and I learned how to get away from the business and spend time with friends and family, but only after I knew the company would make it. I don't see myself as this wealthy guy who runs a publishing empire. I'm the same person I've always been, just with a good business under me."

# Cashing In

Then again, some Gen E millionaires make their fortunes and split, deciding that a change of scenery and a change of pace is the best medicine for enjoying themselves. At Chicago's famous Field Museum, 34-year-old Tim Krauskopf works under the shadows of a 60-foot Brachiosaurus and 3,000-year-old Egyptian mummies, where he streamlines the facilities' computer network and database photograph archives.

It's a dream job for Krauskopf, who founded Spyglass Software, a company he launched while a student at the University of Illinois. Spyglass developed Microsoft's Internet Explorer Web browser. Krauskopf's stake when Spyglass went public: $14 million. But why, when he recently decided to step down as president of Spyglass, did he choose to spend time with mummies and dinosaurs instead of bikini-clad beauties on the French Riviera? "Maybe the Field Museum is my French Riviera," answers Krauskopf. "To me, the Field Museum has a mystique. I stroll into work under a dinosaur's tail and step into the coolest place in the world to work."

It's not often that corporate staffers can complain to a multimillionaire about a balky disk drive and have him drop what he's doing to fix the problem. But that's the case at the Field Museum, where Krauskopf puts in 40-hour work weeks just like everyone else.

"It's impossible to say there's a downside to being young and rich," Krauskopf says. "You know, I figured I was destined to keep riding this remarkable trajectory. Then I left Spyglass, and that trajectory flattened out. But you still have this tremendous urge to repeat; people expect you to repeat. But you've got to re-evaluate and determine—realistically—what's next. That's when you can have a lot of ups and downs. That's the moment."

Krauskopf revels in his newfound anonymity. He doesn't wear a bulging Rolex, and he doesn't show up at the museum commissary looking to buy a pack of gum with a $100 bill. Few of his co-workers know that he's attending post-graduate classes at Northwestern University, either, just like thousands of his peers. "I guess the biggest change is that I can park in the expensive short-term lot at O'Hare Airport when I travel. Now that's a nice perk."

# Chapter

The last thing a 28-year-old business owner is thinking about is estate planning.

# What Do You Do
# For An Encore?

They say the best two days of a boat owner's life are the day you buy your boat and the day you sell it. The same goes for those Gen E business owners who long for the day they can leave their company in capable hands and go sailing off the coast of Bimini or Costa Rica. Some sell because they want to—they are fed up with 80-hour weeks and can't resist the prospect of a multimillion-dollar payday. Some sell because they have to. Adverse market conditions, poor business decisions or simple burnout often cause young business owners to hang the "for sale" sign on their front door.

While everyone's circumstances are different, those are the two main catalysts that spur Gen E business owners to sell their businesses: the need for cash and the need to move on, to divest themselves of a solely owned business and take on another career or lifetime challenge. In Chapter 10, we heard from Kristin Knight, the owner of Creative Assets in Seattle, who is still struggling with the dilemma of whether to sell her business or decrease her role so she can devote more time to starting a family. We also heard from Gregg Levin, owner of Perfect Curve in Boston. Levin isn't interested in selling his business yet, but he figures he will eventually. He doesn't expect to hand the business off to his offspring; when the time his right, he'll cash out and start something new.

Being so young makes Gen E unique among business owners when it comes to selling their businesses. Otherwise confident and self-assured young business owners can be uncertain about the future of their companies simply because their own futures are so far down the road. When Gen E business owners write their list of long-term visions and goals, they assume they'll be around to see those goals achieved. Older company founders—in their 40s and 50s, say—usually expect to retire in 10 to 20 years, and they develop succession plans for their businesses early on. If older entrepreneurs do decide to sell, it's often for tax purposes—to thwart Uncle Sam from collecting on the onerous estate planning taxes that haunt older, wealthier Americans. The last thing a 28-year-old business owner is thinking of is estate planning. It's right up there with the

"Young business owners can be uncertain about the future of their companies simply because their own futures are so far down the road."

possibility of needing adult diapers or stocking up on Viagra.

Then again, it's equally true that socially conscious Gen E business owners can be less likely to want to sell their businesses. To Gen E, selling a business might mean a diminished role as a civic figurehead, less able to launch public service and philanthropic initiatives; it could mean a loss of perceived power and cachet in the community. To the traditionally idealistic youth of America, losing a prominent social platform to espouse noble causes is no compensation for garnering big bucks by selling your shop and conceivably drifting off into the social and political shadows.

No matter how you reach the decision, selling your business is a difficult step, and this chapter will guide you through it. Be clear about your motivations and make sure it's the right thing to do. Most reasons to sell fall under one or more of the following categories:

- **Emotional:** This is the most common reason. Owners are bored or burned out; some have other interests and would rather spend their time, energy and money pursuing them; and others simply don't want the stress of running a business anymore.

- **Lifestyle changes:** Many business owners grow tired of the long hours running a business requires, which keeps them from doing other things they'd like to accomplish. For some, it's the desire to spend time with or start a family; others have new business ideas they'd like to try; some may have health concerns that force them to slow down; and still others may decide it's time to retire—whether they're 35 or 65.

- **Personal economics:** Often business owners want to liquidate or diversify money that is tied up in the business. They may still desire to participate in the business under a management contract with a new owner.

- **Business economics:** A growing company requires the business owner to put a significant amount of the profits back into the company to support increased inventory and receivables. When this is not desirable, it may be an opportune time to sell.

Whether circumstances force them to sell, or they merely want out, many young entrepreneurs find they just can't bear to sell their own businesses, and if they do, they wind up jumping into another entrepreneurial effort, unable to shake the desire for the adrenaline rush of owning their own company. Others may decide to sell but then stay on as part of the business—while they are relieved of the burden of daily decision-making, they can still make serious cabbage as a high-ranking consultant, board member or even vice president.

Then there are those entrepreneurs who never consider selling at all and who instead wind up expanding their businesses through a merger or acquisition. To end the chapter, we'll look at the other side of the equation: how to buy companies.

# 10 Signs That You May Have To Sell

For centuries, gypsies, seers and other spiritualists have made a good living gazing into crystal balls and telling people whether a piano is going to fall on their heads or if true love is lurking around the corner (sometimes both on the same day, and with the same result). Debate continues to rage over the veracity of such predictions, but remember, even the Titanic had a fortune teller on board.

However, a young business owner doesn't have to read tea leaves to see into the future. There are some corporate danger signs you can learn to recognize that can help tell you if agony, catastrophe or the end of your parking privileges is on the horizon. If your company exhibits three or more of the following signs, attributed to Tal Briddel, president of Phoenix Management Services, you may want to consider whether it's time to jump ship and sell your business:

**1** **Your company is experiencing repeated losses.** Recurring losses are bad enough, but when you're financing your losses with additional debt, the problem becomes even more critical. Develop financial goals, sound forecasts, a strategy to achieve the goals and a short-term plan to meet your immediate cash flow requirements.

**2** **Your industry is experiencing a downturn or an explosion in growth.** Neither of these alone is cause for panic, but each should trigger an aggressive response from your company. Do you know what's going on in the market? Are you responding to industry trends? Your company must be equally prepared to handle a downturn, upswing or new product rollout by the competition.

**3** **Your company is experiencing capacity issues and high overhead.** Analyze your overhead costs—including administrative, labor and fixed costs such as buildings and vehicles—

to determine where you can modify spending. If your company has excess capacity in three of five locations, challenge your managers to balance the work flow better.

**4** **Access to a key product line or supplier is evaporating.** If such a loss is on the horizon for your company, you'd better be evaluating alternative suppliers or products and addressing the short-term impact of the loss on your company. While an aggressive response may be warranted, careful consideration should also be given to slowing overhead and distribution costs.

**5** **Your company is branching out into new and unrelated business lines.** Expanding your product line can be good, but be cautious of forays into areas totally unrelated to your core product or service. You may not have the expertise to sustain the new push. More important, make sure you've properly planned the expansion.

**6** **Your company manages for income and not cash flow.** Most companies fail to ensure they have enough in their checking accounts to meet their monthly obligations. They focus instead on short-term income—a sure-fire recipe for failure. While quarterly income is a valued benchmark by Wall Street's standards, don't overemphasize it at the expense of cash flow.

**7** **Your company is experiencing very rapid growth.** Paradoxically, companies can grow themselves into trouble. The cash flow from increased sales may be insufficient to meet your working capital requirements needed to support those sales. Consider borrowing against receivables and inventory and allowing the "financeability" of those assets to support the growth.

**8** **Your company has failed to differentiate its product.** Whether you provide a product or a service, you must differentiate it from your competition. There are only three ways to do that—by service, quality or price—and even then, you must be smart about how you market your differentiation.

**9** **Your company is overly reliant on one product or one customer.** You may be successful now, but what will happen at the next economic downturn? Invest in research and development and marketing, so that you're ready to augment your core product and attract new customers. But pay attention to number 5 above; don't enter product lines or markets that you know little about.

**10** Your board of directors (or advisors) is not actively involved in the management of your company. A good board will probe, ask tough questions, stay informed, expect reasonable responses to their questions, demand access to your senior management and stay abreast of industry trends— in short, it will push you to be a better leader. If your board isn't doing that, recruit a new one.

## Competition Drag

For Matthew Glitzer, 31, the founder and former president of FeMail Inc., a $1 million women's pharmaceutical supplies company, the key issue in selling his business was the competition. Glitzer felt he couldn't compete with the larger players. As his stress mounted, the idea that he might sell his business to one of those larger competitors seemed more and more appealing.

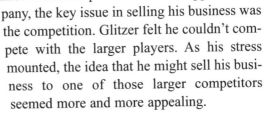

"Women's pharmaceutical supplies is a very competitive field," explains Glitzer, whose company specialized in supplying mail-order fertility drugs. "I saw 150 new players come into the market in 1997 and 1998, and almost immediately I noticed profit margins squeezed in what was already a low-margin business." By early 1998, Glitzer was feeling the price pinch. "I was giving away some of my gross profit to my supplier so they could do fulfillment for me, and they approached me about buying the company outright. I thought about selling, evaluated my current lifestyle and the lack of control I was experiencing running the company in this new business climate, and I thought it was a good time to sell."

Just as Glitzer decided to sell, two more companies expressed interest in FeMail. The heavy courting commenced, although Glitzer makes no bones about what the process was like. "Selling your business sucks on a lot of levels," he says. "First, it's your baby—you founded and grew the business and had some good memories doing that. Then there's the physical process of selling the business. Your idea of a timetable is not the bidder's idea of a timetable, so you do a lot of waiting. I hated that. Once I made the decision to get out, I wanted to get out."

One decision Glitzer made that he later regretted was to negotiate for himself, without a broker, agent or lawyer representing his interests. "I was used to doing things myself—hell, I started the business without a notion of what I was going to do to grow the business and that turned out fine. But negotiating on your own is extremely difficult," he says. "Even if you are in a great financial position, the potential buyers will try to take advantage of you at every turn." One of the chief weapons that the bidders used against Glitzer was time. "As I said, once I wanted out, I wanted out. So the bidders figured they could get a better price for the business and better control of the negotiations if they simply bided their time and tried to wait me out. They knew I was ready to go and took full advantage of that. A good broker might have hid the fact that I was anxious to sell, but there I was, fully exposed."

Fortunately, Glitzer wound up selling the business at a good price to the supplier who made the original offer. "That was a good decision. The money was fair, and I was selling to someone I knew, a company that already had all of our records and documentation in their database. Our customers wouldn't miss a beat and that meant a lot to me." Ironically, the new owners made a successful last-ditch effort to keep Glitzer on board to help run the show. "I wound up taking the offer and becoming a vice president of my own com-

## A New Coat Of Paint Doesn't Hurt, Either

**I**f you are looking to sell, freshen up the business a little to make it more attractive. Here are some tips from top brokers on how to approach the potential sale of your business:

- Refocus your perspective from saving taxes to building profits. While it's a generally accepted practice to allocate revenues to a wide range of fringe benefits to lower taxes, the aim of reduced profitability doesn't help when a sale is contemplated.

- Rethink the way the assets on the balance sheet look. Sell off unproductive real estate. That way, you'll realize additional cash even before the sale of the business.

- Mentor a replacement who can assume command if you or a new owner is disabled or absent.

pany," he adds. "It was a funny feeling, but again the money was good and a lot of the pressures of making decisions was taken off my shoulders." As of early 1999, Glitzer had no plans to launch another start-up.

# The Sales Pitch

So how do you do it? How do you cash out your business for a price that would make the Sultan of Dubai strap on a drool bucket? Here are the most important factors that come into play when you plan to sell your business.

## Don't Go It Alone

There are as many ways to sell a business as there are liberal arts majors at the average marketing meeting. Generally, the idea behind selling your own business is to tout your business, locate the most qualified buyer and obtain the best price and terms to complete a transaction. Sounds simple, right?

Ha. The process, as Glitzer found out, is arduous, time-consuming and frustrating. In FeMail's case, the process was complicated by the lack of a negotiating advisor who could speak for and protect the company during negotiations. The number-one rule is: Don't go it alone. After all, you don't fill your own cavity, do you? You go to a dentist and scream for Novocain like the rest of the civilized world. And drilling teeth has got nothing on selling your business, so why would you enter into negotiations without an experienced negotiator on your side? Selling your business is not the time or place to learn a new skill. Hire an experienced lawyer, business broker or other agent who can go to bat for you and get the most money possible on the sale of your business.

## Everyone Into The Pool

More and more businesses are deciding it's time to cash out. A recent survey by a business brokerage company says that the average price paid for companies went up 8 percent to $458,000 in 1998, from $423,000 in 1997. VR Business Brokers also says the amount of time it took to sell a business went down to 174 days in 1998, from 192 days in 1997. The average down payment for a company remained the same, at $80,000.

An advisor or negotiator generally represents the seller of a business and tries to find and bring a qualified buyer to the seller. In exchange, the broker receives a commission on the sale, roughly around 3 percent to 5 percent of the selling price (although in some more high-profile cases, 10 percent fees are not uncommon), plus, in some cases, a retainer. The retainer fee is paid in advance or as a monthly installment by you, the seller, to help pay some of the up-front expenses related to marketing your business. This fee varies and is based on the size of the company being sold and the marketing to be performed. The retainer fee may be credited against the commission paid to the broker during the sales process. The broker's commission is paid only when your business goes bye-bye. The commission may be a percentage of the total sale price or a set fee. Often there is a minimum fee regardless of the selling price.

## What Your Broker Can Do For You

The services performed by your advisor go beyond dragging prospective buyers by their lower lips to your office and extracting a big, fat check from them. A broker wears a lot of hats. He or she is a combination accounting, public relations and marketing specialist, although most brokers don't give legal or accounting advice. Your broker may put together a business valuation, an asset appraisal, a marketing package and a confidentiality agreement; he or she will also screen prospective buyers, give tours of your facilities and even represent you in negotiations. A listing of business brokers can be found on the International Business Brokers Association's Web site (www.ibba.com).

The business valuation, perhaps the most important document during a sale, may be provided by your advisor or by someone he or she brings aboard for whom preparing these is a specialty. While education, professional affiliations and credentials are not mandatory in the business valuation field, your agent shouldn't be shopping for candidates at the racetrack or the local Laundromat. Above all, experience should be the most important consideration when hiring a business evaluator. Additionally, if your company assets are a large percentage of the sales price, then you may find that an asset appraisal is a valuable and desirable investment. The business evaluator can help there as well.

A broker also earns his or her money by pulling together a comprehensive marketing package to best display your business to prospective buyers. As the Big Cheese, you should always review and approve the presentation before it is distributed—a single typo in a marketing package can cast a shadow over your company's credi-

## Fun With Franchising

Franchising is one alternative for expanding a successful business. Franchises are generally of two varieties. The franchisee purchases the rights to a single location or buys a master franchise to develop an area (that is, multiple locations, which may then be subfranchised, within a given geographic territory). When a business is franchised, a contractual relationship (joint venture) is set up between the successful established business (the franchisor) and the hopeful buyer (franchisee). This contract is based on the key elements of the original concept that are necessary to duplicate the success of the original business in any number of new locations. The contract will often include a sublease on a location, any changes you want to make to the building's exterior, a complete package of leasehold improvements, a furniture and fixtures assortment (all with logos and trademarks), an initial inventory package, an initial training package and an ongoing support system comprised of accounting, promotion and general expertise in all aspects of the business's management.

In return for providing this turnkey, proven success package, the franchisor requires an initial franchise fee and will expect to enjoy the daily profits of the business by means of a royalty (normally, anywhere from 2 percent on the gross sales revenue to 10 percent of the net depending on the nature of the business

> "In **theory**, the franchisee **owns** his or her business, but, in **practice**, the franchise contract **removes** most creative freedom from the operation of that **business**."

and the degree of involvement required of the franchisor). It is also not uncommon for franchisors to expect from 3 percent to 5 percent of a franchisee's revenues to be contributed to a companywide advertising and promotion budget to promote the business concept and corporate identity. In theory, the franchisee owns his or her own business, but, in practice, the franchise contract generally removes most creative freedom from the operation of that business.

bility. That killer silicon chip your firm developed won't seem so hot if your sales package boasts that it's 266 "kegahertz." (True story: One financial software company's press kit claimed that the company was gaining market share fast, reaching "critical ass" in one year. Of course, they could always change the company's mission to making canned chili instead, but the idea is to eliminate those minute mistakes before the public—and potential buyers—see them.)

A confidentiality or nondisclosure agreement, which your broker can help you prepare, is an important document that you should ask all suitable prospects to sign: It assures that the prospect will not talk to your employees, suppliers, customers or their favorite bartender about the sale until an appropriate time. It is very important that prospective buyers not disclose any information about your business to others, except to seek the advice of their counsel, who also must not disclose any sensitive information about your business (and all your business information should be considered sensitive, even the quality and selection of the lunch menus kept in your desk).

Your business broker will also screen prospective buyers to make sure only buyers with the requisite skills to run your company and the financial ability to purchase it are considered. I worked on a trading desk for the late, great Kidder Peabody Inc., a prominent Wall Street brokerage firm that was bought out by General Electric in the late 1980s. Nobody can beat GE at building refrigerators or making clock radios, but their ability to trade securities was questioned by many at the brokerage house. In one of the most famous quotes in Wall Street history, one Kidder trader, upon hearing the news that GE had tapped an engineer to run the brokerage, said, "Great, just what we need—a good tool-and-die man." Needless to say, 70-year-old Kidder Peabody went under within five years. The GE-Kidder match wasn't made in heaven, and a good business broker can ensure that a potential suitor matches up well with you and can keep your business around for a long time.

Your business broker can also be expected to act like a real estate broker and show your "house." Facility tours are generally arranged and conducted by the broker. He or she will answer questions about your business from potential buyers and generally showcase your business in its best possible light. Plus, you don't have to clear out of your building when a prospect comes by for a look-see, as you would if you were selling your house.

Your broker may handle negotiations. If so, keep in mind that, although the broker generally represents just you, the seller, he or she has a vested interest in completing the sale and will work toward an accord.

# The Heart Of The Deal

While you can lean on a skilled broker to navigate much of the rocky terrain that covers the sales process, you're going to have to roll up your sleeves and pitch in as much as you can. If you neglect your duties as the owner, you could find that the price you get for your beloved business will leave you feeling as flat as the cheap champagne you'll have to buy for your post-sales celebration. Here's a closer look at the areas of the sales process you'll need to know.

## Business Valuation

During a business acquisition, both buyer and seller are concerned with price. Each party needs to determine what they feel is the value of the company. Every business is unique, so setting a price for one is something of an art.

If a business is overvalued, the business will not sell, and if it is undervalued, you, the seller, may not receive the price that you should. Nobody wants that to happen. There are three basic approaches to assessing the value of a business: 1) value based on earnings, 2) value based on assets, and 3) value based on an industry comparison. An analyst may use one or all approaches depending upon what is appropriate for your company and then conclude with an opinion based on his or her findings and experience in the market. You have the final say about what price to ask, but again, if it is overpriced, the business will not sell.

According to Nevin Sanli, president of Sanli, Pastore & Hill, a Los Angeles business acquisitions consulting group, determining the value of a business is one of the most complicated and most crucial tasks. "The question, 'How much is your business worth?' is often asked in times of transition and great uncertainty," says Sanli. "The decisions taken based on the valuation can have serious consequences."

Says Sanli, a business valuation is needed when:

● a partner or shareholder wishes to buy out other partners or shareholders;

- an individual or a business contemplates a merger, sale or acquisition;

- litigated matters such as shareholder disputes, divorce and breach of contract require expert witness testimony on business valuation issues; or

- estate and gift taxes must be determined upon the death of a shareholder or owner of a business or upon gifting of an interest to family and friends.

Consult a business broker or business acquisitions attorney for more detailed information on valuing your business. The above methodologies are only a snapshot of the basic financial formulas you can use to price your business. Remember, valuation is more art than science. Your ability to negotiate for a more favorable valuation and terms will ultimately depend on your strategy, market niche, the degree of competition, management strength, entrepreneurial vision, leadership skills and other factors that attract investors and lenders.

## Qualifying A Buyer

Most serious prospective buyers have specific investment criteria in mind that fit with their skills, lifestyle and personal goals. The generalist, who looks at every business opportunity on the market, is performing an exercise in self-discovery at your expense. Each prospective buyer should sign a nondisclosure and nonpiracy agreement that is prepared by your legal counsel before he or she is provided with proprietary information. Then your agent should provide you with the prospect's personal financial statement and a resume to show he or she has the means to buy the business and the ability to operate it successfully.

## Seller's Documentation

As a business seller, you must provide the following documentation to your broker so he or she can successfully represent your business. Again, all information should be held in the strictest confidence.

- Financial statements for the last three years, including income statements and balance sheets. (Your company must be audited or be capable of being audited for its most recent two years of operations.)

- Sales projections for the current year, plus two additional years.

- Aging of accounts receivable.
- Explanation of nonrecurring expenses.
- Tax returns for the last three years, if applicable.
- If the business owns substantial assets in the form of land, property, equipment, stocks and other investments, include any recent appraisals or other relevant information to its value.
- Information relative to any outstanding or pending legal disputes.
- Leases: If any business property is leased or rented, a current copy of the lease is required.
- Contracts and agreements: A current copy of all contracts is required, as they may have to be renegotiated. (It is possible that no renegotiation will be required if a company's stock is sold.)
- List of assets (furniture, fixtures and equipment): This list is provided to help with the valuation and is provided to prospective buyers. The depreciation schedule—another list calculating the value of your furniture and fixtures, and so on, over time—is a good source of this data.
- Inventory value: This is the value, or cost, of your current inventory. Compiling this list will give you a good idea of what's laying around your warehouse or inventory storage area, making it a bit easier to clear out obsolete inventory.
- Owner's job description: This is desirable to show the duties of the owner. This will give the broker or advisor an additional tool with which to prequalify prospects.

## Closing The Deal

Agreeing on a final price is a delicate process. Be prepared to bargain, and don't be surprised if initial offers are below expectations or contain terms that are simply unacceptable. If you think you're being low-balled, don't get into a snit. Better to respond with a reasonable counteroffer rather than letting emotions get the best of you. When you do get an offer you can live with, make sure you get an attorney and an accountant to review all the documents.

# Building An Empire 101

Since opening their Orange County, California, restaurant delivery service in 1993, the owners of Restaurants on the Run—Michael

Caito, 30, Anthony Caito, 28, and Matthew Martha, 28—have turned an initial $10,000 investment into an $8 million business.

The trio has astutely capitalized on a growing trend: Americans, too busy to prepare home-cooked meals, are increasingly dialing out for delivery—and not just for the same old pizza, but for every kind of cuisine. Noting that 51 percent of all restaurant-prepared food is eaten off premises, the Restaurants on the Run gang convinced a bevy of Southern California restaurants to let them deliver food to harried households. For a hefty 30 percent cut, Restaurants on the Run would deliver gourmet-style food to the masses and provide restaurants even more access to those masses. It was a win-win situation for everybody until demand exceeded the company's capacity for deliveries.

"We were really in a bind," says Michael Caito. "We never really had a business plan or an organization chart, so our 'flying-by-the-seat-of-our-pants' approach came back to haunt us." Caito and company hired a consultant to help them solve their capacity problem, and one idea he hatched took hold—buy a local delivery service to help meet demand. "It was a great idea," says Caito. "We had the resources to do something like that, and the fit was perfect. We wound up buying a delivery service company in a market we were not already in and it worked out. We brought the owner of the business on board and found a great deal of value in what he had to say about delivering food to homes and, increasingly, businesses. Today, more than 65 percent of our sales are due to corporate deliveries."

Like FeMail's Glitzer, the owners of Restaurants on the Run handled the negotiations themselves, but unlike Glitzer, they were none the worse for wear for forging their own deal. "Sure, we did some background research," says Anthony Caito. "We talked to a lot of other restaurant owners, and we talked with our consultant. But we really handled the acquisition ourselves and actually enjoyed the process. It was a great learning experience."

## Expand Or Die

Let's face facts: Every company, large or small, whether a mom-and-pop shop or an IBM, is concerned about growth. Companies never stand still for very long, especially young, energetic ones; it's either expand or expire, with very little room in between. Consequently, a major portion of Gen E's time is devoted to plan-

# Do-It-Yourself Detective

**I**f you've got your eye on buying a particular business, take a tip from Sherlock Holmes. A good gumshoe will find out all he or she can about a prospective company during what Harvard Law School types refer to as the "due diligence" process. Quite simply, that means finding out all you can about a company for sale.

Here are a few areas to cover when researching a company you're considering buying. Ask a lawyer or buy-side business broker to help during your fact-finding mission.

● Accounting services contract (last three years if possible)
● Accounts payable records (ditto)
● Accounts receivable records
● Advertising agreements with media companies
● Asset list (including maintenance records, warranties, invoices, title, operating instructions)
● Bank account statements (including deposit receipts and checking account statements with canceled checks, preferably for the last three years)
● Contributions and dues records (to corporate charities and industry organizations, again for last three years)
● Corporate minutes book (previous year)
● IRS tax returns; personal property taxes; municipal, employment and unemployment taxes
● Credit card company agreements
● Customer agreements (wholesale)
● Employment contracts
● Equipment lease agreements
● Equipment operating manuals
● Equipment suppliers list
● Financial statements for last three years
● General ledger
● Insurance policies (including property, liability, medical, business interruption)
● Inventory list with invoices
● Leasehold agreements

- Licenses and fees
- List of employees
- Loan agreements
- Maintenance records/receipts and agreements
- Noncompete agreements
- Personnel policies (including vacation, sick leave, maternity, commission)
- Records of litigation outstanding/notice of litigation pending
- Sales receipts for last 12 months
- Sales receipts on sales of capital assets (last three years)
- Stock certificates
- Supplier agreements and contracts
- Travel and entertainment details (last three years)
- Utility and telephone bills (last three years)

ning and implementing activities that hopefully lead to their companies' growth.

Look what happened to Scott Korn, the 35-year-old founder and owner of York Paper, the wildly successful, $70 million paper products manufacturer in Conshohocken, Pennsylvania. Korn was just 26 years old when he rolled out York Paper in 1989, after spending two years at another paper company where he found his ideas on expanding the company falling on deaf ears. "Even then I knew you just couldn't stand still," explains Korn. "I got so frustrated I decided to go start my own company so I could implement my own ideas about growing and expanding a company—my company."

With a $17,000 nest egg, much of which came from the sale of his sports car, Korn set out to prove to himself he was right in leaving the corporate world. Working 15-hour days, Korn was able to convince paper mills he could deliver high-quality paper faster, better and cheaper. By 1993 his hard work was showing dividends—sales were already at $14 million.

By 1994, revenues were at $25 million and Korn began wondering whether his company should branch out into other industry sectors, like paper recycling. "I thought long and hard about buying a paper conversion company, and then ultimately decided against it," he says. "I think acquisitions are an excellent way to grow your company, but only after you've exhausted other options, like building a new division yourself." That's exactly what Korn did, buying a host of machines that unroll paper, cut it into specific sizes and rewind it, one sheet overlapping the next. "One machine could handle a roll nearly 12 feet in diameter and cut 5,000 sheets per minute."

Since then, York Paper has dipped its toes several times into the acquisition waters, only to pull back at the last moment. "I'm constantly looking for good opportunities to add value to the company," says Korn, who was in the midst of acquiring a paper products company in early 1999. "But it has to be exactly the deal we want. When my management team tells me that a company might be a good acquisition for us, we act fast. You have to be decisive when you're trying to expand your operations."

As Korn's experience shows, buying a company is only one of several options in expanding a business. However, the way you expand is also partly determined by what aspect of the business you want to expand, which is another crucial decision. According to Jeff Jones, a business broker and appraiser for the past 20 years, and president of Certified Appraisers Inc. in Houston, business owners have three main choices for what direction their company can grow:

- Expand in your existing market by getting a share of new business growth.
- Expand into new product and service lines that are compatible with existing lines.
- Expand into new geographic markets.

"All the methods of growth require planning, time and resources that include people, inventory, equipment and money," says Jones. "Because most small to midsized businesses have limited resources, if the wrong decisions are made in the attempts to grow, the results can be disastrous."

## Acquiring Minds

Expanding through acquisition is one of the fastest ways to grow, and it has been a method frequently used by large closely held and publicly held companies. For many of the same reasons large companies buy existing businesses, small to midsized companies can often benefit from this practice. "Perhaps the best reason is to provide synergy to your existing business," offers Jones. "Due to synergism of the combined resources of both companies, sales and profits can often be increased. Sales increase due to the combined marketing efforts, and costs can often be reduced as a result of greater purchasing power, combined facilities and additional skilled employees."

The acquisition of existing businesses in new geographic markets also enables young companies to expand into new markets by leapfrogging two to five years over start-up operations. Most companies find it easier to expand from an existing base of business rather than build from scratch, especially in geographic markets that are not as familiar as the home market.

If you want to roll out a new product line, just as Korn did with his paper conversion operation, buying another company may be the best and fastest way to do so. Opening up related lines of products that can be sold to existing customers of the acquiring company can lead to sales growth without adding significant overhead costs. By way of acquisition, a company can obtain new product or service lines within its existing geographic markets. This works especially well if your company has available space, can obtain new products and services not otherwise available to your customers, and has the staff, time and ability to handle the additional lines.

Here are some other tried-and-true reasons to buy an existing business:

- You can review a company's existing track record as reflected in profit-and-loss statements, tax returns and other financial records, which can all be very helpful in determining expansion plans. Growth potential can be measured based on actual experience rather than the conjecture associated with start-up ventures.

- The need for additional working capital is reduced due to the immediate cash flow being generated by the acquired company.

- The opportunity to gain skilled employees who are familiar with the business operation and market is a major benefit of any acquisition.

- Gaining established customers significantly reduces the time it would otherwise take to attract an adequate number of customers to support the overhead of a new operation.

- Obtaining existing licenses and permits can often reduce the

# The Sandwich Generation

**H**ot bread. Hot concept. That's Cosi Sandwich Bar, the *Zagat Restaurant Survey's* No. 1 rated sandwich shop in New York City, and it's coming to a street near you, if it's not there already. "The foundation of the Cosi sandwich is the bread—a hearth-fired flat bread called 'pizza romana,'" explains Jay. "Batches of this thin, crusty bread are baked continuously throughout the day in an immense, iron-clad, brick oven located in the middle of the restaurant. Cosi Sandwich Bar's bread is always straight from the oven."

In 1993, Shep spent a year abroad studying in Paris. He discovered a little sandwich shop on the Rue de Seine near the Sorbonne in Paris. The sandwich shop, Cosi, owned and operated by Drew Harre, a one-time violin maker and wine taster, immediately won Shep over. Unbeknownst to Shep, a year prior, his brother Jay had fallen in love with Cosi when he was in Paris.

After a conversation on the phone, Jay flew to Paris and he and Shep approached Monsieur Harre about opening a Cosi shop in the United States. "We just walked into the place one day and asked to meet the owner," says Jay.

The Cosi concept was imported stateside by the

**Jay Wainwright, 28**
**Shep Wainwright, 27**

*Company:* **Cosi Sandwich Bar**
*Location:* **New York City**
*Year Started:* **1993**
*Start-up Costs:* **$30,000**
*1998 Revenues:* **$1 million**
*1999 Projections:* **Lips are sealed**

brothers Wainwright and was an immediate hit. In 1998, *Nations Restaurant News* named Cosi Sandwich Bar one of the eight "Hot Concepts" in the restaurant business. And *Zagat Restaurant Survey*, New York City, has named the Cosi sandwich shop No. 1 for both 1996 and 1997.

PHOTO COURTESY: COSI SANDWICH BAR

"We're a cut or two above what customers are used to getting," Jay says. "We get a lot of workplace professionals who want something different." And they do—Cosi is not your parent's sub shop. Toppings include fresh seasonal vegetables, original housemade spreads like "Sun Dried Tomato" and "Eggplant Feta," meats and cheeses, including the "Cosi made mozzarella." Among the special Cosi Sandwich Bar offerings are the tangy "Tandoori Grilled Chicken," exotic "Singapore Grilled Turkey Breast" and the refreshing "Goat Cheese and Cucumber" combination.

Through early 1998, Cosi had 14 stores operating in the United States, including new locations in Boston, Chicago and Washington, DC. "We basically had a conviction that we would sell a lot of these sandwiches in the United States," says Jay. "But that was about it—we had no master plan. We thought we'd just figure out how the food business and the lunch business works and then we'd go from there. That's pretty much what happened."

## Menu

**How to order:** mix and match any one, two, or three of our ingredients

Cosi one 5.95
1 ingredient

Cosi two 6.95
2 ingredients

Cosi three 7.95
3 ingredients

### Ingredients

**Chicken**
West Indian curry chicken
tandoori grilled chicken
pesto grilled chicken

**Turkey**
roasted plum turkey
smoked turkey

**Beef & Ham**
baked Virginia ham
roast beef

**Spreads**
pico de gallo salsa
sundried tomato

time and cost of completing applications, gathering information and conforming to required regulations.

● Sources of capital to purchase existing businesses are more readily available than for start-up ventures. It is very common for the owner of an acquired business to finance part of the purchase price. Banks and other financial institutions prefer to lend money for existing operations that have a proven track record.

## Looking For The Belle Of The Ball

Finding profitable businesses for sale at reasonable prices can be done; it just takes a great deal of patience, stamina and preparation. Also, knowing where to look for companies that might be for sale helps.

Each week hundreds of businesses are advertised in local newspapers, *The Wall Street Journal* and trade publications. By regularly checking these publications, it may be possible to find a business that meets your criteria; however, owners are often reluctant to openly advertise their businesses for sale, so other methods may need to be employed.

Suppliers may be good sources of information regarding businesses for sale within the industries that they service. If you call or write to your suppliers and vendors and make them aware of your acquisition criteria, several prospective sellers may surface that are not actively on the market, but would consider selling.

Finding profitable businesses for **sale** at reasonable prices can be **done**; it just takes a **great deal** of patience, stamina and **preparation**.

Using direct mail to contact business owners whose businesses meet your general acquisition criteria can generate potential seller prospects. This method is frequently used by business brokers to seek out business owners who desire to sell. A shortcoming of this method is that you are contacting owners who may not be actively willing to sell, and therefore, their motivation to sell may not be very strong, which often results in unacceptable prices and terms of sale.

Business brokers usually represent sellers, and as such they can be a valuable resource of businesses for sale. Their full-time job is

# 10 questions

**Name:** Marcia Kilgore
**Age:** 30
**Company:** Bliss, oh-so-chic day spa
**Location:** New York City
**Web Site:** www.blissworld.com
**Year Founded:** 1996
**Start-up Costs:** $400,000
**1998 Sales:** $11 million
**1999 Projections:** $15 million

**1. What was your first entrepreneurial venture?**
Personal trainer

**2. At what age did you start it?**
18

**3. What did you learn from the experience?**
To focus on my clients, offer the best service possible, and not dwell on the small mistakes

**4. What age were you when you made your first million?**
I'll let you know!

**5. What was your first job (as an employee)?**
Worked in a children's center

**6. Did you go to college?**
Yes, majored in business.

**7. What age were you when you started your first "real" full-time venture?**
20

**8. Who is your role model?**
[Humorist/writer] Patrick McManus because he can take seemingly normal situations and find the humor in them

**9. How many businesses have you started?**
Six

**10. How many were successful, and how many failed?**
Six were successful, and none failed.

to contact business owners and find those who are motivated to sell. Brokers usually help business owners looking to buy to determine a reasonable value for a business, and can often assist in finding financial resources for the acquisition. Furthermore, business brokers will have knowledge of a variety of businesses for sale, and can help eliminate those for which the price does not make any economic sense. The broker's fee is typically paid by the seller based on the market price of the business; it is not additive to the market price. However, there are a growing number of business brokers who represent only buyers, and for a fee will actively search out businesses that meet your acquisition criteria. If there is an immediate need to make an acquisition, hiring a broker to do a comprehensive search will produce the quickest results.

Searching the Internet is the newest method for finding businesses for sale. A keyword search will turn up more than 200 Web sites indicating a listing of businesses for sale, like *Entrepreneur* magazine's Business Resale Network (www.br-network.com), a listing of thousands of businesses for sale, with additional resources and information. Many business brokers have also set up their own home pages and provide a list of businesses for sale at their Web sites. Some of these sites are national and international in their scope. One such site is Bizquest (www.bizquest.com), in which more than 200 brokers provide information on businesses for sale. Many local business brokers also have their own Web sites.

Growth through acquisition is a proven way both to get into business and to make it grow. While in the past, finding profitable businesses and then getting them financed were major problems, today there are excellent resources to assist in an acquisition search and plentiful sources of debt and equity capital. Public and large private companies frequently use the acquisition method of growth, and now many small to midsized companies are finding that it is often less expensive and more profitable to buy an existing business rather than to start from scratch.

# Chapter

# 11

"You have to be strong and believe in your idea and be able to focus."

# From The Frontlines: Top Tips For Aspiring Entrepreneurs

Maybe Gen E will be the first to invent a time machine. From the sound of it, they sure could use one. Ask nearly any young entrepreneur what they would have done differently—if they could go back in time and launch their business all over again—and you'll get a wish list as long as my 4-year-old daughter's letter to Santa Claus every December.

# Artfully Hip

Take Cristina Bornstein, a 31-year-old native New Yorker, artist, former bartender and current co-owner of Tony & Tina Vibrational Remedies, one of the hippest cosmetic companies in the industry. Along with partner Anthony Gill, 32, Bornstein started the business in 1997 after they held a conceptual art show in which one featured piece using nail polish caught the eye of the public.

"It happened so fast in a creative sense, and sometimes I wish I had that time back so we could do some things differently," Bornstein says. "In February 1997, our business partner called us three weeks after the art show—not about starting a cosmetic company but about traveling and getting our artistic message across to the cosmetics industry. She'd also mentioned she knew some guys who were looking to invest money into a new business idea, and said she thought of us."

The idea of taking their art commercial struck a chord in Gill and Bornstein, who overcame some early doubts about compromising their artistic integrity and went the Full Monty by launching their own line of nail polish and other cosmetics, backed financially by their investors. Working quickly, the duo filled about 290 bottles of polish with some of their most outrageous colors and announced the formation of Tony & Tina Vibrational Remedies. "By May we had developed full nail polish product lines."

The company's name was a hit as well. "There's a Broadway play called 'Tony 'n' Tina's Wedding,' and our friends were constantly making jokes about it," recalls Bornstein. "We got a lot of attention from the name, so that worked out for us by default, I guess." Soon Tony & Tina Vibrational Remedies was being carried by Bloomingdale's and Nordstrom, among other heavy-hitting retailers. Other distribution outlets came aboard with greater difficulty. "I wanted to get us into the [nouveau chic] Bliss Spas," says Bornstein. "I was going there for a waxing one weekend, and I knew that if we got into Bliss, we could write our own ticket. I brought some nail polish samples in. They said no, and I said, 'Gee, I guess you don't want to see something new.' That caught their attention, and some of their staff asked to look at our polish. They flipped out and said they wanted our polish in their catalog within 48 hours. So we also wound up with Bliss, along with Bloomingdale's and Nordstrom."

Sounds like a booming success story, right? Think again, says Bornstein. "It took us a long time to get on the path we wanted and do things the way we visualized, which I guess is the case for most young entrepreneurs," she says. "We didn't have a lot of business experience and things happened so fast we got caught up in the whole experience without thinking every decision through."

Outside interference and bad advice was the chief barrier to the company's growth—and to Bornstein's personal fulfillment with Tony & Tina Vibrational Remedies. "My advice to young entrepreneurs getting into retail—or any business for that matter—is to beware of false prophets. You are going to find that a lot of people—investors, distributors, vendors—promise you a lot of things. But at the end of the day, if those promises don't materialize, then it's you as the owner of the company who's left to make amends. So you have to be strong and believe in your idea and be able to focus. Once you do that, you can minimize outside interference and distractions and you trust yourself, which is the most important thing a young entrepreneur can do."

## Tips From The Trenches

**M**atthew Glitzer
**FeMail Inc. (pharmaceutical supplies), on knowing your business upfront:**

"My company's start-up was bumpy for a variety of reasons, but the primary one was that I didn't fully understand my business. I did something that most entrepreneurs don't do—start a business in an industry I didn't know. All I had was a marketing idea. I tried to catch up on research, but the pharmaceutical industry is a closed-mouth industry. That lack of industry knowledge slowed me up enough to where I had to get a part-time job to eat. So it was a long learning curve for me, longer than it needed to be. My advice? Research, research, and then research some more."

# Great Skates

Few Gen E business owners would argue the point that you must stay true to yourself and to your vision of your business, but certain challenges can only be understood once you've been through the crucible of experience.

For the three founders of Sector 9 Inc.—Steve Lake, 28, Dave Klimkiewicz, 29, and Dennis Telfer, 31—the issue was cold, hard cash. Specifically, the infuriating lack of the green stuff just as they were trying to get their business, manufacturing skateboards, off the ground. "If we could go back in time and start Sector 9 all over again," says Lake, "we'd do a better job of managing our cash flow."

In the early 1990s, Lake and his buddies lived in La Jolla and were going to college at San Diego State. "We've been surfers and skateboarders our whole lives. We used to ride skateboards down hills to the beach to go surfing," recalls Lake. "Dennis had a big snowboard and wanted to add some wheels, which he did to our utmost jealousy. We wanted the same great board, so we got busy creating our own." Tracing out a piece of plywood in his back-yard, Telfer perfected his new board, adding fiberglass and air-brushing the board with a "9-Ball" insignia. "We used to call each other '9-balls' because we were always goofing off."

Soon Telfer made a similar board for Lake and the two set out on the rolling streets of La Jolla. "The boards caught fire from day one," says Lake. "People would stop us on the streets and ask us to make them a skateboard. So we started making these 4-foot-long skateboards for $25 apiece on Dennis' pool table. Sector 9 snowballed from there. We were doing something that nobody else was doing—resurrecting skateboarding—something that had been extinct since the 1970s."

By 1993, they were making hundreds of boards in Telfer's backyard. "I'd just graduated from college," Lake says, "and I was debating selling phone systems up in San Francisco or continuing making and selling the long skateboards with my buddies. At about that time we'd been approached by a few stores whose employees had seen our stuff and who wanted to sell our boards. I think that was the point where we looked at each other and said, 'Hey, maybe we can make a run at this as a legitimate business.' So we brought in Dave Klimkiewicz and the three of us decided to go for it."

They named the company Sector 9—after the "9-ball" moniker—and set up shop. However, selling to retailers proved to be much more difficult than selling to their contemporaries on the street. "We got laughed at in the beginning," says Lake. "I think retailers saw skateboarding as nonfunctional and stuck in that small-board, small-wheel logjam of the '70s. They didn't understand that we were taking a different approach with bigger boards and bigger wheels that glided real nicely, almost like a snowboard's ability to glide on the snow. But nobody was buying into our vision."

No retail orders meant that cash was hard to come by—and without cash they couldn't buy tools and supplies or pay for trips to trade shows to hawk their wares. Months passed and the trio grew frustrated. Ultimately, they wrote a business plan and got a $10,000 loan from Lake's parents, which at least solved their most pressing short-term cash needs. "My parents were dubious but very helpful," recalls Lake. "So we took the money, made some more samples, created a catalog and went to the key industry trade shows."

At the 1997 Action Board retail show in San Diego, Sector 9 pushed their boards hard. They were $2,000 in the red after their brief spending spree, and there was no margin for error. Either the company would sell some boards at the show or Sector 9's brief life might soon be over. Then, at the show, a Japanese businessman ordered $8,000 worth of skateboards, ponying 50 percent up front. "He cut us a check right there, and we turned the corner," says Lake. "We got some more orders at the show, and things started to roll from there." By the end of 1998, Sector 9 had earned $4 million, boasted a staff of 40 employees and saw a flurry of competitors enter the market. Nobody is laughing now.

Sector 9 has taken off—its products are distributed in 1,400 stores and 40 coun-

## War Story

**K**atrina Garnett
**Crossroads Software Inc.,
database software developer**

"I think one of the worst experiences I encountered was in building my first board of directors. When you're raising capital, you have to be careful whom you put on your board. That was not the case for me when I started out—there was some friction there that I definitely could have lived without."

tries—but Lake says they still wrestle with money problems. "We wear a lot of hats at the company and one of mine is chief financial officer. Even though things have gotten better, I'm still juggling numbers and trying to keep the cash flow rolling," says Lake. "My advice to aspiring young entrepreneurs is to learn up front how to handle money, instead of learning along the way, as we did. It could mean the difference between your business succeeding or not."

# Voices Of Experience

As the saying goes, you can't go home again—and you can't go back in time and start over. But you can learn from the experiences of others like Tony & Tina Vibrational Remedies and Sector 9. If you prefer your lessons the easy way, peruse the list of tips and wise warnings below, which have been culled from the experiences of successful entrepreneurs like Bornstein and Lake. They cover a wide range of issues in no particular order, such as checking credit ratings of vendors, hiring an attorney, applying for trademarks and patents, getting insurance, creating and using Web sites to sell, tracking the effectiveness of advertising, hiring a consultant, spotting billing scams, leasing office space, staying healthy and much more.

Going into business is hard enough. Listen to those who have been there, and make it a little easier.

## War Story

### Greg Levin
**Perfect Curve, custom-made baseball cap holders**

"After we developed the Perfect Curve cap holder, we wanted to show people we could be more than a one-product company. So we built a 'Gozonta'—a flexible retention cord that skiers would use to keep their caps on if they blew off going down the slopes. The idea was great, but I didn't package it well, didn't research it well and didn't display it well. The product only had a shelf life of six months. We thought about fighting for the Gozonta, but it would have cost us about $15,000 to redesign and repackage it. I thought 'no way.' That was an expensive lesson learned."

## Check Out Your Customers

Before signing contracts with new clients or vendors, it helps to have some insight on their creditworthiness.

Do they pay on time or deliver as scheduled? Visit Dun & Bradstreet (D&B) online for answers.

Connect directly (www.dnb.com) or through the AOL WorkPlace, which provides business information on thousands of companies (www.D&B@AOL.com), to access your choice of reports on a given company. D&B's cornerstone product, the Business Information Report ($85), usually includes a company summary, its D&B rating, operation performance, payment patterns, company news, recent financial history and an overview of the company's history. If you need a few key vendors, on whom your business will depend, these reports can take some of the guesswork out of choosing the best ones.

Another resource, the Business Background Report ($21), provides information on a company's history, the business background of its management, recent news items and a business operation overview. It does not include credit information.

The reports, which are updated daily or as needed, may also be ordered by phone; call D&B at (800) 765-3867.

## Bank On It

Wondering if your neighborhood bank is friendly to small businesses like yours? You can find out in *Small Business Lending in the United States*. This annual Small Business Administration report ranks the lending performance of more than 9,300 banks by state and identifies the ones that are small-business friendly. According to the report, commercial banks are among the largest sources of credit to small businesses, with $120 billion in small commercial and industrial loans outstanding in 1998.

An easy-to-use tool for locating loan sources in your community, the complete report may be accessed via the Internet at www.sba.gov. Or visit www.entrepreneurmag.com/money/best-banks/ for a listing of banks. To purchase a hard copy of the complete study ($60), call the National Technical Information Service at (800) 553-6847 and ask for PB98133101.

## Hook Up With A Legal Eagle

When it comes to starting your own business, Uncle Sam will be right there—prodding, poking and bothering you for money and with all sorts of regulations. The government increasingly affects every aspect of small-business operation, from relationships with landlords, customers and suppliers to dealings with government agencies over taxes, licenses and zoning.

The best way to ensure you've got everything covered is to hire an attorney with small-business expertise who can give you advice in these key areas:

- **Business structure:** Should you form a sole proprietorship, partnership, corporation or limited liability company? Do you know the advantages and limitations of each?

- **Written documents:** Does your lease state who pays for utilities, maintenance and repairs? Do you have an option to renew? Can you sublet? Your leases and other written documents—purchase agreements and employment contracts—should be drafted in clear, precise language and spell out each party's expectations and responsibilities.

- **Co-ownership agreements:** What happens if your partner wants out of the business? Do you have a buy-sell agreement to purchase his or her interests? Does it contain a "noncompete" clause so he or she can't open up a similar business down the block?

- **Licenses and ordinances:** Does your industry require you to be bonded or insured? Will you need professional or product liability insurance?

- **Employee relations:** If you hire independent contractors, do you know how to classify them so you're not penalized by the IRS? Have you prepared an employee handbook outlining your firm's policies and procedures? What about trade secrets you want to protect?

- **Future planning:** Have you drafted a will or trust to protect your business assets and your firm's continuity in the event you die or become disabled? Even though you're in the bloom of youth, as a business owner you should have a will.

Having a lawyer at your disposal doesn't mean calling on him or her every 15 minutes for counsel. It's not practical, economical or even necessary to contact a lawyer about every business decision you make that could have legal ramifications. Handle the most routine matters on your own. For example, if you plan to run a home-based business, you can check zoning laws and land-use restrictions on your own to ensure that your business complies. If a relative wants security for the money he or she is lending you, simply sign a promissory note, available at most stationery stores.

Another option: Sign up for a prepaid legal plan. Often compared to HMOs, these services give you access to a set amount of legal services and consultation time for a monthly fee as low as $20.

When you find a lawyer you're comfortable with, be prepared to get what you want in terms of legal help. Follow these steps:

- **Discuss fees.** Once you have found the right lawyer, ask whether he or she charges an hourly rate or a fixed fee. If charges are by the hour, set a cap so you know the maximum you will be spending.

- **Do some legwork.** Keep accurate records, do preliminary research and write out a draft of any agreement you want your attorney to finalize.

- **Use paralegals.** Ask your lawyer about using paralegals for routine legal tasks, like researching public records and drafting documents. Their hourly rate could be half what your attorney charges.

- **Educate yourself.** Call special-interest publishers Nolo Press (800-955-4775) or PSI Research/The Oasis Press (800-228-2275) to obtain a catalog of legal books and software programs for business owners. Also check into legal seminars offered by your chamber of commerce, local business association or university extension service. They can help you learn the basics of legal issues affecting your business.

## One Is The Loneliest Number

Many Gen E business owners start out with a limited budget. That means keeping employee costs to a bare minimum. You may, in fact, only be able to hire one employee. When you only have one person working for you, keeping him or her motivated presents special challenges. Your employee has no one with whom to exchange ideas, discuss work problems or share a coffee break. Nor does he or she enjoy the momentum that working with others can bring.

The good news: One doesn't have to be the loneliest number— not if you make a concerted effort to keep your solo employee energized and happy. Here are some tips to do just that:

**1** **Ask for input.** When employees are asked for their ideas and opinions, they will feel vital and involved—and you will have a highly motivated employee. Make sure to tell your employee if you end up using his or her advice, and why. The next time you ask for an opinion, your employee will be more eager to give it.

**2** **Be upfront.** Employees become bored and critical when they don't know what's going on and feel left out. Keep your employee regularly informed about your company, and about what you are thinking in terms of the business. Give the person a chance to air any concerns he or she may have. Even small decisions can have a large effect in a two-person office.

**3** **Be accommodating.** When you rely on one employee, you may begin to feel that you can't go a day, or an hour, without that person. Remember to make special allowances, such as giving him or her time off to attend a class or take a child to a doctor's appointment. Always try to be flexible.

**4** **Set the tone.** Establish the ground rules from the start so your employee is aware of your boundaries. Make sure your employee knows how much authority or responsibility he or she has and clearly understands your expectations.

**5** **Always reward achievement.** When your employee has an idea that helps you sell to a fussy client or resolve a vendor problem, give him or her praise, thanks—and financial rewards. Before long, your employee will become your strongest ally.

## Make Your (Trade) Mark

Trademarks and patents can be vital to protect your ideas and your business. It can take a while to gain that kind of protection, but once you do, it's worth it. Just ask Andy Rose.

"I was a bartender and bar manager for several years when I came up with the idea for the DirectRoot," says Rose, the 31-year-old owner and founder of Andros Enterprises, a garden-supply business in Scottsdale, Arizona. "I was not looking to invent something or start my own business; it just kind of fell in my lap. I had one 6-foot-tall plant that I knew had to be carried into the bathtub once a month for a good soaking—top-watering plants are very inefficient, as you never know exactly where the water is going, usually right down the side of the pot to collect in the drip pan. When I picked up the plant to move it, I rammed it against the ceiling and broke the top off. Frustrated, I thought, 'There has got to be an easier way to water a plant effectively without having to move it.' Light bulbs started flashing. I dug a little hole in the dirt and poured water into that instead. It kind of worked. I then started scheming and devising, and ended up buying a syrup bottle, cut the top off, poked holes in it, and buried it upside down in the plant. What do you know? It worked!

"The idea seemed so simple and obvious that I decided to apply for a patent. I went to one of the largest firms in Arizona, and after a $1,000 patent search, was told that the idea probably was not patentable, but that I probably wouldn't be infringing on anyone else's. Not very encouraging. I consulted another patent attorney who came recommended from a fellow entrepreneur and good friend, and now I'm sitting on no fewer than four patents, two of which are amazingly strong." Rose's DirectRoot Water Spike is selling so well it's all Rose can do to keep up with demand. "Now that we've proven that it sells, we are slated for dozens of new accounts this spring, including RiteAid Pharmacy, QVC and the Home Shopping Network. We have also shipped an entire container to Australia, and do great business in both Canada and the U.K."

Rose says always look out for number one. "Protect your product at all costs. There are people out there who want to steal your idea." That may mean getting a registered trademark to help protect your unique product or name from unscrupulous interlopers, charlatans and other corporate creatures of the night.

## Tips From The Trenches

**K**atrina Garnett
**Crossroads Software Inc. (database software developer), on making decisions:**

"When I started my company, all I had were some blurry ideas and the notion that as an experienced corporate manager, I knew how to make decisions. Ha! I'd thought I made difficult decisions in the corporate world, but they were nothing compared to the ones I was making running my own show. My advice? Make the tough decisions and don't look back. As long as you've thought things through and have kept the company's interests at heart, you'll be OK."

A trademark includes any word, name, symbol or device, or any combination, used to distinguish the goods of one manufacturer or seller from the goods of others. A trademark should be used to protect a new product or logo before you bring it to the marketplace. A patent can be more abstract and is most often used to protect an idea or invention. Using trademarks in combination with patents can give your product a substantial market advantage.

Registering a trademark with the U.S. Patent & Trademark Office costs only $245—far less than getting a patent. The cost for either can rise to $1,000 or so if you use an attorney, though it shouldn't be more than that for a small company. Patents and trademarks can last as long as you want, provided you are deemed patent- or trademark-worthy. Some are only for three years or so, and some are for 20 years.

For more information on trademarks, check out the following resources:

● **The U.S. Patent & Trademark Office:** (800) 786-9199 or www.uspto.gov

● **Trademark search firm Pop Data Technologies:** (800) 576-2723 or www.trademarksrus.com

● **Government Liaison Services Inc.:** (800) 642-6564 or www. trademarkinfo.com

## Be In Good Hands

One of the biggest mistakes a young business owner can make is to take a pass on insurance, specifically personal disability insurance. Since many young business owners start out alfresco, with nobody else committed to or knowledgeable about the business, protecting your business investment against personal illness or injury is a top priority.

Think about it. If you were injured or suddenly became seriously ill tomorrow, could you afford to keep your business running for six, eight or 12 months until you were able to return to work? That means paying your rent, utilities and other ongoing expenses and hiring someone to work temporarily in your place. And could you meet your personal obligations: home mortgage, car payments, grocery bills and other family needs?

Unfortunately, disability insurance is at the bottom of most Gen

E business owners' to-do lists. Take my advice—bump it to the top.

There are three types of disability coverage. Income replacement coverage replaces income you've lost due to an injury or illness. Business overhead expense coverage pays ongoing business expenses while you're unable to work. This includes rent, phone, utilities, employee salaries and other costs of running a business. If you have a partner, you'll want to consider the third type of disability coverage: buyout protection. If you are disabled for an extended period of time, it provides the money for your partner to purchase your interest in the business.

Premiums for your disability insurance policy depend on the type of coverage you want, your age and the level of risk an insurance company assigns to your business or industry. Other considerations are whether you want to protect yourself in the event that you can't perform any type of work, the length of time you'll wait before receiving payments (the longer you wait, the lower your premiums), and how long the contract will run—for one year or until you retire.

As a general rule, disability insurance premiums range from about $75 to $150 per month for policies that replace 40 percent to 60 percent of your income before you were disabled or injured.

For information about what type of disability insurance might be right for you, consult your insurance agent. Also check with

## Tips From The Trenches

**K**ristin Knight
**Creative Assets Inc. (creative staffing agency), on finding a mentor:**

"When I started my business, I had very little practical business experience, especially when it came to accounting. One of the best things I ever did was bring in a minority partner with a background in running a business; one who knew all the nuts and bolts. Some financial partnerships are very difficult but ours was not. He had a wealth of experience in the staffing industry that I didn't have. He was more than an advisor—he was a mentor. He did a great job of offering insights and suggestions. And he was always quick to say it was my company, which is rare. My advice? Don't go it alone when you don't have to. Bring someone on board as an investor, a board member or even a partner who has experience you don't and who has your company's best interests at heart."

your local chamber of commerce, trade organization or small-business association to find out if any of them offer disability coverage to members.

# Web Sites Made Easy

Building the perfect Web site for your emerging business needn't be an onerous task. Remember, it's an important doorway into your business; it's a place where you can establish a vivid public identity and make a powerful marketing pitch for your company. "I'd recommend being as creative as you can without losing sight of the goal that you're out to sell a product," says Tony & Tina's Bornstein.

Bornstein cautions against trying to become the Mardi Gras of the Internet. Too many bells and whistles can drown out your company's message. Plus, your top concern is that your site is compatible with the hardware and software that your customers are using. Not everyone has the Cray Supercomputer needed to handle that multimedia tribute to Britney Spears that you've always wanted to add to your site.

To create the right site, start by charting the demographics of your potential visitors. Are they women or men? What ages? What types of businesses do they operate? What are their income levels? How often do they upgrade their computers? Find these things out from trade association Web sites, by setting up a test site to gather information, or by mailing questionnaires to your customers. Using this information, a Web site designer or consultant can match your site to your customers' sophistication level.

## War Story

**E**ric Strauss
**Crazy Carrot Juice Bar**

"I got lucky once in spite of myself. To raise some capital for the company, I launched a plan to sell some of my company to about 200 investors, in the form of company stock. I kind of hacked my way through it, not impressing too many people with my sales pitch. At the time it was such an amazingly tedious process that I never thought it would work. But people were kind to me and helped with my pitch and helped me perfect my business concept. Thanks to that, I was able to ramp up and get into some banks and some corporate investors quite successfully. I wound up getting 30 investors, like I said, in spite of myself."

Think simple. Most nontechnical companies should keep their sites low-tech. So who gets to use all the fun stuff? Computer-related companies, mostly. More important for most entrepreneurs are the three hallmarks of a good site: 1) attractive, simple graphics; 2) coherent organization and presentation; and 3) value-added content. Only after those basics are in place should you consider adding high-tech extras.

Here are some more pointers to help you build a great Web presence:

**1** **Choose a name for your Web site carefully.** The name of your site is extremely important. Stick with names that are easy to remember and spell.

**2** **Chat it up.** Enter online "chat rooms" frequently, and aim to get in on discussions where you can offer advice in your field of expertise. To build strong relationships that can pay off down the line, strive for one-on-one interactions with Web users.

**3** **Content is king.** Keep in mind that better content makes for a better Web site. Never compromise on the quality of your content—that's what draws people in.

**4** **Take it easy.** One of the most common mistakes people make when marketing online is to use techniques that come across as pushy. The Internet is a medium where members appreciate a delicate touch.

**5** **Keep promising something new.** Your Web site should constantly promote what's coming up in the near future so users will return again and again. Keep adding to and improving your site from the day you launch it.

**6** **Offer to provide content to others.** Electronic newsletters and magazines are always in need of new information. One of the best ways to create an online presence is to e-mail sites and volunteer content on a regular basis.

**7** **Respond rapidly.** If people visiting your site have questions, reply within a day or two, or you're liable to lose them as customers. Fast response is the single most important factor in retaining Web users.

**8** **Keep it simple.** When interacting online, brevity is the rule. Learn to express yourself concisely so you don't waste people's time.

**9** **Be patient.** It's unlikely you'll achieve the results you want online right away. Try not to be turned off when people don't respond immediately; follow up several times with potential prospects.

**10** **Link with like-minded sites.** The more gateways to other sites you have, the better. Try to find free links, or "trade-outs," where you offer a link to another business' site and that company provides one in return. It's possible to offer hundreds of links, but make sure they all appeal to your target audience.

**11** **Be consistent.** Don't expect results if you market your business online only occasionally or haphazardly. Maintain a constant presence so you'll build a solid reputation in the online universe.

**12** **Market your Web site in other media.** If you advertise in print media, write columns for industry publications or engage in public speaking events, be sure to always mention your Web site.

# Web Cyber-Sales: If You Sell It, They Will Come

If you plan to sell your wares on the Web (and who isn't these days?), you can use your Web site as a consumer cyber-center as well as place ads on other well-traveled Web sites. If you do plan on selling on the Internet, here are a few points to keep in mind:

**1** **Read Internet newsletters.** The Internet is an evolving environment. To keep abreast of new developments and stay current on new Web sites aimed at their target customers, some Gen E business owners read dozens of free online newsletters. Try looking for newsletters that target Webmasters or discuss e-commerce or Web-site promotion. One such newsletter, www.virtualpromote. com, gives advice and alerts readers to the many shady offers for Web business assistance prevalent on the Internet.

**2** **Be patient and work hard.** Your early months on the Internet may yield little fruit. Remember that people aren't going to just magically appear at your site. Links with other sites are often needed to draw them in. (Links enable users to jump from one site to another.) I know time is precious for an entrepreneur, but try to spend a few hours per week reading online newsletters and looking for and establishing links with other sites aimed at your target market.

Expect about six months to start getting your site mentioned in stories, chat rooms and newsletters with links to your site. It may take nine months or more of networking before you reach what's regarded as the magic number for a successful Web site: 1,000 hits, or visits, per day.

**3** **Link with sites that target your audience.** Links allow an Internet business to avoid paying for costly advertising, which may or may not get results, and the best sites to link with are those that already target your desired customer. Young entrepreneurs who sell vintage automobiles, for example, would want to establish links with car aficionado Web sites and any other sites that affluent males between 30 and 60 years old visit frequently.

Once you find sites aimed at your target market, contact the owners about the possibility of adding links to your site. When doing this, be careful only to establish links with legitimate sites that provide a benefit to their visitors. Most sites want to know how many visitors your site gets per day before establishing a link. Once you reach the magic number of 1,000 hits per day, major sites are more willing to link with your site, thus boosting your site traffic tremendously.

Finding enough sites aimed at your target market is the key to selling successfully on the Internet. Most businesses need at least 500 to 1,000 hits per day. You can't get that number unless there are: 1) a huge number of potential customers, 2) many sites targeted at that customer, and 3) target customers with a strong desire to search for information.

**4** **Give something away.** Free stuff is always a draw. A young entrepreneur selling children's educational software could provide a few samples that people could download for free. This won't cost the entrepreneur much, if anything, and it helps get the company's name out to the target market. It's also a huge traffic-builder at linked sites, which can also mention that free kid's software is available.

**5** **Find an Internet service provider (ISP) focused on Internet businesses.** Internet businesses need three important features from their ISPs: 1) the ability to download at least 20GB to 25GB of data per month, 2) accurate tallies of the numbers of hits, visitors and link transfers, and 3) a very low percentage (less than 0.5 percent) of downtime during peak business hours. Most ISPs can't provide this level of service, so check with your provider before building your site. You might have to switch several times before finding one that works for you.

## Tracking The Wild Ad Campaign

Advertising is an expensive marketing tool—but how can you tell whether it's working? It's important to monitor the effectiveness of your ad campaigns and to verify that every one of your precious dollars is being put to good use. Try to determine which ad medium is most effective and what kinds of ads (size and type) perform the best. This reduces waste and helps you plan your future advertising efforts as efficiently as possible.

To help track your advertising results, get interactive with your audience. For example, your ad could ask respondents to call or write for a free booklet. Then track responses by building devices (such as numbered codes) into your marketing materials that help you identify where your respondents are coming from, or even what specific ad on what specific day they are responding to. You can track print advertising responses by using a special telephone number or extension or have mail-in responses go to a specific mailbox. If you have the same ad in three different magazines, give each one a different code that respondents must enter to receive the free material.

"I think you have to get as creative as possible and do as much follow up as possible," explains Caryl Felicetta, the founder and co-owner of Argyle Studios, a creative services and marketing company. "You can have the most carefully designed and best executed ad cam-

### War Story

**John Carmack**
**Id Software, video game manufacturer**

"Oh boy, where do I start? I could have handled leaving my last employer a little bit better. I made some big mistakes there, like doing work for Id right out of my employer's office, and I wasn't too private about it. So there was a lot of twisting and shouting from their side, and with good reason, too. They had grounds to be as mad as hell—and they were, too.

"I also think we got pounded financially on our first release of Doom, but I've learned not to dwell on it. Besides, we learned a lot and by the time Quake came out we did a lot better."

paign in the world, and it will fail if you don't provide the necessary follow up."

Felicetta recommends entering all the response data into a good contact management database so that even after you've closed the sale, you can maintain contact with your customers by mail or phone on an ongoing basis. Some companies that track ads plug respondents' information into their computer with a coded symbol so they become a part of the company mailing list.

## A Consultant, A Consultant, My kingdom For A Consultant

Even Mafia dons have consiglieres, so why not hire a consultant? Sometimes consultants get a bad rap in the business media for overcharging and underproducing, but consultants often don't get the credit they deserve. A good consultant can provide an objective evaluation of your business, identify problem areas and recommend strategies for solving them. Plus, consultants offer plenty of flexibility, no matter what your business or what your needs, from accounting, management and marketing to improving your writing or customer-relations skills. "I think [consultants] are OK if you know what you're getting," says Matthew Glitzer, vice president and founder of FeMail Inc., a women's health-care supplies distributor. "If you can get good advice without having to pay a salary, then that sounds like a good deal to me."

Indeed, when weighed against the cost of a full-time employee's salary—plus benefits—the expert advice of an independent consultant can be a worthwhile bargain. Here's what to look for when deciding on a consultant:

1 **Understand a consultant's role.** A consultant is an advisor, not a magician. If your marketing campaign hasn't increased sales for the past six months, don't expect a consultant to turn business around overnight. If someone promises to do so, be skeptical. You want a consultant who is knowledgeable in your industry or field and can offer a workable long-term solution, not a quick fix.

2 **Identify your needs.** Determine what you want to accomplish, quantify it into specific goals and write it down. A consultant can't read your mind, and the more specific your goals, the

more specific your results. Not pleased with the results of your marketing campaign? Tell your consultant exactly what you want to accomplish: Don't just say that you want to create more sales, for example, but that you want to increase sales by 10 percent or more this year in three target markets and to create a more unified brand identity.

**3** **Know what you'll commit.** Provide your consultant with whatever resources you can to help him or her do the job. Consider background materials on your business, plus any office equipment, space, supplies or employees you can make available.

**4** **Establish fees up front.** Some consultants charge flat rates or bill by the hour, the day or the project. Others charge a contingency fee, in which the amount paid is based on the results. For instance, if a consultant reduces your operating expenses by $10,000, he or she might receive 10 percent of the savings as the total fee or as a bonus in addition to a flat rate.

The average full-time consultant charges $95 to $150 per hour. Some charge much less. Just remember: You get what you pay for.

**5** **Develop a list of questions.** Interview several prospective consultants before making a final decision. Find out what experience they have in your industry, if they've handled similar problems, and if they can give you full confidentiality and represent you without conflict of interest with their other clients.

**6** **Check references.** Ask a prospective consultant for three recent references—and call them. Find out if the consultant accomplished what was promised, if he or she communicated regularly and if the company would hire the consultant again. Letters of recommendation are nice, but they don't always tell the whole story. Ask for the names of past clients who run businesses similar to yours.

**7** **Put it in writing.** A handshake just won't do. Make sure your written agreement spells out clearly the services to be performed, the starting and ending dates, the fee and how it will be paid, expenses you agree to pay and services you will provide. If you have an attorney, ask him or her to review and approve the agreement.

For more information on hiring a consultant, check out these resources:

- The Institute of Management Consultants maintains a free referral service for certified management consultants who've completed the institute's professional accreditation program, completed an ethics exam, signed a code-of-ethics agreement and undergone a screening process. Contact the institute at 521 Fifth Ave., New York, NY 10175, (212) 697-8262 or www.imcusa.org.

- The Association of Management Consulting Firms provides a free referral service, categorized by industry and specialty, to help businesses of all sizes select consulting firms. Call (212) 455-8231 or visit www.amcf.org.

- You can also find consultants through trade associations in a particular industry. The American Society of Association Executives (ASAE) can refer you to these trade groups. Write to the ASAE at 15175 I St. NW, Washington, DC 20005, or call (202) 626-2793.

- The Service Corps of Retired Executives (SCORE) is an organization of some 12,400 retired business owners and executives that provides free consulting for small businesses. Call (800) 634-0245 or visit www.score.org.

- Small Business Development Centers (SBDCs) are one-stop shops set up by the Small Business Administration to give entrepreneurs free or low-cost advice, training and technical assistance. There are more than 50 centers, at least one in each state and territory. Call (800) 8-ASK-SBA or visit www.sbaonline.sba.gov.

## Tips From The Trenches

**G**reg Zedlar
**Cardstar.com (niche greeting card manufacturer),
on having patience:**

"Take the time to do your research and think things through. The worst decisions we ever made were the ones that were rushed. One time we went and printed 110,000 catalogs without bidding out the process. Instead, we opted for what we saw as a bargain rate. To our horror, everything went wrong. The catalogs were the wrong format, the wrong print size, the wrong everything. We wound up losing $20,000 to fix everything. My advice? Do your homework, explore every option and take time to think decisions over. It's a money saver."

# A Pocketful Of (Part-Time) Miracles

Need extra help for just a few months? Having trouble getting everything taken care of in the office, but don't want to fork over big bucks for a full-timer?

"Hey, I hired my father to provide advice and keep an eye on the budget," says Gregg Levin, 30, owner of Boston's Perfect Curve, which makes custom-made baseball cap shapers and holders. "He didn't ask for a lot of money, and I have to admit it's fun telling him what to do."

There are several creative ways to get more help without breaking the bank. For instance, bring an intern aboard, such as a high school or college student who works for little or no pay in exchange for valuable work experience. You'll need to make some time to train them, and then keep a close eye on their work, but you can't beat the price.

Draw up a detailed description of your internship, and then promote it at the career placement center at your local high school or college. The National Society for Experiential Education in Raleigh, North Carolina, provides information on starting internship programs; call (919) 787-3263, ext. 21.

Or, get someone with loads of experience and lots of time on their hands. Senior citizens can bring a wealth of real-world expertise to the job, and though retired, many are eager to keep their

## Tips From The Trenches

**M**ichael Caito
**Restaurants on the Run (restaurant delivery service),**
**on expanding your business:**

"The biggest mistake we made was expanding too quickly and going into too many markets. Looking back, we should have waited a bit and gotten more experience. In restaurants, when you hook up with someone like a California Pizza Kitchen, they want you to grow and expand with them. It took us a couple of years to catch up, and we were lucky that we had the chance to do so. My advice: Develop a good business plan with an organization chart so everyone is on the same page. Also consider hiring a consultant who can teach you about developing your own unique business" hands busy in the business world. Check with senior centers in your community and your local branch of the American Association of Retired People (AARP).

If you need individuals with targeted skills, like a graphic designer or annual report writer, freelance contractors might be just the solution. Or if your business relies on skilled work, consider starting your own work apprentice program. That'll help you mix practical classroom instruction with a year or more of on-the-job training. You'll be working with entry-level talent you can train and eventually hire full time as your business grows. Jobs for the Future is a Boston-based organization that's geared toward helping entrepreneurs establish successful job-training programs. For help or advice, call them at (617) 742-5995.

## Scam Alert

It happens all too often: You get a bill in the mail for services or equipment you're not sure you ordered. It seems wrong, but then again the bill has all your correct information, it's not that much money, and you don't have time chase down all the supporting paperwork—so you just pay it, falling for one of the oldest tricks in the book. It's relatively easy for con artists to get your vital business information off the Internet or through your competitors and begin invoicing you for fabricated services. Amazingly, many charlatans who engage in this practice get away with it.

Shady characters and unscrupulous snake oil salesmen run a number of scams geared at separating business owners from their money. To help you protect your business, here's a quick peek at five common scams and how to avoid them:

**Scam #1:** Office supply rip-offs. If the offer sounds too good to be true, it probably is. Dishonest peddlers lure their victims with claims of a liquidation sale or a shipment mistakenly labeled with your company's name that you can have at a greatly discounted price.

Other con artists might claim to be conducting an office equipment survey. After you innocently provide information about your copy machine, for example, the individual will call back and pose as your new supplier or authorized dealer for the products you use for your copy machine. You'll place an order, pay them the money and never see a part.

**Solution:** Whenever possible, do business with local suppliers. Try to do business with people you know in the community. You should also make it a rule never to buy from a new supplier by phone or mail before you check out the company's background and references. Insist on written purchase orders, don't accept c.o.d. shipments, and don't pay cash for a shipment.

**Scam #2:** Phony invoices. Knowing small businesses don't use elaborate accounting systems, scam artists often use phony invoices to great advantage. Here's how it works: The swindler calls your company to get your name and other information. Then he or she sends an invoice for an amount just small enough not to attract attention. The invoice might be for goods you never ordered or for advertisements in bogus publications.

**Solution:** Set up a system of checks and balances to weed out the bogus bills. Every order should be given a shop number. And then, when an invoice is received, pay it only if it has a matching shop number.

**Scam #3:** Sneaky solicitations. "I get a lot of junk mail,"says John Mueller, owner of The Idea Factory in Menomonee Falls, Wisconsin, maker of the Rinse Ace. "And when I get what appears to be a bill, I examine it closely." That type of eagle eye can thwart a popular scam that involves what look like invoices for directory listings or advertisements but are really solicitations, with this disclaimer in very fine print: "This is a solicitation. You are under no obligation to pay unless you accept this offer." Sending solicitations with such a disclaimer isn't illegal. But many business owners miss the small print and pay anyway.

**Solution:** If a "bill" arrives by second-class or bulk mail, beware. It's probably a solicitation. When you receive a "bill," match it with a purchase order for the product. If you can't find one, chances are you never ordered the item.

**Scam #4:** Charity pleas. Want to support your community by donating money to build a home for abused children? It sounds like a great cause, but the charity may not be legitimate. "Oh gosh, we used to hear from everyone," says Tim Krauskopf, founder and former president of Chicago-based Spyglass Software, which developed Microsoft's Internet Explorer Web browser. "You want to help where you can, but you just don't have the time to check everybody out as thoroughly as you'd like."

**Solution:** Be cautious. Some solicitors use names that closely resemble those of well-known organizations. Before you give, check with the local charity registration office of your state attorney general's office and with your Better Business Bureau. If a caller offers to send a "runner" to pick up your contribution, pleading that the group needs your money now, hang up the phone. It's a scam.

**Scam #5:** Technical difficulties. A repair technician might offer you a free inspection of your office equipment to ensure that it's in good working order. That's fine, unless the technician surreptitiously damages your otherwise healthy equipment and then performs high-priced work to "fix" it.

**Solution:** When someone solicits you, ask for references. If you decide to accept the offer, insist your equipment remain at your business while it's being inspected or repaired. If you must send your equipment in for repairs, request that damaged parts be returned. If you suspect foul play, call another technician for a second evaluation, and contact the Better Business Bureau (BBB) if you've been ripped off.

You don't have to be a BBB member to receive its free pamphlets, which cover everything from telemarketing schemes and credit card laundering to tips on charitable giving. Contact your local BBB for information.

If you've been scammed, you can report the incident to the National Fraud Information Center in Washington, DC, where counselors will help you file your complaint. Call (800) 876-7060 or visit www.fraud.org.

## Tips From The Trenches

**Jody Kozlow Gardner**
**Co-founder with Cherie Serota of Belly Basics (maternity wear), on partnerships:**

"We think that partnerships can really work for a company, but you've really got to work at it. Don't be afraid to disagree, and always pull your weight. If you do that, you'll find that bouncing ideas off each other really helps. We think it would be very hard to launch an entrepreneurial effort on your own. Our advice: There may be some bickering, but a good partnership will lead to a better product."

# Lease Logic

Steve Lake, one of the co-founders of the skateboard maker
Sector 9, thought he'd found nirvana when he located a nice place
for his company to build their skateboards. Soon, a rift developed
over the issue of trash disposal—specifically, who was going to pay
for it. The issue became so contentious that Sector 9 was almost
forced to vacate the premises before a compromise was reached.

Headaches of that nature can be avoided by confronting sensitive areas during lease negotiations. Here are some tips designed to
keep both landlord and tenant happy as clams.

**1** **The overall lease:** A lot of small-business owners don't read
the lease and don't understand it. It's your responsibility to
understand what you're getting into. The lease document is the
rulebook. Whatever is in there, you're stuck with.

Like any contract, the lease should be reviewed by an attorney. Most attorneys can review a lease in less than an hour, so it's
not a big expense, and it's a safety valve for potential problems.

How do you determine whether a lease is a good deal or
not? Many leases state a base rent per square foot, but this rate
can be misleading. Sometimes it includes space that's not use-
able, such as corridors and elevators, and this makes it difficult
to compare two leases for two different spaces. Instead, look at
the total amount to be paid. Sometimes a space that's slightly
smaller with a higher price per square foot may work out better for your business because it's more efficiently laid out.

**2** **Length of the lease:** Many new business owners want a short
lease or no lease at all. That way, if the business is unsuccess-
ful, they aren't on the hook for thousands of dollars for space
they are no longer using.

However, it may be difficult to get a short lease if you're in
a tight housing market. When space is scarce, many landlords
won't settle for leases shorter than five years. Short of working
out of your garage, the only recourse you have is to move to a
part of town where rents are cheaper but where your neighbors
may not subscribe to Martha Stewart Living.

**3** **Tenant improvements:** You may want to save money by making improvements yourself, but most leases require the landlord's permission. Submit your plans before you sign the lease.

**4** **What's included and what's not?** Too many small-business owners focus on dollar amounts without considering what they get for their money. Some tenants pay for utilities and a percentage of common-area maintenance. Many law firms have a gross lease, which includes all expenses, but some tenants sign a triple net lease in which they pay their own property taxes, insurance and maintenance. In such cases, the base, no-frills rent is less. For my money, base rent is a better deal when you're just starting out. Just keep control of the thermostat and wear a sweater in January.

Also watch for nonmonetary clauses. Will heating and air conditioning be shut off after business hours or on weekends? This may be important if you plan to work odd hours.

**5** **Subleases and allowable uses:** If you decide to move or find that you're using just part of your space, you may want to sublease or assign the lease to another business. Most leases won't allow this without the landlord's approval.

Most leases also specify the type of work you can do on the premises. Landlords tend to make this "allowable use" as narrow as possible. In most cases, negotiate to make it broader, to allow for future expansion of your business.

**6** **Pass-through expenses:** A common trap for tenants is the annual increase in operating costs, or "pass-throughs." Often landlords will ask for a 4 percent or 5 percent annual increase to protect the landlord against inflation.

These days, the increase often is more than the inflation rate because the soft real estate market of the early '90s forced landlords to forgo any rent increases for a long time. Watch for inaccurate calculations of operating costs; overcharging tenants 10 percent to 15 percent is not uncommon.

Leasing a commercial space poses some risks, but by paying attention to these six points, you can protect yourself and get your business off on the right foot.

Before you go out to negotiate that lease, here are some lease terms you should know:

- **Lessor:** landlord
- **Lessee:** tenant
- **Right of first refusal:** before vacant space is rented to someone

else, landlord must offer it to the current tenant with the same terms that will be offered to the public

● **Gross lease:** tenant pays flat monthly amount; landlord pays all operating costs, including property taxes, insurance and utilities

● **Triple net lease:** tenant pays base rent, taxes, insurance, repairs and maintenance

● **Percentage lease:** base rent, operating expenses, common-area maintenance, plus a percentage of tenant's gross income (most common for retailers in shopping malls)

● **Sublet:** tenant rents all or part of space to another business; tenant is still responsible for paying all costs to landlord

● **Assign lease:** tenant turns lease over to another business, which assumes payments and obligations under the lease

● **Anchor tenant:** major store or supermarket that attracts customers to a shopping center

● **Exclusivity provision:** shopping centers can't lease to another tenant who provides the same product or service that existing tenant does

● **CAM:** common-area maintenance charges, including property taxes, security, parking lot lighting and maintenance; may not apply to anchor tenants in retail leases

● **Nondisturbance clause:** tenant cannot be forced to move or sign a new lease if building or shopping center is sold or undergoes foreclosure

Once you find a place to put down roots, here are some questions to ask before signing the lease:

**1** Does the lease specifically state the square footage of the premises? The total rentable square footage of the building?

**2** Is the tenant's share of expenses based on the total square footage of the building or the square footage leased by the landlord? Your share may be lower if it's based on the total square footage.

**3** Do the base-year expenses reflect full occupancy or are they adjusted to full occupancy? (That is, real estate taxes based on an unfinished building are lower than in subsequent years.)

**4** Must the landlord provide a detailed list of expenses, prepared by a CPA, to support increases?

**5** Does the lease clearly give the tenant the right to audit the landlord's books and records?

**6** If use of the building is interrupted, does the lease define the remedies available to the tenant, such as rent abatement or lease cancellation?

**7** If the landlord does not meet repair responsibilities, can the tenant make the repairs, after notice to the landlord, and deduct the cost from the rent?

**8** Is the landlord required to obtain nondisturbance agreements from current and future lenders?

**9** Does the lease clearly define how disputes will be settled?

## Quick Picks

You can access dozens of commercial online databases where you can get the full text of important business documents. Here's a sampling:

- **American Business Disc:** Valuable information on thousands of U.S. businesses, including address, phone number, sales, number of employees, contact names and more.

- **Commerce Business Daily** (http://cbd.savvy.com): Full text of announcements issued by the Department of Commerce on contracts, procurements, requests for products, research and service needs of U.S. government agencies.

- **National Trade Data Bank:** Collection of databases produced by the U.S. government on domestic commerce and international trade.

- If you have access to a university or law school library, check out **Lexis/Nexis** (www.lexis-nexis.com): This exhaustive online database is divided into two parts. Lexis covers U.S. and state legislation, court cases, bills and legal issues. Nexis provides articles from business newspapers, magazines, periodicals and company annual reports.

## For Future Reference

Following are the most useful reference books you'll find at your public library:

- *Business Information Desk Reference:* Where to Find Answers to Business Questions (Macmillan): This tells where to find information on almost any business topic, from finding funds to starting a business.

- *Encyclopedia of Associations* (Gale Research): This guide lists thousands of associations for practically every industry imaginable.

- *Encyclopedia of Business Information Sources* (Gale Research): This bibliography has 24,000 citations on 1,100 subjects, listing directories, encyclopedias, yearbooks, online databases, trade groups and professional societies.

- *Gale Directory of Publications and Broadcasting Media* (Gale Research): This is a listing of newspapers, magazines and radio and TV stations by geographic area.

- *Industry Surveys* (Standard & Poor's): These publications cover 69 major domestic industries with prospects for future activity.

- *Thomas Register of American Manufacturers* (Thomas Register): This comprehensive guide lists thousands of product manufacturers.

## Finally, Be Healthy

One of the chief complaints of the entrepreneurs interviewed for this book had to do with time: there isn't enough of it. Running a business gobbles up every waking moment, leaving you precious little time for yourself, whether to hit the gym for some stress-relieving exercise or to hit the couch for some much-needed downtime. But Gen E business owners value their bodies and souls just as much as their bank accounts and so they are striving to make more time to break a sweat or take a mental health day. "Getting away from the office is harder and harder," says Kristin Knight, 31, CEO of Creative Assets, a staffing agency in Seattle. "You try to take as much time for yourself as possible, but you really only wind up stealing away hours, or even minutes at a time."

Looking and feeling healthy is easier than you think. All it takes is a little adjustment. So close your laptop, get off your tush and follow these five steps:

1 **Walk:** Use coffee breaks at business meetings and conventions to take a brisk stroll—not enough to break into a sweat but enough to loosen your muscles. A five- to 10-minute walk will

raise your heart rate, increase your oxygen intake, burn additional calories and increase your metabolic rate. Your body will feel energized and your mind sharp.

**2** **Stretch:** Take two or three minutes every hour to stretch your upper body, shoulders and neck. You can do a simple routine while sitting at your desk.

**3** **Avoid sugar:** The sweet rolls and cookies often found at conferences may taste great, but the sugar they contain provides only a short-term energy boost. Sweets act as a natural depressant in the long run.

**4** **Limit caffeine and alcohol:** Coffee, tea, wine and alcoholic drinks will dehydrate you and limit your ability to focus.

**5** **Drink water:** The amount of water you drink each day should equal, in ounces, one-half your body weight. If you weigh 140 pounds, that's 70 ounces, or seven 10-ounce glasses, each day. So take a water bottle with you and fill it—and drink it—regularly.

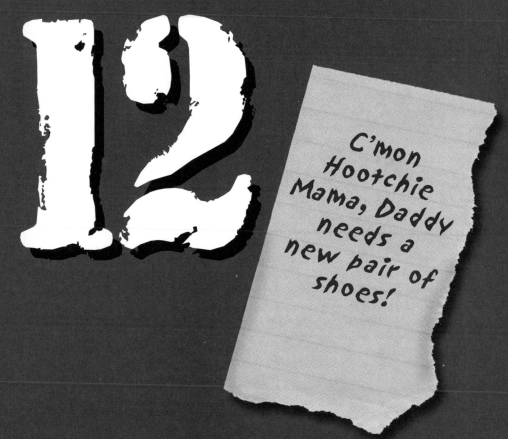

# Chapter
# 12

C'mon Hootchie Mama, Daddy needs a new pair of shoes!

# Austin Or Bust:
# The Best Places To
# Launch A Business

S oftware companies located on the cusp of pristine Pacific Coast beaches. Concierge services in the heart of major metropolitan areas. Web design firms rubbing up against tony college campuses. These are the places that Gen E is setting up shop.

Generation E business owners seem less likely than their corporate ancestors to roll out the welcome mat in a place simply because it offers the best tax base or is nearest to the interstate. Sure, financial incentives and easy access are issues that matter to young entrepreneurs, but their motives for choosing a locale to start their companies go way deeper than that.

More than any other generation, quality of life is critical for young entrepreneurs. Why rent office space near exit 9 off the turn-pike when you can set up digs next to your old college campus or in a hip warehouse in the art district downtown? New blood wants to be close to new blood, and Gen E's could care not a wit about the suburban office parks where their parents work. That's why city digs are so popular with Gen E; preferably digs in cities with a buzzing nightlife, high culture and a plethora of college graduates to staff their upstart firms.

The cities listed below are high profile, brand-name places, easily recognizable by any reader. That's not meant to disparage wonderful, lower-profile locales like La Jolla, California, and Madison, Wisconsin, which offer comfortable living for many young entre-preneurs. For the purposes of this chapter—and to assuage the denizens of places like La Jolla, who begged me not to draw attention to their small but fair cities for fear of crowds—we'll stick to describing the best big cities with 500,000 or more citizens.

The 17 cities that made the cut not only offer the civic "can-do" attitude that make entrepreneurs of any age feel welcome, but they also have character and personality and a sense of their place in the world. Residents wake up and know they are someplace exciting and attractive, a place where people want to be. No city is perfect, but those listed below offer a special pull to young entrepreneurs. Let's find out why.

# Atlanta: A Georgia Peach

For young Americans who think New York is too big, too cold or simply too much, Atlanta is proving to be a popular option. The combination of Southern hospitality and big-business appeal is simply too hard to resist for many young entrepreneurs, especially those in the white-hot communications and manufacturing sectors.

What's not to like? The home of the 1996 Summer Olympics offers Gen E business owners plenty of what they need: a low-cost business climate, plenty of educated workers and a vibrant nightlife that borrows more from Dixie neighbor New Orleans than it does from northern lights like New York or Boston.

According to Georgia's Department of Labor, the state's population is expected to grow from about 7.1 million in 1994 to about 8.2 million in 2005. More than 50 percent of these people are expected to be transplants from other states and countries. More than 586,000 new jobs have been created in Atlanta in the past decade. Atlanta has led the nation in four of the last five years, generating 88,400 jobs in 1996 alone. In the past three years, more than 700 companies moved to Atlanta. In spite of the influx, the city continues to offer competitive wages and a relatively low cost of living.

Atlanta's multifaceted economy is supported by a variety of industries. United Parcel Service's (UPS) headquarters is here, and light manufacturing continues its hold, thanks to local Ford and GM plants. Other healthy markets include service, aerospace, trucking, construction, retail, software, technical and personnel. The latest U.S. Census Report ranks Atlanta eighth in the nation for the number of women-owned businesses and fifth for minority-owned businesses.

Atlanta's transportation infrastructure has come a long way as well. In 1978 there was no nonstop international air service from Atlanta. Now it is home to the world's second-busiest airport, following Chicago's O'Hare, and it

PHOTO© TONY STONE IMAGES/GREG PROBST

served more than 63 million passengers last year. Atlanta also continues to be a centrally located interstate and railroad hub, making accessibility one of its biggest drawing points.

Finding good employees shouldn't be much of a problem. The Department of Labor projects an increase in the number of young workers trained in popular fields such as marketing, advertising, public relations, computer-related jobs, education and nursing. Already, the job market is healthy, with the Metro Atlanta Chamber of Commerce reporting that Atlanta's unemployment rate has been hovering around 3.3 percent.

**Upside:** Great climate and a "can-do" civic culture that attracted the 1996 Summer Olympics to Atlanta. Educated, diversified work force means great pickings for entrepreneurs starting new businesses. Emory University, Moorhead College and Georgia Tech nearby inject an ample shot of youth into mainstream Atlanta.

**Downside:** Nightlife is improving all the time, but it could be better, with the city rolling up the sidewalks, so to speak, after 6 p.m., although the action spills over into the tony 'burbs like Buckhead. Plus, Atlanta is becoming such a high-profile beacon to young college graduates, real estate prices are beginning to spike upward at an alarming rate.

## The Inside Scoop

**Population:** 397,000
**Best hotel room:** Ritz-Carlton Atlanta, (404) 237-5500
**Hottest table:** Mumbo Jumbo, (404) 523-0330
**Best place for a business drink:** Martini Club, (404) 873-0794
**Most visited museum:** High Museum of Art, (404) 733-4400
**Counties within metro area:** Clayton, DeKalb and Fulton
**Median price of a three-bedroom house:** $158,000
**Projected job growth to 2001:** 10 percent
**Annual sunny days:** 219

*Source:* Fortune *magazine*

# Austin: Urban Hip, Texas-Style

The funny thing about Austin is that, culturally, it's closer kin to Berkeley, California, or Cambridge, Massachusetts, than it is to down-home neighbors like Houston and Dallas. No big oil money

and no cowboy culture in Austin, just a place where free spirits and counterculture rebels can settle down and open a mighty fine business.

Austin is where Generation Xer Michael Dell launched his little mail order computer business that could. Dell Computer is now the region's largest private employer, adding a staggering 100 to 200 jobs each week. Michael Dell and his posse of Dellionaires have irreversibly altered the Austin scene from sleepy college town to booming techno hub. Led by Dell, the most prominent wealth creator in town, software firms have flocked to Austin, their numbers ballooning from 177 in 1989 to more than 600 by 1999. Of the 57 publicly held companies in Austin, 32 have gone public since 1994. Such companies are accomplishing the unthinkable—drawing some of the best minds from high-tech bastions like Silicon Valley and Boston's Route 128 technology corridor to come to live and work in sunny Austin. For local entrepreneurs, it all began with Michael Dell, but Austin is becoming more than a one-horse town. "Dell is like the anchor store in a mall," says one young and local entrepreneur. "It's driving so much of the economy and providing a sense of excitement and growth."

Austin's high-tech industry is definitely here to stay. Motorola Inc., the city's largest employer, has been in Austin since 1974. Overall, semiconductor manufacturers have invested more than $7.5

## Best Places To Live In North America

1. Cincinnati
2. Seattle
3. Philadelphia
4. Toronto
5. Raleigh

*Source:* Places Rated Almanac

billion in plants and equipment here in the last 25 years. Dell Computer Corp., with headquarters in nearby Round Rock and the area's second-largest employer, employs more than 9,500.

In the high-tech sector, the manufacturing giants may be growing, but it's the hundreds of rapidly expanding software firms following in their trail that are really lifting off. The number of software companies has tripled in the last five years (to more than 600), and their payrolls have soared as well, to more than 17,000. Two software start-ups are typical of the trend: Smart Technologies Inc. grew from 15 to 140 employees in just 18 months, while Vignette Corp. rose from two employees to more than 80 in the same period. New shopping districts, restaurant rows, office complexes and subdivisions are spreading in and around the bluffs leading to the Hill Country. Now it's possible for newcomers to live, shop and work without ever coming downtown.

**Upside:** Hook 'em Horns! Nearby University of Texas provides plenty of skilled and knowledgeable workers to local companies. Happy Hour option: Instead of quaffing a few margaritas at one of the many local watering holes, Austin business owners can bring staffers to the city's Congress Avenue Bridge, where every night from April until October the world's largest colony of free-tailed bats swoop en masse skyward in search of food (of the insect variety).

**Downside:** Ouch! A sales tax rate of 8.25 percent is fairly stiff. Public transportation is pretty much limited to buses.

## The Inside Scoop

**Population:** 587,000
**Annual population growth rate:** 3 percent
**Climate:** 300 sunny days per year, but they're hot ones. Summer temps are in the 90s.
**Unemployment rate:** 3.7 percent (1998)
**Median price of a new house:** $148,000
**Great place for dinner and drinks:** The Oasis, (512) 835-7208

*Source: Austin Chamber of Commerce*

# Boston: Athens-On-The-Charles

Four hundred years old and counting, Beantown remains a favorite of young entrepreneurs, despite its chilly climes and sometimes onerous tax situation. Graduates from local A-list colleges like Harvard, MIT, Brandeis, Babson and the University of Massachusetts who go on to launch their own businesses are willing to put up with a snowstorm or two and a heftier tax bill to stay local. Young entrepreneurs in Boston are a lot like their neighbors there—hearty souls who feel the pull of history every time they walk outside in the morning. It's  difficult to travel 200 yards in Boston without stumbling over a historic or cultural landmark—Harvard Yard, Fenway Park, the Olde Trinity Burial Grounds and the beautiful Public Gardens in Boston Common, where blue-blood Brahmins have strolled side-by-side with working-class heroes for well over 200 years now.

No doubt about it: Boston has the brains. Its colleges and universities produce thousands of bright young entrepreneurs, whose brash start-ups often grow to great prominence in technology, finance and medicine. It's a great city to get sick in as well—Boston has twice as many doctors per capita as the average U.S. big city.

PHOTOS COURTESY: GREATER BOSTON CONVENTION & VISITORS BUREAU

It's difficult to think about Boston in a business sense without thinking about software and mutual funds, the linchpins of the local economy. Almost a fourth of the country's mutual fund assets—including those of Fidelity, Putnam and State Street—are managed in Massachusetts, with the vast majority in Boston. Altogether, Boston's financial institutions manage about $1.4 trillion and provide more than 80,000 jobs, 9 percent of all jobs in the city. A new, $50 million annual tax-incentive

**Upside:** The urban boutiques keep repopulating themselves with highly educated people. The most successful companies are knowledge-intensive companies that need to be able to recruit bright, talented people out of good universities. In Boston, there's no shortage of great workers. Also, Boston may be the best walking city in the United States. It's only a 10-minute stroll from Boston Harbor to Boston Common, and only another 15 minutes to Fenway Park and a Red Sox game. The bleachers at Fenway are the biggest outdoor bar in the United States, so be forewarned. If the Yankees are in town, it can get ugly.

**Downside:** Boston, one of the smallest major cities geographically in the United States, isn't cheap. At $33 a square foot for Class A space, Boston has the second-most-expensive commercial real estate (following New York). On the bright side: Boston's violent crime rate is at its lowest since 1973, the murder rate is at a 30-year low, and no juvenile had been killed by gunfire in 28 months through 1998. Also, Beantown offers a lot of generals, but not many soldiers. If your company needs regular, dependable help at lower skill levels, set up shop somewhere else. Lastly, Republicans are as rare in Boston as Big Foot sightings. If you're conservative politically, you're viewed by the locals the same as a Junebug, fit only to be squashed.

## The Inside Scoop

**Population:** 549,000
**Counties within metro area:** Cambridge and Gloucester
**Median price of a three-bedroom house:** $168,500
**Best hotel room:** Four Seasons, (617) 338-4400
**Hottest table:** Mistral, (617) 867-9300
**Best place for a business drink:** Rowes Wharf, Boston Harbor Hotel, (617) 439-7000
**Most visited museum:** Museum of Science, (617) 723-2500
**Projected job growth to 2001:** 3.7 percent
**Annual sunny days:** 205

*Source:* Fortune *Magazine*

plan for mutual fund companies will help these industry giants stay put. That's good news for new businesses, from deli caterers to software doctors, who feed off the gargantuan local finance industry.

Boston is also giving Silicon Valley a run for its money as a mecca for technology and venture capital, thanks (again) to its unparalleled network of 68 colleges and universities. No other American city benefits from such a concentration of brainpower—companies created by MIT graduates alone account for more than a third of the city's manufacturing employment. Local technology companies received $1 billion in venture capital last year. Statewide, the number of software companies soared from 800 in 1989 to well over 2,500 in 1999, with most concentrated around Boston. (Silicon Valley has about 2,000.)

# Cleveland: A Remake By The Lake

It wasn't too long ago that Cleveland was the butt of a thousands jokes. With a decrepit downtown area that resembled a demilitarized zone, it was called the "Mistake by the Lake."

Not anymore. During the past decade, Cleveland has become fun, inexpensive and more prosperous than ever. In recent years, the average Clevelander enjoyed a 30.4 percent jump in personal income. Office rental rates have dipped nearly 16 percent in the last five years. And to top it off, Cleveland recently added a pair of major jewels to its crown: In 1994 the city unveiled its $450 million Gateway Sports Complex, home to baseball's Indians and the NBA's Cavaliers. The following year Cleveland became the permanent home of the Rock and Roll Hall of Fame, beating out New York, Memphis and a host of other cities for the honor.

Like Boston, the "feeder factor" is high. The city's rel-

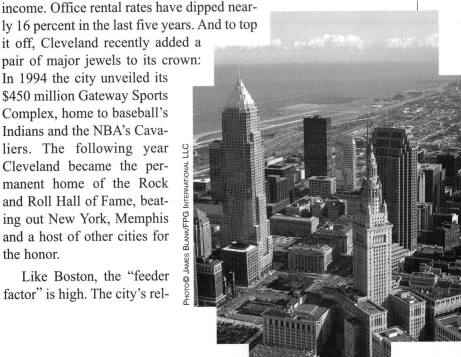

PHOTO © JAMES BLANK/FPG INTERNATIONAL LLC

atively low cost of doing business has attracted the nation's eighth-highest concentration of Fortune 500 companies to the Greater Cleveland area, including giants like TRW (No. 135), Eaton (No. 207) and KeyCorp (No. 241). The median age of residents is 34.5 years, so you'll have plenty of company if you decide to open a business there.

Upside: In a few short years, it's gone from defunct steel town to most-livable city. Its revivified manufacturing base is complemented by new service industries. Old-fashioned Midwest optimism and cheery manners are prevalent in Cleveland.

Also, well-established universities set up specialized research-and-development centers, then spin off dozens of advanced-technology companies. City and state governments realize the importance of entrepreneurship and recognize that the future of the region lies in small business. For example, Cleveland's Council of Smaller Enterprises, which is affiliated with the city's chamber of commerce, helps entrepreneurs by offering cut-rate prices on everything from group health insurance to office supplies.

Downside: In some industries, there are strong unions, which can make it hard on young business owners if they want to. Plus, the Rock and Roll Hall of Fame has yet to induct Madonna.

## The Inside Scoop

**Population:** 493,000
**Best room:** Ritz-Carlton, (216) 623-1300
**Hottest table:** Mallorca, (216) 687-9454
**Best place for a business drink:** Great Lakes Brewing Co., (216) 771-4404
**Most visited museum:** Rock and Roll Hall of Fame and Museum, (216) 781-7625

*Source:* Fortune *magazine*

# Denver: A Mile-High Buzz

A Super Bowl champion football team and a scenic landscape may get Denver some great press, and youth may come here for the snowboarding and eclectic lifestyle, but there's a great deal more to the Mile High City than those attributes. The city has made great strides in the 1990s to attract new businesses, and this is what pays off for Gen E business owners in the long run.

A new convention center built in 1990 on time and under budget went a long way toward boosting the city's morale and providing newcomers with a sense of commitment from city elders. Despite some glitches, the new $4.2 billion Denver International Airport—the first new airport built in the United States since 1974—is now bringing more people to the city than ever before.

Denver's economic rebirth has created other issues for the city. In 1991 immigration surpassed emigration, and the growth has been nonstop ever since. Housing developments are creeping into the foothills of the Rocky Mountains. Modern office parks tower over what was once scrubland. In the Cherry Creek section, small postwar ranch houses are coming down to make way for elegant townhouses and condominiums.

This could be a recipe for disastrous urban sprawl, but the city has been vigilant about inventing ways to keep people coming to the city center. Most spectacular, perhaps, has been the conversion of the Lower Downtown area, or LoDo as the locals call it. This once-decaying collection of vacant warehouses is now bustling with microbreweries, sleek restaurants and hip, exposed-brick lofts. The transformation began in the late 1980s, but it took off exponentially when the Colorado Rockies baseball team came to Denver in 1993 and chose to locate its stadium in LoDo. Ambitious plans are now underway to extend LoDo into the barren wasteland of railroad tracks and empty space that separates it from the Platte River. Over the next 10 to 15 years, more than 6 million

## Top 4 U.S. Mountain Cities

1. Salt Lake City/Ogden, UT
2. Phoenix/Mesa, AZ
3. Las Vegas, NV/AZ
4. Denver, CO

Source: Dun & Bradstreet and Entrepreneur magazine

square feet of development will occur in the area, including offices, shops, apartments and a riverfront park.

Denver also has the opportunity to counter sprawl by taking advantage of available land near the city limits. The 4,700-acre site of the old airport is ripe for development. And the 27-square-mile Rocky Mountain Arsenal, where the federal government once made nerve gas and pesticides, has been designated a wildlife refuge, which will open in 2007.

## Good Business Is Local

Sure, Internet Web sites like Amazon.com and Ebay are making money hand over fist. But don't get too caught up in global marketing yet, say business writers Hal Pickle and Royce Abrahamson in their book *Small Business Management* (John Wiley & Sons).

As my mom used to say, "Don't forget to keep the home fire burning!" (Or maybe it was "Get the hose! The cat's on fire again!" I can never remember which.) But Pickle's point is that a good marketer hones in on his or her geographic market first. Even in the age of the Internet and E-commerce, that's pretty good advice. As Pickle says, "The community or trade area where you will operate your business is generally that geographic domain from which you will draw the major portion of the customers needed to support your business on a continuing basis." According to the authors, the trade area can usually be divided into three distinct zones of influence:

1 **The primary trading area:** The geographic area within the community where you will be able to exert the most influence. This is usually defined as the greater metropolitan area where your business is located. It usually accounts for 75 percent of sales.

2 **The secondary trading area:** The geographic area that is immediately beyond the primary trading zone, such as your county and state. The secondary trading area usually accounts for 15 percent to 20 percent of sales.

3 **The tertiary trading area:** The rest of the United States and the world. This area is outside both your primary and secondary trading areas, but it still holds customers who patronize your business. The tertiary trading area usually accounts for around 5 percent of sales.

In Denver, central homebased entrepreneurs needn't look far to find other like-minded folks in the Mile High City. Networking events are publicized in local newspapers almost every day, and the chamber of commerce offers a program called BusinessPlus for the small-business community. The program provides small-business training on everything from dealing with government regulations to time management. Additionally, just 10 miles east in Aurora is the Rocky Mountain Home-Based Business Association, and 25 miles to the west is the Mount Evans Home-Based Business Association. The state of Colorado also offers a business start-up program called Leading Edge that was customized to meet the specific needs of homebased entrepreneurs.

**Upside:** Fast growth. More than 700,000 people have flocked to the Denver area in the last 10 years. If you believe its chamber of commerce, Denver is also the most highly educated city in the United States. Ninety-two percent of the population have high school diplomas and 35 percent have at least a bachelor's degree. The national average is 82 percent for the former and 23 percent for the latter.

**Downside:** Arggh!!! More baby boomers on average live in Denver than anywhere else in the country. That means more Range Rovers and more "Relaxed Fit" Gap jeans.

## The Inside Scoop

**Population:** 516,000
**Cost-of-living index:** 4 percent above the national average
**Median household income:** $41,539
**Per capita income:** $29,280
**Best hotel room:** Brown Palace, (303) 297-3111
**Hottest table:** Sostanza, (303) 292-4682
**Best place for a business drink:** Cruise Room at the Oxford Hotel, (303) 628-5400

*Source: Fortune magazine*

# Indianapolis: Little Pink Houses For You And Me

When John Mellencamp sang about little pink houses in his 1987 homage to his home state of Indiana, he likely never realized how big little Indianapolis would grow. The city of Indianapolis has evolved into a growth dynamo, with what real estate agents would call a great "ground floor" opportunity for young business owners to come downtown and set up shop.

Indianapolis made a commitment to improve its downtown in the late 1970s, when the unofficial motto of the declining central district was "You can't build a suburb around nothing." Since 1990, the public and private sectors have invested more than $2.5 billion to develop the city's downtown, and the results are sports facilities, historic preservation projects, high-rise office buildings, beautified parks and green spaces, apartments and single-family homes. Indianapolis' downtown now ranks high on the list of places nationally known for shopping and entertainment.

Downtown's millions of visitors and 12,500 residents enjoy a convenient package of amenities: more than 300 retail businesses, 200 restaurants and bars, 19 museums and galleries, 30 hotels, a thriving shopping district and a gleaming new convention center. Downtown Indianapolis also has an action-packed schedule of festivals, events and performances, and everything within downtown's Mile Square is easy walking distance. That makes it a convenient place to live, work and be entertained. It's also a big draw for meetings and convention business, which, according to Indianapolis Convention & Visitors Association, has increased an average of 18 percent each year since 1984.

PHOTO © JAMES BLANK/FPG INTERNATIONAL LLC

Downtown Indianapolis reached a notable milestone in 1995 with the opening of Circle Centre, a focal point in the revitalization of downtown. The $319.5 million shopping and entertainment complex—800,000 square feet, with a sales average of $400 per square foot, far above the industry average of $230 per square foot—motivated more than 12 million visits in its first year alone. And it contributes greatly to downtown's continued growth.

## Top 5 U.S. Central Cities

1. Indianapolis, IN
2. San Antonio, TX
3. Austin/San Marcos, TX
4. Fort Worth/Arlington, TX
5. Dallas, TX

*Source: Dun & Bradstreet and* Entrepreneur *magazine*

The revitalization of downtown Indianapolis and its increasing popularity has triggered the demand for office space and the increased occupancy of Class A and B space to its highest level in eight years. The demand for downtown living is also high. Downtown apartment and condominium occupancy is nearing 100 percent.

To spur innovation in city government through privatization, the current mayor, Stephen Goldsmith, has opened certain city services to competitive bidding. The Indianapolis International Airport, for example, is now operated by the British Airport Authority, with a projected savings to the city of $105 million over 10 years. When the Pentagon announced plans to close its Naval Warfare Center in 1995, the city countered with a proposal to privatize the facility in order to save the 2,200 jobs it provided. The following year, Hughes Technical Services took over the site and has since promised to increase the number of jobs to 3,000 in the next five years.

Altogether, since 1992 the city has generated more than 25,000 new jobs and retained more than 100,000 existing ones, resulting in a drop in the unemployment rate to 2.7 percent, the lowest in three decades. The availability of work has attracted people from all over, creating, for the first time, a diverse ethnic community. All of this means opportunities for subcontractors and support businesses, vendors and partnerships and an even more attractive environment for other employers and national and international visitors to Downtown Indy.

**Upside:** New infrastructure that any young Hoosier would love. Indy's new Circle Centre is home to 75 specialty shops, nightclubs and restaurants, a nine-screen theater and a virtual reality playground, and it has enclosed walkways that connect to six hotels, the Indiana Convention Center & RCA Dome and Churchill Downs Sports Spectrum satellite wagering facility. The architecture of the structure blends new construction with restored facades from 130-year-old buildings. The Centre has 2,500 full-time employees and accounts for a 2.4 percent rise in convention bookings for 1997.

Also, a $20 million IWERKS CineDome and Festival Plaza and a $2.5 million state-of-the-art ScienceWorks Gallery opened at The Children's Museum, already the world's largest. A $10 million IMAX 3-D theater, one of only 12 in the world, opened at White River State Park. Total 1998 attendance at major downtown attractions, theaters, museums and sporting events surpassed 1995 numbers by 38 percent and reached more than 15.4 million visits. Now the city that couldn't generate a suburb is looking more like "Trendy Indy."

**Downside:** The closest ocean is 700 miles due east. In Indy, the locals don't care. But if you're from either coast, believe me, you'll notice.

## The Inside Scoop

**Population:** 818, 014
**Proximity:** More than 65 percent of the U.S. population lives within a 700-mile radius of Indianapolis.
**Number of hotel rooms:** 15,500
**State retail tax:** 5 percent
**Median price of a house:** $122,000
**Best hotel room:** Canterbury Hotel, (317) 634-3000
**Hottest table:** Palomino, (317) 974-0400
**Most visited museum:** Children's Museum, (317) 924-5431

Source: Fortune *magazine*

# Las Vegas: Neon Nirvana

C'mon Hootchie Mama, Daddy needs a new pair of shoes!

Who can deny the adrenaline rush of leaning over a craps table throwing the roll of your life? Gambling is a main reason why 32 million visitors come to Vegas annually, but the sunny days and bullish business climate make staying in the Southern Nevada desert a safe bet for young entrepreneurs. On a percentage basis, Las Vegas has ranked among the top 10 U.S. cities in job creation and population growth since 1990. The city remains a big attraction for gambling and nongambling upscale vacationers, and as the host of Comdex—the annual technology blowout—it's easily the nation's top convention destination. The city has 4.8 million square feet of meeting space and plans to expand its convention facilities nearly 30 percent by 2000. Not only that, but Vegas also intends to add another 20,000 hotels rooms to its unmatched total of 109,608.

While Vegas will always be the home of the $1.99 buffet, Sin City has grown up. Now high rollers can buy $8,230 alligator bags from Fendi and feast on broiled Gulf escolar at Emeril Lagasse's tony New Orleans Fish House. Then there is the $300 million worth of masterpieces by Monet, Kline and other artists at the Bellagio, Steve Wynn's new $1.6 billion, 3,005-room extravaganza. Or how about the Venetian, where guests can take gondola rides on an indoor canal and get hydrotherapy treatments at a branch of the world-renowned Canyon Ranch Spa?

This injection of snob appeal is part of Vegas' effort to wean itself from gambling. The city's casinos are reinventing themselves

to lure the nongambling upscale vacationers who have eschewed Vegas in the past. It's working: Only about 50 percent of the newer hotel-casinos' revenues come from gambling, a big change from the days when rooms and restaurants generated mere pocket change. Thrill seekers pumped almost $25 billion into the city's economy last year.

**Upside:** Compared to New York, Los Angeles or Toronto, Vegas isn't yet a truly big city, and most of its growth is new: At the start of the 1990s, the metropolitan population was nearly half what it is today. So there's still time to get in and launch a new business on the cheap. There's lots of labor, inexpensive or otherwise: The number of jobs rose 8 percent in the last two years. Not only is business growing in Las Vegas, but most of the new companies are small, so your company can grow with its customers.

**Downside:** Not a lot of culture that doesn't eventually involve the services of a cardiologist and a Greyhound Bus reservations clerk. Plus, the curse of any frontier town, namely, that a lot of people arrived only yesterday. It's strictly cash or credit here—no personal checks.

## The Inside Scoop

**Population:** 327,000
**Annual number of visitors:** 32 million
**Number of new residents (annual average):** 50,000
**Unemployment rate:** 4 percent
**Number of new businesses launched in 1998:** 17,000
**Taxes:** No corporate income, franchise, inventory or personal income taxes
**Percentage of new companies that are high-tech:** 50 percent
**Sunny days (annual average):** 300
**Number of parks:** 90
**Number of golf courses:** 25

*Source: Las Vegas Chamber of Commerce*

However, Vegas today is a mecca not just for tourists and conventioneers but for a growing number of software and biotechnology companies as well. Low costs and nonexistent state taxes have lured new companies to town. A recent $315 million expansion of the slot-machine-filled McCarran International Airport has increased Vegas' daily nonstops to cities like Phoenix (35), the Bay Area (37) and Los Angeles (57). Those L.A. flights take only an hour, which helps give Vegas an unmistakable "Left Coast" air about it.

# Los Angeles: Touched By The City Of Angels

L.A. is still the place where dreams come to live and where they come to die. Beneath its glossy veneer is a hardscrabble town where movie moguls cut deals behind each others' backs and where the difference between the "haves" and "have-nots" is about as distinct as in any city in the United States except New York.

In biblical terms, L.A. is more the City of Apocalypse than it is the City of Angels. Fires, earthquakes, riots and a permanent brown smog are the norm. But so are lush mornings, tropical afternoons and golden sunsets.

However, for entrepreneurs, L.A. is a veritable treasure trove of opportunity. Government officials have been bending over backward to welcome business to Southern California and erase the negative images fostered by the race riots of the mid-1990s and the scandal of the O. J. Simpson murder trial.

Since 1993, crime is down 40 percent, thanks to new "get tough" law enforcement measures, and murders have declined by 47 percent over the same period. Local government officials succeeded in balancing the budget after years of overspending, and today Los Angeles is one of the most financially stable big cities in the United States. Since 1995, 300,000 new jobs

PHOTO© TONY STONE IMAGES/KEN BIGGS

have opened in the city, and plans are well underway to upgrade the area's hot transportation spots: the harbor and L.A. International Airport.

A new civic initiative, called Business Improvement Districts, enables small businesses to get more services from the city, like street cleaning, for a small fee. Civic leaders have also gone public with a commitment to make sure every local business and home is connected to the Internet to take advantage of the online commerce boom.

Upside : Great weather, beautiful beaches and a sense that you're where the action is. The film industry rules L.A. culturally, drawing a never-ending supply of tourists who tramp through Beverly Hills and nearby Hollywood for a glimpse of Tom Hanks or Julia Roberts. This could be a plus or a minus, depending on your perspective, but if nothing else, setting up shop in Tinseltown provides plenty of cachet and conversation starters on dates.

Downside : There may be big improvements civically, but there's still a slight whiff of that old L.A. "business as usual" attitude, especially when it comes to entrepreneurs. Los Angeles was the last of the top 10 cities in the country to give the green light to homebased businesses.

## The Inside Scoop

**Population:** 3.6 million
**Average high temperature in July:** 76 degrees
**Average low in January:** 45 degrees
**Average annual days of rainfall:** 35
**Median price of three-bedroom home:** $194,000
**Unemployment rate:** 7.6 percent
**Number of library books per capita:** one for every 72 people
**Number of four- and five-star restaurants:** 50
**Average commute time for city residents:** 26.4 minutes
*Source:* Money *magazine*

# New York City: Big, Bold And Beautiful

It's still a helluva town, but my, how times have changed.

New York City has undergone a facelift that would make Joan Rivers blush. Beaten down in recent years by high crime, high taxes and surly cab drivers, Gotham has roared back under the astute leadership of Mayor Rudy Giuliani. The mayor has streamlined city spending, eased the tax burden on companies who do business in the city and offered an olive branch to visitors and residents in the form of a highly publicized civility campaign, which now has criminals saying "thank you" after snatching your pocketbook.

PHOTO © VCG/FPG INTERNATIONAL, LLC

In truth, Giuliani has put more police officers on the streets and successfully changed the way cops go about their work—introducing an initiative known as CompStat that incorporates up-to-the-minute data with intensive crime analysis to pinpoint patterns in each city precinct.

A better quality of life is, of course, very good for business. After years of watching Fortune 500 companies abandon the city for the 'burbs, New York has secured commitments from 34 major companies—including Paine Webber, Conde Nast and Merrill Lynch—to stay at least 15 years. Taking a cue from the big boys, many smaller companies are deciding to hang around, and new businesses like Belly Basics and Cosi Sandwich Shops are popping up 'twixt the skyscrapers every day.

PHOTO © PHOTODISC

New York is genuinely keen on seeing new businesses open up in town. The city's Economic Development Corp. persuades start-ups to relocate to the Bronx and helps them take advantage of tax incentives and other savings. By retaining and recruiting companies, New York has finally reversed a decade of job loss in the city. Since 1993 the private sector has created 173,600 jobs. Riding Wall Street's long winning streak, the securities industry alone generated 16,200 new jobs during the same period.

New York is also back as a mecca for visitors, young and old. Tourism reached an all-time high recently with 31 million visitors in 1998, a 21 percent increase over 1990. And a 30 percent reduction in the hotel tax has helped lift hotel occupancy to more than 80 percent.

In part, tourists are responding to the cleanup—and commercialization—of certain old haunts, most notably Times Square: Here, entertainment has traditionally been preceded by the word "adult," but it has become as family-friendly as Disneyland. (Some argue that it has become Disneyland, with a Disney store and the-

Upside: The biggest, baddest, most bodacious city on earth.

Downside: The biggest, baddest, most bodacious city on earth.

## The Inside Scoop

**Population:** 7.3 million
**Number of companies:** 103,000
**Number of employees:** 1,450,000
**Annual number of visitors:** 32 million
**Annual number of conventions:** 190
**Number of hotels:** 230
**Number of hotel rooms:** 60,000
**Average cost of dinner for two in Manhattan:** $60
**Number of Broadway theaters:** 35
**Annual number of visitors to Metropolitan Museum of Art:** 4.5 million
**Number of bookstores:** 500
**Number of Fortune 500 firms with headquarters in New York:** 50

*Source: New York Chamber of Commerce*

ater on 42nd Street.) Not to
mention the crop of shop-till-
you-drop megastores, such as
NikeTown, Virgin Megastore
and the Warner Bros. Studio
Store, which have opened
cavernous spaces in the past
five years. From Chelsea to
Murray Hill, Gaps and Barnes
and Nobles are as ubiquitous
as delis.

## Top 5 U.S. Northeastern Cities

1. Middlesex/Somerset/Hunterdon, NJ
2. Monmouth/Ocean, NJ
3. New York, NY
4. Pittsburgh, PA
5. Boston, MA/NH

*Source: Dun & Bradstreet and* Entrepreneur *magazine*

A "can do" mentality has found its way down Old Broadway.
Now if they can only do something about those cabdrivers. . . .

# Phoenix: Desert Bliss

Freeze frame, 1969: The city of Phoenix was barely a blip in the
Arizona sagebrush. The city's population was a third of what it is
today, and there were almost no big corporations. The economy
was driven largely by tourism, drawing snowbirds from the East
and Midwest who came in search of abundant winter sunshine and
golf.

Fast forward to 1999: The city's population is 1.3 million.
Fueled by this surge in growth, the economy is booming, with high-
tech as the largest economic growth sector. New residents are arriv-
ing daily, and yet job creation has kept pace. Employment has
grown by 174 percent over the past 20 years, compared with 50
percent nationally. Indeed, for the past four years, Phoenix has been
the fastest-growing large labor market in the nation.

Even Phoenix's suburbs have shared in the wealth. Chandler, a
town just southeast of Phoenix, has become a mecca for technology, particularly semiconductor production. In 1996, Intel opened
the world's largest chipmaking plant here, and Motorola and SGS
Thomson have facilities as well.

City leaders say that Phoenix is handling its growth admirably,
especially relative to other high-growth cities. Data gathered by
accounting firm Arthur Andersen shows Austin workers spend
about 46 minutes commuting to work, compared with 49 for
Phoenix workers. But in Austin, the commute time is increasing

about 11 percent per decade. In Phoenix, the commute is growing more slowly, by about 3 percent per decade.

Phoenix has become a beacon to young entrepreneurs. In a recent issue of *Fortune* magazine, Phoenix scored best in the U.S. for new business growth, scoring 93 out of a possible 100 points. One possible explanation is that Phoenix does not have a single dominant corporation, leaving ground for smaller start-ups. Phoenix also has a young entrepreneurial work force that is more mentally in tune with the idea of taking a business solo. Call it the wild, wild West's pioneer spirit, but there's definitely something about Phoenix.

**Upside:** Unspoiled, breathtaking beauty as far as the eye can see. The Sonoran Desert is nearby, and the Grand Canyon is an easy day's ride. Great civic transportation, with an airline known as the "hub of the Southwest." Climate is wonderful, with average daily temperatures at about 72 degrees and more than 320 sunny days per year. Its decent convention center—renovated to the tune of $32 million in 1995—boasts 300,000 square feet of exhibition space.

**Downside:** Except for the fact that it's hotter than hell in the summer, none that I can think of. Not the place to go if you hate golf and spectacular sunsets, I guess.

## The Inside Scoop

**Population:** 1.3 million
**Annual growth rate:** 2.65 percent
**Average high temperature in July:** 107 degrees
**Average low temperature in January:** 44 degrees
**Average annual rainfall:** 7 inches
**Airport traffic:** 12 million annual visitors fly in and out of Phoenix Sky Harbor International Airport
**Number of hotel rooms:** 41,000
*Source: Phoenix Chamber of Commerce*

# Portland: Singin' In The Rain

*Question:* What has Portland got that your city does not?

*Answer:* How about a growing and diversified economy, a well-educated and stable work force, excellent transportation services, low utility rates, a wide availability of low-cost land already zoned for business and a strategic location on the Pacific Rim?

Portland is one of those "cool" cities that seems to maintain its hipness year in and year out. Pittsburgh and Buffalo may rise and fall in favor, but every year Portland has a place on those ubiquitous "best cities" lists. It's not hard to see why. Metropolitan Portland is the economic center of Oregon and southwest Washington, and it's home to some 49,000 businesses. The metropolitan area has a stable economy that is linked directly to its diverse industrial base. Unemployment in 1997 was 4 percent, down from 4.5 percent in 1996.

People are getting wealthy in Portland. Since 1990, there has been a 120 percent increase in the number of households making more than $500,000. The city also has seen a 240 percent increase in the number of homes worth more than $500,000 and a 26 percent increase in professional jobs.

For the allegedly laid-back Pacific Northwest, the city works hard to lure new businesses. Portland continues to improve on infrastructure, working on a light-rail transit system to lessen congestion throughout the metropolitan area. Additionally, greater emphasis is being placed on school-to-work and welfare-to-work programs. And, spurred by the not-for-profit Oregon Entrepreneurs' Forum (OEF), Portland is taking care to nur-

PHOTO© TONY STONE IMAGES/CHUCK PEFLEY

## Top 5 U.S. Western Cities

1. Portland/Vancouver, OR/WA
2. Seattle/Bellevue/Everett, WA
3. San Jose, CA
4. Riverside/San Bernardino, CA
5. San Diego, CA

*Source: Dun & Bradstreet and* Entrepreneur *magazine*

ture its fast-growing companies through business mentoring and the Oregon Emerging Business Initiative, sponsored by the OEF.

Nicely diversified, the greater Portland economy is nevertheless rich in high-tech businesses, not surprising when you consider nearby microchip monolith Intel Corp. In fact, the high-tech sector provides the roots the city has long needed. Twenty years ago, this industry hardly even existed here, and today, it is the largest employer in the state. Local technology manufacturers like Intel court a multitude of satellite suppliers, while a recent wellspring of investment capital has given birth to many cutting-edge companies, particularly in the software and multimedia segments.

**Upside:** Cost of living is great for a city this nice. Compared to cities like San Francisco, Washington, DC, and nearby Seattle, Portland is a much cheaper place to live. And what are you really giving up by living there?

**Downside:** While close proximity to the Pacific Rim has been good to Portland over the long haul, with a bevy of new Japanese, Korean and Indian businesses opening their doors in recent years, the Asian Tiger hasn't been as kind in the late 1990s. The continuing downward economic spiral of Pacific Rim nations has hurt Portland in recent years.

## The Inside Scoop

**Population:** 491,000

**Climate:** Mild, with an average high of 66 degrees in the summer and an average low of 38 degrees in the winter.

**Average annual rainfall:** 37 inches

**Outdoor recreation:** Camping, fishing, hiking, river rafting, biking, skiing, wind surfing and kite flying; Portland has 9,400 acres of parks.

**Major private-sector employers:** Oregon Health Sciences, Intel Corp., Kaiser Permanente, U.S. Bank of Oregon, Legacy Health System, Tektronix Inc., Freightliner Corp., Safeway Inc., Wells Fargo

*Source: Portland Chamber of Commerce*

# Raleigh-Durham: Turning Over
# A New Leaf Along Tobacco Road

Apparently, in North Carolina good things come in threes. The cities of Raleigh, Durham and Chapel Hill are all within a 20-mile radius. A trio of universities—Duke, the University of North Carolina at Chapel Hill and North Carolina State University—mark the three corners of the area's famed Research Triangle Park. Founded in 1959, Research Triangle Park is the fourth-oldest research park in the United States, covers about 6,800 acres

## Top 5 U.S. Southeastern Cities

1. Raleigh/Durham/Chapel Hill, NC
2. Jacksonville, FL
3. Orlando, FL
4. Atlanta, GA
5. Charlotte/Gastonia/Rock Hill, NC/SC

Source: Dun & Bradstreet and Entrepreneur magazine

and is located centrally between the three cities. The Triangle is home to 130 companies employing 37,000 individuals.

Inside the Triangle, dozens of companies concentrate on three major industries—tech, biotech and telecommunications—and constantly swap brainpower with the local universities, making these schools a lot more than your typical self-contained ivory towers. Today, the Triangle is an international magnet, drawing not just IBM and Cisco but multinational giants like Japan's Sumitomo.

For entrepreneurs, clinical research, telecommunications, biomedicine and software are perennial growth industries that make this one of the country's most active business communities. Venture capital investment has picked up, though there's still room for improvement; local officials, deciding to take the mountain to Mohammed, are venturing into Boston and Silicon Valley to woo investors. The state government has also gotten into the act by increasing pension investments in venture capital from $30 million to $100 million.

However, space in the Triangle is tight, and the communities are having a hard time keeping up with growth. A number of employment initiatives, including the Durham Work Force Partnership and Marriott Pathways to Independence, may provide needed relief for the employee shortage in nonskilled jobs. And bonds have been approved to finance new schools and road improvements. But change will not happen overnight. Consequently, some economic developers are encouraging new businesses to locate in nearby communities—rather than directly in the Triangle—to alleviate congestion.

As new companies arrive, so do people: Raleigh-Durham's population rose by a whopping 18.4 percent between 1990 and 1999. The influx of new talent has also given salaries a big boost—average income in the area shot up by almost 30 percent during the

**Upside:** Great college town, with three universities within a 15-mile radius. Climate is fine, with shorter summers and winters, and longer springs and autumns. No lack of resources for young entrepreneurs, with all three colleges offering courses on entrepreneurship. Housing costs are low compared to northern neighbors Richmond and Washington, DC.

**Downside:** Not much. The area is conservative, politically and religiously. The first question you may be asked by a native is which house of worship you belong to, which many consider a positive. Business-wise, the Triangle may outgrow itself in the next few years, so if you're not ready to move soon, it may be too late.

## The Inside Scoop

**Population:** 500,000
**Average annual snowfall:** 7.5 inches
**Average annual rainfall:** 49 inches
**Best hotel room:** Sienna Hotel, (919) 929-4000
**Hottest table:** 518 West, (919) 829-2518
**Best place for a business drink:** 42nd Street Oyster Bar, (919) 831-2811
**Most visited museum:** North Carolina Museum of Life and Science, (919) 220-5429

*Source:* Fortune *magazine*

same period. The influx of talented young workers makes Raleigh-Durham a mecca for young entrepreneurs.

It's also difficult to find a better city for raising kids. An innovative countywide school program gives every Raleigh family the option of sending their children to school on a year-round basis. And in 1999, two new museums—one devoted to international culture, the other to natural science—opened their doors. That should give even the unfortunate kids who spend their summers stuck in a classroom something to smile about.

Also in 1999, the Research Triangle opened a new arena for the North Carolina State University basketball team and the transplanted Hartford Whalers (now the Carolina Hurricanes) NHL team. A performing arts center opened to great fanfare, and the World Special Olympics and the United States Golf Association Open tournament will arrive in nearby Pinehurst.

# Salt Lake City: The Rise Of The Stormin' Mormons

To visitors from either coast, Salt Lake City is a strange place. Order a martini after work, and the bartender will explain that you'll have to buy a "private club membership" first (and that's just to buy a drink—complimentary lap dances are not part of the deal).

Salt Lake was founded on July 24, 1847, by a group of Mormon pioneers—148 to be exact—led by Brigham Young. The famous California Gold Rush of 1849-50 brought many settlers to the area who chose not to continue to the West Coast. Nineteen years later, the driving of the Golden Spike at Promontory Point joined the Union Pacific railroad from the West and the Central Pacific railroad from the East, bringing more settlers bound for Salt Lake City.

Between 1900 and 1930, the population of the city nearly tripled. City parks were built and sewer and street lighting systems were installed. The Great Depression halted the area's growth, but the boom started again after World War II. Many military installations revitalized the economy. Also, war workers and soldiers spent their money in the city's restaurants, ballrooms, shops and theaters. As in the rest of the country during the 1960s, there was mass exodus from downtown to the suburbs. The ZCMI Center shopping mall was constructed to counteract the movement, but it wasn't until the 1970s that the downtown area fully expanded. Classic older buildings were renovated, new businesses and shopping malls were constructed, and city planners implemented many beautification projects.

The 1980s brought more growth to the city with developments like the expansion of the Salt Palace, the Salt Lake International Center and the Triad Center and Research Park at the University of Utah. The 1990s have added steps toward expanding the airport, building a downtown sports complex and improving citywide transportation. The city's skyline has been modified with the completion of a $70 million expansion of the Salt Palace Convention Center, which includes a 36,000-square-foot ballroom and a 1,000-foot-tall glass-and-steel tower. The John W. Gallivan Utah Center is a blockwide plaza where the work of 15 Utah artists is permanently displayed.

The city's high-tech business community is pretty progressive as well. Salt Lake's University of Utah Research Park has spawned dozens of homegrown companies, such as Evans & Sutherland, a $159 million computer graphics company that did the special effects for "Star Trek: The Next Generation." It's also home to biotech outfits like TheraTech, whose transdermal testosterone patches (sort of like the Viagra of the male hair-growth industry) made the cover of *Newsweek*.

Software companies used to dominate the city's tech scene, but now hardware manufacturers are gaining a foothold as well. In

PHOTO © TONY STONE IMAGES/CHUCHK PEFLEY

1998, Gateway opened a new PC factory that will employ 1,300 people by the end of 1999. And Intel is seriously considering Salt Lake as the site for a new 7,000-employee research facility. The city is home to a progressive high-tech business community; the

**Upside:** The Olympics are coming to Salt Lake, giving the city a boost in civic pride. Unfortunately, allegations that Olympic officials were bribed to lure the games to Utah has placed a damper on things. However, Utah has the highest literacy rate of any state. Transportation is smooth as well. There's easy access in and out of Salt Lake City: Locals say that a tie-up on the interstate is when traffic slows to 25, and the airport can sometimes feel abandoned, it's so easy to get in and out of.

Gen E's may like the fact that, overall, Utah is expected to continue to have the youngest population in the nation. Utah's median age in 1995 was 27.1 years; in the year 2010 it is projected to be 30.5 years, compared to the national average of 38.4 years. And Utah will continue to provide lots of local customers. Utah has the largest average family size of any state in the nation at 3.13. Salt Lake City's average household size is 2.33, while Utah's average household size is 3.06. Utah's statistics vary dramatically from the national scene, where the average persons per household has declined in every state since 1980.

**Downside:** If you're a night owl, Salt Lake City is no hoot. If you do go out, you'll be the only one in the office bleary-eyed the next morning.

## The Inside Scoop

**Population:** 190,000
**Median household income:** $35,138
**State income tax:** 7 percent
**Corporate franchise tax rate:** 5 percent of net taxable income
**Average annual temperature:** 51.8 degrees

*Source: Salt Lake City Chamber of Commerce*

University of Utah Research Park has generated scores of computer and biotech companies; and Salt Lake City is the site of the 2002 Winter Olympics, an event that will significantly boost its economy.

In fact, the city is almost perfect except for the disturbing lack of nightlife. The sidewalks roll up exactly at 5 p.m., and even if you venture out to one of the city's bars or microbreweries, chances are you'll have the place to yourself. During the day, residents are griping about the traffic jams caused by a $1.5 billion highway expansion and the construction of a $313 million light-rail system.

Salt Lake City is a media maven, having been described as "vibrant, vigorous and visionary." Take, for instance, 1998, a typical banner year. Salt Lake made *Entrepreneur* magazine's list of the top 30 cities to launch a business in; *Fortune* magazine listed Salt Lake on its top 10 list of the best cities in America for business; *Western Blue Chip Economic Forecast* and *American Demographics* magazines refer to Utah as "one of the top three economies in the nation"; *Adweek* magazine identified the city as "poised to become a city of the future"; and Prentice Hall's *Places Rated Almanac* placed Salt Lake in the top 10 most livable metro areas in North America. With these accolades and others, Salt Lake's future continues to look bright.

## Find Yourself A City To Live In

**T**o conduct an analysis of your local community—or of the place where you are considering relocating—to see if your product or service has a good chance of thriving, you will need to consider many factors. The most important questions to answer are the following:

● Is the population base large enough to support your business?

● Does the community have a stable economic base that will promote a healthy environment for your business?

● Are demographic characteristics compatible with the market you wish to serve?

● What are the attitudes of outlooks of people within the community?

Your local chamber of commerce can help you with the population and economic numbers, and even the demographic layout of your community. The personal stuff—how residents feel about certain businesses or whether they'll buy your product—is something that you're going to have to get by going out and mixing it up with your neighbors.

# San Jose: Suddenly Silicon

San Jose is the tale of two cities—one part is strictly beer and burgers, the other dry martinis. The Drew Carey side runs along El Camino Real, the 60-mile main artery of Silicon Valley, which is lined with vintage strip malls, cheesy motels and cheap taco joints as far as the eye can see. Surrounding Carey-ville is the James Bond part of town—the bucolic campuslike corporate offices of the big-deal technology companies that have become the symbol of entrepreneurial wealth in the '90s. It's a mix of town and gown that proves uniquely alluring to entrepreneurs with an edge.

Young businessfolk approve not only of San Jose's cosmopolitan structure—or lack of one—but also the city's resiliency. San Jose is the prototype, the real deal, that every high-tech campus across the country seeks to emulate. Silicon Valley has more than held its own against a wave of Silicon Deserts, Silicon Beaches, Silicon Alleys and the other wannabes that threaten to usurp its position as ground zero for techno-innovations. It is constantly reconfiguring itself—from its early boom in defense and semiconductors, to PCs, biotech, and now the Internet and software. More than 3,500 new businesses were registered here in 1997 alone; since 1992, the area has added more than 200,000 jobs.

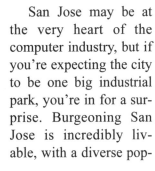

San Jose may be at the very heart of the computer industry, but if you're expecting the city to be one big industrial park, you're in for a surprise. Burgeoning San Jose is incredibly livable, with a diverse pop-

PHOTOS COURTESY: SAN JOSE OFFICE OF ECONOMIC DEVELOPMENT

ulation, a start-up-happy business climate and plenty of warm, clear days. San Jose's role as the technology capital of the United States gives it a leg up on most cities when it comes to telecommuting because companies there don't suffer from technophobia.

When San Jose workers put down their notebook PCs, there are plenty of places to relax, including (go figure) the Tech Museum of Innovation, the symphony and the repertory theater. And despite San Jose's nerdy legacy, it's taken to pro sports like a fish to water. Don't miss the hockey-playing Sharks—there's nothing like an arena full of techno-types cheering to the theme music from Jaws.

**Upside:** Close to San Francisco. Plus, San Jose is a techie's dream. You couldn't swing a dead PC without hitting a computer science major.

**Downside:** Can't get out of San Francisco's cultural shadow and probably never will.

## The Inside Scoop
**Population:** 874,000
**Counties within metro area:** Palo Alto and Sunnyvale
**Median price of a three-bedroom house:** $225,000
**Projected job growth to 2001:** 8 percent
**Annual sunny days:** 257
*Source: San Jose Chamber of Commerce*

# Seattle: Tossed Salad And Scrambled Eggs

There's a legend about Microsoft that reveals the work culture in many Seattle companies. It goes like this: Bill Gates is walking behind a Microsoft employee who complains, "These 12-hour days are just killing me." Gates quips, "So you're working half days again, eh?"

In a city where 18-hour workdays are common, entrepreneurship plays an enormous role. And thanks to the hundreds of businesses that have sprung up around Gates's little software venture, Seattle is a start-up lover's dream. Workers are highly educated and culturally sophisticated, and there is a Starbucks on every corner. What's more, the overall cost of living in Seattle is a lot lower than its high-tech neighbors to the south, and Washington state has no income tax.

Yep, Frasier Crane's new hometown may not be a place where everybody knows your name, but they'll likely know the value of your company's stock option plan. There's an aura of success in Seattle, but woe to the newbie millionaire who takes himself or herself too seriously—it's not chic to flaunt your stock options here. It's a city where every day is casual Friday, and where denizens are surrounded with breathtaking nature just walking to work. Back around 1990 the downtown area was almost completely abandoned. Now it's been completely revitalized, with a new concert hall and a new Seattle Art Museum. This has helped lure NikeTown, Planet Hollywood and FAO Schwarz as well.

A newer twist in Seattle's business community is the uptick in locally based venture capital firms. Until now most of the start-up capital for the city's fledgling biotech companies and "Baby Bills"—as the spin-offs founded by Microsoft alums are known—has come from Silicon Valley and beyond. Now a cluster of local firms is stepping in and putting Seattle's entrepreneurial energy to work.

One thing that's stayed the same is the city's legendary quality of life. The opportunity to be 45 minutes away from skiing and 20 minutes away from great hiking and to marry that lifestyle with a great entrepreneurial environment is unparalleled. Yet Seattle is hardly Manhattan-in-the-woods. For one thing, the nightlife is surprisingly sedate. And the "Don't Californicate Washington" bumper stickers still spotted around town point to a more significant problem—the city's ever-thickening traffic jams. Determined not to let its popularity get the best of it, Seattle recently committed to building a $3.9 billion rail and bus system.

**Upside:** Great coffee, great seafood, great microbrews, great scenery, great atmosphere for start-ups...Great Caesar's Ghost! Why don't I live there?

**Downside:** Great buckets of rain pouring down on your head with alarming regularity.

## The Inside Scoop

**Population:** 540,000
**Median price of a three-bedroom house:** $173,344
**Projected job growth to 2001:** 10 percent
**Annual sunny days:** 136
**Best hotel room:** Four Seasons Olympic, (206) 621-1700
**Hottest table:** Axis, (206) 441-9600
**Best place for a business drink:** Oliver's, Mayflower Park Hotel, (206) 623-8700
**Most visited museum:** Seattle Art Museum, (206) 654-3100

Source: Fortune magazine

# Toronto: Millionaires, Molsens And Maple Leafs

Ready for some good times, eh? Then move to Toronto to launch your fledgling business. Besides being one of the friendliest, most cosmopolitan cities you'll ever find, Toronto today is one of the most diverse cities in the world. The area has dozens of well-preserved neighborhoods, many of them old streetcar suburbs similar to Atlanta's Virginia-Highland or New York City's Brooklyn Heights, and they are revitalizing the shore along Lake Ontario.

For years Toronto's been the darling of environmentalists and enlightened social engineers, who saw this neighbor to the north as a kinder, gentler alternative to U.S. urban decay. But an economic downturn in the early 1990s forced Toronto to reevaluate itself as a business capital. As it emerges from recession, Toronto is not only remarkably clean and well-organized but also more responsive to business.

Despite economic sluggishness in the past decade, Toronto has cemented its position as Canada's premier city. Its stock exchange has benefited greatly; last year it had a market capitalization of $950 billion, making it the ninth largest in the world. Companies moving to Toronto are fueling a real estate renaissance—the commercial vacancy rate fell from 15 percent in the third quarter of 1996 to 10.4 percent in 1998.

The city continues to invest in amenities, too. The 1989 creation of Rouge Park, North America's largest urban park, has added even more recreation facilities to this already green-filled city. Culturally, Toronto is coming into its own; touring artists' bookings were up from 488 in 1992 to more than 1,500 in 1998. There's a new highway to ease traffic congestion and a four-mile subway extension.

And there's more change in the air. On January 1, 1998, Toronto woke up to a new form of municipal government. Called Mega-City, the new structure consolidated Metro Toronto and the outlying suburbs under one authority. The business community is generally in favor of the new structure because it promises to streamline services, save money and reduce taxes, which can be as much as 15 percent higher than in the United States.

Toronto also has one of the highest levels of transit ridership in

North America; the SkyDome stadium opened in 1989 with only 400 parking spaces. Transit broke even in Toronto until the 1970s, when it began serving the suburbs. Even now, only 20 percent of the Toronto Transit Commission's operating budget is subsidized, one of the lowest rates in the world.

**Upside:** Plenty of affordable office space and some of the friendliest people you'll ever meet in your life.

**Downside:** It gets cold up in Toronto in January, but no colder than Detroit or Boston. The currency rate issue is still tough for U.S. business owners, but the gap seems to be tightening a bit in recent years.

## The Inside Scoop

**Population:** 4.3 million
**Best hotel room:** Four Seasons, (416) 964-0411
**Hottest table:** Adega, (416) 977-4338
**Best place for a business drink:** Al Frisco's, (416) 595-8201
**Most visited museum:** Royal Ontario Museum, (416) 586-5549

*Source:* Fortune *magazine*

# Vancouver: Big Bucks In The Land O' Canucks

Nestled comfortably between snow-capped mountains and the Pacific Ocean, Canada's third-largest city is one of the world's most spectacularly situated metropolises. Year after year, boasts the local civic organizations, the breathtakingly beautiful British Columbian port is among the top three cities worldwide in travel destinations.

In December 1997, the Corporate Resources Group, a global business relocation consultant in Geneva, Switzerland, rated Vancouver as the most livable major city in North America and the world. Auckland, New Zealand, was ranked second, Toronto third and Montreal 15th.

Vancouver is the largest city in the province of British Columbia, situated in the southwestern corner of Canada. It is located approximately 25 miles north of the Washington State border and is surrounded on three sides by water.

I hate to sound like a travel agent, especially when I don't get any commissions, but there really is something for everybody in Vancouver, especially for nature lovers and recreationists. It's an ideal base for sailors, rock climbers, skiers and other sports enthusiasts, all of whom can get active within an hour's drive of the city core.

Even the city's downtown looks more rural than some of the tony suburbs of Denver or Minneapolis. Stanley Park, on the edge of the downtown, is one of the world's great urban parks. And on English Bay in the nearby West End, sandy beaches are literally minutes away from downtown's chrome-and-glass office towers.

As Canada's major Pacific Rim port, Vancouver is one of Canada's most ethnically diverse cities—with substantial populations of Chinese, South Asians, Indians and Europeans. It's also ideally situated—roughly midpoint on the West Coast of North America, and equidistant by air from London and Tokyo.

Vancouver is known to be wet, but it's also particularly "cool." "The X-Files" TV series was shot here (among several other shows) before moving to L.A. in 1998. You'd hardly know it, but Vancouver is now North America's third-largest film production

PHOTO © TONY STONE IMAGES/BARRY ROWLAND

center, after L.A. and New York. And there's a much-used nude beach within walking distance of the University of British Columbia campus.

Upside: Absolutely magical panoramic view of the British Columbia Rockies from just about anywhere in town. Smart work force, but they won't work late.

Downside: The cost of retail space can be high. To break even in a high-traffic mall, you'll have to generate $1 million in sales each year. If you are planning to import from another country, customs and carriage costs will need to be factored into your pricing. In addition, make sure you get information on building codes and restrictions. In the United States, it's permissible to have your retail business and residence in one location, but Canadian regulations prohibit this.

The cost of labor is also a consideration. In many countries, it's not unusual for people to stay late without expecting to be paid for overtime; in Vancouver (heck, in all of Canada), anything more than eight hours a day requires paid overtime.

## The Inside Scoop

**Population:** 543,871
**Apartment vacancy rate:** 1.4 percent
**Office space:** 40 million square feet
**Office space vacancy rates:** Downtown, 8.3 percent; suburban, 5.6 percent
**Unemployment rate:** 8.1 percent
**Job growth:** 2.53 percent
**Average hotel occupancy:** Downtown, 77 percent

Source: Vancouver Chamber of Commerce

## World's Best Business Cities

1. Singapore
2. San Francisco Bay Area
3. London
4. New York
5. Frankfurt
6. Hong Kong
7. Atlanta
8. Toronto
9. Paris
10. Tokyo

*Source: Arthur Andersen*

## Most Desirable International Headquarters

1. Singapore
2. London
3. New York
4. Washington, DC
5. Toronto
6. Frankfurt
7. Brussels
8. Hong Kong
9. Dallas
10. Chicago

*Source: PHH Fauntus*

PHOTOS© PHOTODISC

# Chapter

# 13

What industries make Gen E's hearts skip a beat? Well, it ain't plastics.

# Hot Stuff: The Coolest Industries And The Boldest Markets

Before I pulled the plug on the corporate life and went out on my own as a writer, I had a boss who loved to frame his views on business around what got him out of bed in the morning. "I don't know about you," he'd say, "but I'm excited about working smarter and not harder! That's what's getting me out of the bed this week!"

Then he'd whisk the question around the conference table, asking his staffers what got them out of bed in the morning. The sycophants would play along and say, without a shred of dignity, that working hours of overtime for no pay for truly insidious clients was what got them out of bed in the morning. Other, more secure comrades would say that an alarm clock or the warm smell of coffee percolating would get them up and running. One brave soul who didn't last long at the company but earned my undying respect for all eternity answered by saying the job stressed her out so much she never went to sleep at all. Me? I usually stayed silent and daydreamed about where my friends and I would go for drinks after work.

Then I figured out my answer to the question: working for myself—as a writer. My old boss was actually an entrepreneur at heart, and if his staffers never quite figured out his enthusiasm, he was at least ready to jump from under the covers every sunrise and do battle with the forces of commerce in his own way.

What industries make Gen E's hearts skip a beat? Get their adrenaline flowing? Get them out of the bed every morning? Well, it ain't the old stalwarts like insurance companies and widget factories. It ain't plastics. No, today's younger business owners are going where their hearts lead them, and they are often using their old friend technology to get them there. Let's take a look at some of the industries that Gen E is gaga over and see if one of them doesn't wake you up early tomorrow morning, eager to get out of bed and start a business.

# Rubies In Paradise: Jewelry And Fashion Accessories

**Here's The Deal:** Have a knack for creating unusual designs? Then maybe you can carve yourself a niche in the jewelry and fashion accessories industry. Many would-be Cartier's are breaking into the industry by designing and marketing their jewelry at local crafts fairs, farmers' markets, house parties and boutiques.

It's a creative industry that stresses uniqueness and style, not cookie-cutter sameness. Whether you're designing jewelry yourself or selling handcrafted fashions out of your own store (or both), the industry is wide open and always looking for new ideas.

Some basic elements of the jewelry business haven't changed in 50 years. The reasons people buy jewelry remain essentially the same. Platinum is in again and gold is God, but hand-crafted homemade jewelry has developed its own unique cachet with the public. And the bridal business is still a big part of any store's revenues.

In other ways, though, things have radically changed, thanks to the pervasiveness of computers, the dominance of shopping malls, the influx of women in the workplace and the erosion of consumer confidence in virtually every profession.

One serious pressure on independent retail jewelers is that consumers can now use the Internet to research prices, and they're increasingly able to access wholesale deals on gems and jewelry. Not only that, but independent jewelers must often compete against retailers with significantly lower overhead, such as high-volume chain stores, TV shopping networks and, increasingly, Web-based jewelers.

Unless you become one of those Web-based businesses yourself. They are especially practical for techno-savvy twentysomethings and thirtysomethings. Transaction-based jewelry Web sites can be set up for as little as $2,500. Customers appreciate logging on without the annoyance of a salesperson asking, "Can I help you?" Potential customers can print or download pictures, descriptions and prices of, say, a gold tennis bracelet or a 14-karat black cultured pearl necklace, and then run down to a regular jewelry store to comparison shop.

With little overhead, Web retailers can price diamonds and tennis bracelets, and so on, as much as 25 percent to 50 percent less than even very competitive conventional stores. While it's hard to pin down numbers, some virtual stores have grown at a rate of 130 percent a year. And more growth is expected.

Of course, if you want to start off in a shop downtown or if you can swing a mall deal, be my guest, but bear the following facts in mind.

**First Things First:** Find a market that's not heavily saturated with competition. Then pick everyone's brain in the industry and find mentors in other fields who can serve as role models.

**Price Tag:** Start-up costs are relatively minimal; the average upstart jeweler only needs $3,000 in materials to start a jewelry business. But if you prefer a range: $1,500 to $6,000.

**The Price Is Right:** Charge up to $20 for smaller pieces, like low-grade earrings and broaches, and much more for pieces that require more exquisite materials, like gold or platinum. Your costs depend on typical business expenses: manufacturing and equipment costs, rental space or leases, and time-to-market cycles.

**Tools Of The Trade:** Jewelry-making equipment depends on the jewelry you're crafting. But you can count on using clasps, fasteners, string, pins, earring bases and a few small metal-working tools.

**Basic Training:** Believe it or not, there are jewelry classes o'plenty, especially if you live close to a big city. Check out continuing education classes or trade school course catalogs in cities near you. Better yet, apprentice with a jewelry craftsperson if you can. A flair for the dramatic and a willingness to study and experiment with different designs are mandatory. Even if you plan to open a retail shop and avoid the design end of the business, you're going to find that a handiness with jewelry tools will pay off with jewelry maintenance and repair revenue. Need more help? Contact the National Craft Association at (800) 715-9594 or visit their Web site at www.craftassoc.com.

**The Bottom Line:** You'll make $500 and up weekly for the first two years, depending on economic demand and where you sell your jewelry.

**Hot Tip:** Have a catalog sheet and price list on hand at all times. These documents should include ordering information and pricing terms that you can give to customers.

# A Hunting We Will Go:
# Personal Concierge Service

**Here's The Deal:** "Pardon me, but do you have any Grey Poupon? I need it for my client. She's giving a dinner part Saturday night."

Outrageous? Not for a personal concierge. For years, savvy business travelers often turned to a hotel concierge for help in a jam. Whether garnering hard-to-find theater tickets or replacing a lost pair of contact lenses on short notice, a concierge takes pride in saving the day.

Now a growing number of industrious young entrepreneurs are taking the hotel concierge concept to the masses, opening personalized service shops that cater to busy career men and women who don't have the time to whip up a meatloaf or walk the family dog. Errand services are an easy, if always hectic, business to start for first-time entrepreneurs. If you're calm under pressure and can deal with demanding people who may bang their rattles against their high chairs when they don't get what they want, a personal concierge service could be for you.

No one is quite sure how many concierge services operate in the United States, but there certainly seems to be a need. A 1998 study by the Families and Work Institute revealed that American workers are more pressed for time than ever before, with the average worker spending 44 hours per week on the job. In some 78 percent of married couples, both spouses work, leaving no other shoulders to bear the myriad responsibilities of everyday life. For service-minded entrepreneurs, the time crunch may offer some interesting opportunities.

The great thing about the personal concierge business is the thrill of the hunt. There's a bit of an adrenaline kick finding the lowest airfare for a client's vacation. To be a top-tier concierge, you've got to know how to make things happen. Finding a table where others have failed rates highly in the concierge skills set, as does picking up dry cleaning on a moment's notice or handling trips to the Department of Motor Vehicles. Personal concierges have to be prepared for anything: One concierge had to overnight a client's toupee (and glue) from New York to Denver, where the client was about to address a big meeting. Other personal concierges find themselves doing holiday shopping for office-shackled clients, who usually demand hard-to-find items like tee times at Pebble Beach Golf Course or Ballerina Barbie dolls.

### First Things First: Clear up a lot of time to handle the job right. Personal service professionals say that there aren't enough hours in a day to accommodate their clients' needs. No part-timers need apply to this business. Ironically, some time-starved personal concierges wish they could pay someone to handle their errands for them. Tip: Offer new customers discounted rates for gift packages to their friends, co-workers and family. Then follow up.

### Price Tag: Very small. You'll need a good computer and software to keep track of client's records—and two phones: a regular phone and a cellular one that you carry with you at all times. If you already have these items, you can open up shop for the price of a Yellow Pages advertisement and some business cards. So figure about $300 if you already have a computer and about $2,500 if you don't.

### The Price Is Right: Most personal service professionals start by charging a small rate, usually monthly or even yearly if they're really confident. Figure about $300 a month as a retainer to start, then scale it up or down as you see fit, depending on the demands of a particular client. Hourly fees range anywhere from $40 to $75.

### Tools Of The Trade: Telephone system, with cordless phone, dependable voice-mail system and pager. Good computer to handle accounting and to help with correspondence. A daily planner is a good idea, and the patience of a saint comes in handy.

### Basic Training: Just some decent people skills and good shoe leather are all that's needed. You're going to be knocking on a lot of doors, both figuratively and literally. Also, a marketing eye comes in handy. You'll need that to identify your target audience, like dual-income couples and single professionals.

You might want to hop on the National Concierge Association's Web site at www.lpconcierge.com.

**The Bottom Line:** You'll make anywhere from $40,000 to more than $60,000 annually. As a personal concierge, you'll likely be compensated based on the amount of work you put into the job.

**Hot Tip:** Don't forget about the corporate market. Many companies are beginning to provide personal services like grocery shopping and finding day care on short notice for employees. That keeps employees on site and happy and gives employers more satisfied workers. Approach a target company through their human resources department to make your pitch.

# ER for PCs: Computer Consultant

**Here's The Deal:** According to the U.S. Department of Commerce, computer training and consulting is a $66-billion-a-year industry. It's expected to continue growing, as more businesses and individuals remain uncertain about what new technology to purchase or, like me, buy computer equipment they don't know how to use.

Computer specialists are the Godfather's of the cyber age. Customers are forever lining up, checkbooks open, with special requests, and you can pick and choose when and where you want to work. One guy I know in my hometown of Boston works six months of the year in Beantown as a computer consultant during the spring and summer and six months in balmy Singapore the rest of the year, when snow banks are higher than some of Boston's skyscrapers.

PHOTO © PHOTODISC

There's a lot of flexibility in being a desktop doctor, too. You can be hired to diagnose a simple computer malfunction, train people to use software or consult on the design and purchase of computer systems. Your potential client list can include law and doctor's offices, CPAs, financial analysts, retail outlets, department stores, hospitals, hotels and homebased businesses.

The primary goal of a computer consulting practice is to help businesses use computers more efficiently and to improve their bottom lines. When they first enter the market, most consultants deal with small businesses and then ratchet up on the fly. As they progress, consultants earn a reputation and start to attract the attention of larger businesses: banks, accounting offices and insurance companies in need of computer consulting services on a regular basis. The work is the same for all companies, regardless of their dimensions, but serving larger operations is advantageous because most of them have the cost of consulting services built into their budgets.

Most consultants charge either a fixed price for well-defined projects or by the hour for custom programming, office setup, network configuration and other technical services. Because many support their clients electronically by modem, they can build highly professional and efficient businesses from home offices. Homebased shops benefit clients as much as they do consultants, since they don't have to cover traveling expenses. All clients care about is that you're available and you have a pulse when they need help. If you're in your office and can help them within five minutes of their call, that's better than getting to their office a day later.

PHOTO © DIGITAL VISION LTD.

On the computer training side, business is booming as well. According to market research firm International Data Corp., technology-based training is experiencing exceptional growth, with annual revenues expected to climb from $1.9 billion in 1998 to $7.6 billion in 2002. The fastest-growing market segment? E-learning (Internet/intranet-based training)—which should blossom from $202 million in 1998 to $3.8 billion in 2002.

**First Things First:** Computer training and consulting is rapidly becoming a competitive field. Carve out a niche by focusing on one or two target markets and expand from there. You'll need a strong background in computers to understand how various systems operate.

**Price Tag:** Entrepreneurs with extensive computer knowledge have started consulting services for as little as $3,500 to

$5,000, depending on whether you use your existing computer or buy a new one. Most already have the office equipment they need to start in computer consulting. If you don't, be prepared to spend about another $10,000 for computers and software.

## The Price Is Right:

Charge anywhere from $20 for a quick-fix deal over the phone or via e-mail up to $70 an hour for an on-site call. For late-night or early-morning emergency calls, you can slap on a premium.

## Tools Of The Trade:

At the very least, your own desktop computer and up-to-date versions of the software you'll be specializing in. A laser printer and some problem-detection software are mandatory as well. A modem also is necessary to communicate with clients online. A portable computer and printer are a good idea for on-site calls and a media safe (to store backup disks that contain critical client data) is a good investment as well. A portable ATM machine might come in handy to deposit all the cash you're going to make, too.

## Basic Training:

You need a strong knowledge of computer hardware. You may want to specialize in either Mac or PC systems—along with the quirks and most common snafus associated with the most popular software programs. In this business, it's imperative that you stay up to date on the latest advances in technology, and it's important to have adequate equipment yourself—software programs that diagnose problems, such as Norton Utilities, are especially useful.

Joining an association is one way to keep on top of the industry. Try these on for size: Computer Technology Industry Association at www.comptia.org, or ITrain—International Association of Information Technology Trainers—at (410) 290-7000 or www. itrain.org. PC Magazine Online (www.zdnet.com/pcmag/hotlinks/ index.html) is another great resource, offering links to lots of techie information and support.

## The Bottom Line:

Like I've been telling you, it's good news: Some established companies boast revenues of more than $1 million annually. You'll make more if you have a host of corporate clients. If you're making home-office calls, the pay is lower but still good. Plenty of computer consultants who rely on retail businesses make more than $100K per year. A recent survey conducted by the International Computer Consultants Association

(ICCA) showed that three-fourths of ICCA members reported a billable rate between $40 and $60 per hour, and averaged 30 billable hours per week. In general, consultants (including both part time and full time) bill an average of 14 working days per month directly to their clients. This means that monthly gross revenues range between $5,000 and $20,800 per month for successful, well-established, full-time computer consultants.

**Hot Tip:** Take advantage of computer-based advertising avenues such as e-mail and your own Web site. On a Web site, which

you may be able to upload for free from your Internet service provider's server, you might offer possible solutions to some of the most common computer problems or give answers to frequently asked computer questions. This helps establish your credibility as a computer expert and promotes goodwill by offering some advice for free.

# Going Ballistic Over Holistic: Herbal Pharmacy

**Here's The Deal:** Did you know that pharmacists are the number-one trusted professionals after the clergy? I didn't either (I thought struggling writers were). But they are, and one popular trend in the profession is to ditch the Nyquil and Viagra and go organic. More than 75 percent of Americans have used alternative herbal therapies and will do so again, according to the Academy of Natural Healing in New York City. Is it any wonder then that the $30 billion natural healing industry would be attractive to young entrepreneurs with a flair for and interest in all-natural herbal medicines?

Herbs are hot. From echinacea to ginseng, herbal remedies once considered on the fringes of medicine are popping up in pharmacies everywhere. Consumer demand for medicinal herbs is growing phenomenally, culinary herbs are growing strong, and herb farms are springing up across the country to meet the demand.

The driving force right now in the herb market is the interest in alternative health-care products, herbal supplements, herbal medic-

inal products and dietary supplements. Besides selling herbal medicines, some growers also formulate and manufacture their own
herbal products (such as shampoos and skin creams), which are
sold by mail order or at their retail stores.

What differentiates herbal pharmacists from traditional health-
food stores is that owners are trained pharmacists who help customers understand alternative healing methods. Herbal pharmacists
have always been counselors, helping people choose over-the-
counter medications. Now, some entrepreneurs are taking the pharmacy ideal one step further, starting integrated health centers complete with an on-staff medical doctor, natural healer and massage
therapist.

Not every herbal pharmacy writes prescriptions, but all assist
customers in making the right natural product selection that is right
for them and their conditions. The information you provide as an
herbal pharmacist educates customers on the proper use of nutritional supplements and helps guide them toward healthy lifestyle
changes that provide a better sense of well-being and improved
health. In some cases, herbal pharmacists make private consulta-
tions available for customers.

**First Things First :** If you want to go all the
way and deliver prescriptions along with sage advice on the latest
Western, Chinese and Ayurvedic herbal traditions, you should get
your pharmacist's license. However, just because it says "pharmacy" doesn't really mean you have to be a pharmacist. Take a more
"village country store" approach and simply sell over-the-counter
herbal treatments. Start by researching herbal treatments and medicines at your local library or on the Web. Visit herb shops in your
city and others to see what products they are selling and how they
are displayed. Carefully study your future competition: well-established health-food stores and natural-
food and health-goods co-ops.

Sales will be greater for an herbal
pharmacy operating in a mall or near a
hospital or group of physicians'
offices, as it will receive a large number of walk-in patrons or shoppers for
prescription drugs. You can increase
sales if other drug stores do not offer

the same convenience. Free delivery service should be offered at a minimum to shut-in or disabled patients. A five- to 10-mile radius for deliveries is common.

Also, when establishing your shop, try to answer the following questions: How well will the location attract customers? How hard will it be to get customers to come to the store? Would people in the area be interested in buying herbal products? Is there much tourist business, and would tourists be interested in buying herbs, live herb plants, herbal crafts and so on? If you like the answers you get, then you're on the right track.

Price Tag: Not too expensive. You can start an herbal remedies catalog for the price of the writing, illustrations and printing and then order your inventory from a plethora of herbal medicine providers. Cost: about $2,500. For a retail site, you'll pay the going rate for store space in your town (anywhere from $1,000 to $5,000 per month in most cases). Setting up a Web site for orders and deliveries is a good idea. You can roll one out complete with product descriptions and interactive credit card purchase page for less than $3,000.

The Price Is Right: Some herbs like Chinese Energetics and the like can be a tad pricey. But most holistic and homeopathic remedies are easily available and thus relatively cheap. Figure about 25 percent of your budget for inventory. If you're not sure, an herb broker can give you tips about what's in demand and the likely price you'll pay for herbal medicines and products. Remember, prescriptions alone aren't enough to make a buck in the industry. In the general pharmaceutical sector, prescriptions only account for 27 percent of a store's revenues—the rest derive from soap, hair products and the like. Roughly, expect an investment of $2 for every $5 in estimated annual sales. While an herbal pharmacy is not a capital-intensive business, nor a labor-intensive one, some money must be invested into store shelving, equipment and inventory items.

Tools Of The Trade: A personal computer to log data, like inventory and prescription information, and a dependable telephone system with a good voice-mail system to keep the lines of communication open with your customers.

Basic Training: Solid footing in herbal therapies: It's up to you whether that means spending six weeks sleeping under a yak in Pakistan or six years in medical school in L.A. Add to that hands-on education by reading all the natural remedies books on the market as well as getting literature from the various herbal product manufacturers out there (visit www.thomasregister. com). There's no real regulatory framework for marketing herbal remedies other than having a passion for them.

**The Bottom Line:** You can make a nice living marketing herbal remedies, but just don't expect to be swapping shop talk with the Vanderbilts in Newport come summertime. Small herbal pharmacies may have annual sales of only about $500,000—or less. Many herbal pharmacists ply their trade in rural settings, like New Hampshire, Vermont and amidst the sequoias in Northern California and the Pacific Northwest. Living expenses there are smaller, but so is your paycheck. Incomes of $80,000 annually are not uncommon in the right setting, and job satisfaction from industry entrepreneurs is sky high. People in the industry believe they are making a difference in customer's lives, and you can't really put a price tag on that.

**Hot Tip:** If you choose a storefront shop to market your herbal remedies, make sure you capitalize, but don't overcapitalize. You don't want a store that looks too cheap, but you'll wind up with a lot of debt if you overcompensate and go for a bigger, more powerful retail statement. In the herbal remedies business, profits can be slow to come, so watching your budget may be more critical in this industry than others.

# Supersize This:
# Upscale Sandwich Restaurant

**Here's The Deal:** It's fast food by any other name— but that's where the similarities end, say owners of upscale sandwich shops. Research firm Find/SVP reports hectic schedules prevent 34 percent of consumers from cooking meals. That home-meal replacement trend keeps upscale sandwich restaurants busy well into the dinner hour. Not only that, but according to the National Restaurant Association,

more than 65 percent of restaurant customers say menu items at their favorite eateries provide flavors and tastes unlike any they can prepare at home. Consequently, the audience for upscale sandwich shops is mushrooming.

People, especially white-collar workers, are tired of the tuna and mayonnaise pabulum served up in too many pedestrian delis. Upscale sandwich shops try to offer a boutique flavor, doing what hair salons did for barbershops. Upscale sandwich shops often bake their own bread and throw away produce that's more than a day old. The stores are often better lighted with some nice jazz piped in via stereo. Young urban workers often come to check out the opposite sex while they chow down on chicken tarragon salad. Ka-ching!

**First Things First:** Canvas the upscale neighborhood restaurants you haunt and any other ones you visit while you're out of town. Check out the sandwich menus and chat up the kitchen help—the head chef would be preferable—and find out what's inside the gourmet delights they serve. Take notes not only of the menu but of the decor. Read as many gourmet food magazines and visit food trade shows to find out what's new in the sandwich wars. Also, write a business plan—more than most businesses, a restaurant really benefits from one because it's such a cash-intensive, time-consuming business. It'll keep you on track when you get derailed.

**Price Tag:** What separates upscale sandwich shops from the garden-variety deli down the street? For starters, money. Even at the low end, with limited seating, upscale sandwich shops can cost more than $40,000 to start. Figure on another $7,500 to $15,000 if you're buying into some of the new franchises sprouting up on city blocks and in suburban malls.

**The Price Is Right:** The ones I've seen, like Cosi in New York and Au Bon Pain everywhere, charge about a buck or two more than what you'd charge at a typical sandwich joint. And remember, you can't put a price tag on ambiance.

**Tools Of The Trade:** A good-sized oven, a microwave oven and a regular inventory of fresh meats, cheeses, breads, poultry and produce—with plenty of gourmet condiments.

**Basic Training:** Some chef schooling would be nice. Or a stint as a sandwich chef at a good restaurant. But if you've honed your cuisine talents in your home kitchen, and your friends and family say that Julia Child has nothing on you, you'll probably do fine. The National Restaurant Association (www.restaurant.org) can also clue you in on the equipment and regulatory ins and outs of this business.

**The Bottom Line:** Some nicely located upscale sandwich shops garner more than $250,000 annually. With a staff of three or four employees, some owners say they can devote more time to crafting eclectic new menu favorites like tandoori chicken and Norwegian smoked salmon sandwiches baked on European flatbread.

**Hot Tip:** The key to success in the gourmet sandwich business is the same for any restaurant: location, location, location—and of course, a great menu. But even a kick-ass menu can be defeated by a poor spot to open your shop. To avoid that, look for locations on college campuses, downtown districts and, if you can afford it, suburban shopping malls. That's where you'll find the audience for your haute cuisine.

# I'll Have A Squishy, Abu—And Make It A Double: Juice Bar

**Here's The Deal:** They have yet to appear in Homer Simpson's local Quick-E Mart, but all hail the Raspberry Rush and the Guava Oasis. "Smoothies" are the fruity, frothy fountain drink of the 21st century, and juice bars serving them are popping up with the regularity of hairweaves at a game-show host convention. It was a $500 million-plus business at the end of 1998—making the juice craze the latest trend in the beverage marketplace.

PHOTO © PHOTODISC

Fresh ideas—and ingredients—are what this industry is all about. Some juice bars cater to the age-phobic baby boomers and market their juice drinks as the fountain of youth. Others cater to younger customers, setting up kiosks inside their restaurants that not only include cup-holders and magazines but Internet-ready computers.

Juice bars serve a variety of drinks, but the most popular are without a doubt "smoothies," healthy combinations of fruit, fruit juice and yogurt. Healthful additions such as proteins, brans, calcium and bee pollen can be added to these drinks to even further increase their nutritional value.

PHOTO COURTESY: CRAZY CARROT JUICE BAR

Juice bars are popular with consumers because smoothies offer them a healthy and lightweight alternative to fast food. Smoothies taste great, are good for you and can be made in under a minute.

Juice bars are a great business opportunity for anyone wanting to run their own business. They offer ease of preparation, virtually no waste and very little equipment to worry about. A juice bar can be profitable seven days a week, 12 or more hours a day.

Some juice bar owners are marketing their drinks in, uh, unique ways. To a growing number of adult-minded entrepreneurs, juice bars are both all-natural and au naturel. Some juice bars are taking their vitamin-packed, fruit, vegetable and herb beverages and packaging them in an adult entertainment format, creating alcohol-free nightclubs complete with exotic dancing.

**First Things First:** Bone up on health drinks at your local library or via the Internet. Better yet, go check out a juice bar and talk with employees and customers. Tip: When you're considering where you want to open your juice bar, avoid the coasts. The vast majority of juice bars in the United States are operating on the East and West Coasts, leaving a land of opportunity in between.

**Price Tag:** You might want to spice up your Pineapple Paradise with a shot of rum before you check out the price tag on opening a juice bar. Figure in annual rent ($3,300), utilities ($12,000), insurance ($3,600), labor ($25,000), equipment ($15,000) and marketing ($3,500) and you're starting to run into some serious money. Many juice bars are opened for less than $50,000, but if you're in a highly competitive market in a well-populated city or town, the price may rise to about $100,000.

**The Price Is Right:** Many juice bars charge between $2 and $5 per drink. Some also serve sandwiches and bagels for between $1 and $5.

**Tools Of The Trade:** Mainly a commercial rental or leased property, preferably near a lot of foot traffic. Inside your shop, you'll need some basic kitchen equipment like blenders, refrigerators and walk-in coolers. Oh, and lots of aprons.

**Basic Training:** A retail restaurant background is a big plus, maybe as a bartender or manager. A marketing degree comes in real handy when you're competing against a burgeoning number of like-minded juice vendors.

**The Bottom Line:** There's good news, too. Based on an average of 40 drinks sold per hour in your busy store at about $3.50 a pop, you can gross well over $500,000 annually. Some juice bars gross well over $1 million annually. Hey, I'll drink to that.

**Hot Tip:** A "juice consultant" can help you get started on the road to juice bar-dom. These consultants provide everything from site and menu creation and design to tracking and accounting systems for a nominal fee. Check the Internet under "juice bar consultants." There's plenty of companies ready to help you out.

# My Web Page Or Yours?
# Web Site Development

**Here's The Deal:** When the Internet was in its infancy, no one paid much attention to how attractively information was presented online. Today, a cool Web site is the hottest way for a company to market its products and services. That's why companies hire professionals to conceptualize and build their sites; to design the backgrounds, buttons and graphics; and to publish the sites on the Web. With so much off-the-shelf Web-site design software available, your creativity and graphic skills are just as important as your technical ability.

PHOTO © DIGITAL VISION

The work is out there: According to research firm Gartner Group, sales for the Web design industry are expected to exceed $700 million in 1999. But it's no longer enough to simply design Web sites or provide graphics and content. Successful companies offer value-added services such as assistance with advertising, e-commerce or direct marketing.

That said, tech-savvy Web entrepreneurs have a big, built-in advantage over more mainstream entrepreneurs. Companies are stumbling over each other in the race to get on the Web, but many corporate execs are still in the Dark Ages when it comes to high-tech. College students and young high-tech professionals have a tremendous advantage in the computer arena: They grew up with the Internet and pounding HTML and Java code is second nature.

**First Things First:** Research the sites on the Web you like and examine what it is that makes you blink. Look for color blends, interesting ways of expressing content and how the sights are organized for user-friendliness. Incorporate those ideas and blend them with a healthy chunk of your own style and creativity, and you're in business.

**Price Tag:** The average Web design firm can get off the ground for about $1,000 (not including a computer system). A Yellow pages advertisement, some brochures and business cards and a place to work—even if it's your garage—are all you need to get going. That is, along with a talent for toiling in cyberspace.

**The Price Is Right:** Web site development prices are coming down due to increased competition. Still, you can make a good living at it. I've seen small-business Web sites, with only a page or two, billed for about $250 to $500 for the initial setup, plus up to $100 a month for maintenance. Larger companies pay top dollar for top-dollar work. The trouble is, most Fortune 1000 Web sites have been taken in-house. Where they're not, the work can be worth $5,000 a project and up.

**Tools Of The Trade:** A desktop PC or Mac, with software ability to write HTML and Java code. A good, high-speed modem (about $150), Internet portal to get on the Web (about $15 per month) and added phone lines (about $50 monthly). Some marketing brochures, business cards and media ads (about $500 total) should get you off and running. A bedroom or garage to work from and a card table to work on.

**Basic Training:** If you don't know Java from HTML, you can make up ground by taking one of many Web design courses at your local college, library or continuing education program. They're pretty cheap—no more than $500 a whack for an eight-week course, and often cheaper. All you really need is a basic understanding of the Internet and of HTML and Java, the preferred languages for developing Web content.

Last but not least, join an organization like the Association of Internet Professionals. Call (800) JOIN-AIP, or visit www.association.org and check out the cool links for gazillions of great resources.

**The Bottom Line:** You can earn anywhere from several thousand dollars per year to $1 million annually and more. Web design is a volume business—the more clients you attract, and the more pages they want, the more money you will make. Some Web design companies have annual revenues that exceed $10 million.

**Hot Tip:** Many companies create fancy Internet sites, then fail to promote them to potential customers. So here's a side business to mull over: As a Web site consultant, you register the company's site with multiple search engines to increase traffic, arrange reciprocal links with related sites and help the company make purchasing decisions about banner advertising. Start-up cost: $2,000.

# Please Don't Pet The Crocodile, Mrs. Fishbein: Specialty Tour Operator

**Here's The Deal:** Specialty tour operators serve up travel with a twist. Say good-bye to the days of the cattle-call bus tour, when masses of weary visitors were herded through seven countries in six days, stopping just long enough to snap a photo and climb back into their air-conditioned coaches. Today's travelers want to participate in their vacations, not be passive sightseers. They want to explore and experience new things.

This contemporary breed of traveler has spurred the growth of the specialty travel industry. Tourism is the third-largest retail sales industry in the United States, and specialty travel is one of its fastest-growing segments. In 1996 (the most recent year for which figures are available), more than 25 million people—many of them baby boomers with unprecedented discretionary income—traveled on tours, an increase of 22 percent since 1993.

The explosion in specialty travel has given the word "vacation" a whole new meaning. Tour companies catering to virtually every taste and interest imaginable are springing up. No longer content to settle back with a bestseller on the beach, ordinary people can spend a week living the life of a Civil War soldier, taking a Jeep safari through the Arizona desert or learning the elements of espionage. They can rope calves from atop Palomino horses, go on archaeological digs, sample various types of cigars or take cooking classes in Mexico.

As most specialty tour operators will tell you, if it's done right, specialty travel businesses can be started by anyone.

**First Things First:** Entrepreneurs in the specialty tour industry say the greatest challenge is marketing, so getting your hands on some mailing lists is a good place to start. Because direct mail is the most effective way for specialty tour operators to attract clients, many purchase mailing lists from groups that have members who might be interested in their tours. They also maintain Web sites and advertise in national and special-interest publications. So pour some early funding into touting your business. If you're into African safaris, for example, advertise in zoological magazines or target zoo membership lists for your direct mailing and Web marketing. Or, consider an agreement with your local zoo to advertise on their Web site.

**Price Tag:** To start, you'll need $5,000 and up, depending on how much advertising you do at the outset. Much of that goes toward initial marketing efforts, purchasing blocks of tickets and reserving hotel space; the remainder covers office equipment. Big plus: Specialty tours are not capital-intensive businesses once you

hire staff and set up shop. As you go along, charge people in advance and that should cover ongoing expenses, payroll and the like.

**The Price Is Right:** Again, it varies. A surf tour off Maui is going to cost more than a tour of the great yarn factories of northern Maine. Scour the travel brochures of leading global travel firms and see what they're charging for their expeditions. Also, if you have competitors, see what they're charging. The guys who organize the Mount Everest climbing expeditions each year charge as much as $70,000 per climber. Visiting the old barns of rural Nebraska? Well, a couple Greyhound bus tickets and some comped meals at Shoneys are only worth so much.

**Tools Of The Trade:** They vary depending on your tour. If you're starting a company that specializes in high-terrain bicycle tours, then you're going to need some bikes. Ditto surfing vacations and safaris, where a couple Humvees will come in handy. For foreign excursions, though it's not a tool per se, inside contacts in the country or countries you'll be visiting are vital. You're going to need a knowledgeable businessperson or government official to help cut through the inevitable red tape—whether you're going to Mexico, China or Europe.

**Basic Training:** It's good for prospective specialty tour organizers to have experience in the travel industry or a network of contacts at hotels and other destinations. Many specialty tour operators are former travel agents. You at least need an avid interest in the specialty tour field you're considering and some solid marketing know-how. Check out your local community college. Many offer certificate courses in the travel field. Or get on-the-job training by first working for a specialty tour company that offers tours that interest you.

You can also bone up on the industry by checking out organizations such as the American Society of Travel Agents at (703) 739-2782 or www.astanet.com, or the United States Tour Operators Association at (212) 944-572 or www.ustoa.com.

**The Bottom Line:** As with any start-up, profits can be slim initially, especially since you must pay upfront to buy tickets or reserve hotel rooms—sometimes even before you've booked a single client. As the business grows, however, so do annual profits, which can range from $50,000 to more than $100,000, or an average of 10 percent to 15 percent of gross sales, say industry experts. But for people in this business, getting rich quick isn't the primary motive. Making a living doing what they love is the big payoff.

**Hot Tip:** Make your first hire a good sales agent and the second a good travel organizer. Both will pay you back in spades.

# Quit Hogging The Mirror: Cosmetics

**Here's The Deal:** Are you frustrated that the only nail colors at your local cosmetics counter are boring shades like Shimmering Shell or Love that Red? (I know I am.) Then do something about it and start your own cosmetics line and/or beauty store. The cosmetics industry contains a rich palette of possibilities if you know your pastels and polishes.

In general, the cosmetics business is divided up into several sectors, including color cosmetics or makeup, treatment or skin care, fragrances, and health and beauty aids, which is a broad, diverse area that includes everything from shampoo to foot products. The wide range of products also means there are numerous ways entrepreneurs can enter this field: You can manufacture a product, distribute other manufacturers' products, open a retail location, sell wares at local fairs, launch a Web site, publish newsletters on the topic, or even provide services such as facials and makeovers using natural products.

PHOTO COURTESY: RIPE INC.

Out of all the above avenues, for most Gen E's, manufacturing cosmetics is where it's at. While private label manufacturing, in which you create products for store brands, like Bloomingdale's, used to be the way to go, the popular trend of late is to take the route of hot Gen E nail polish companies like Hard Candy and manufacture your own cosmetics with your brand name on the label.

Selling products under your company's name makes you legally responsible for the product in all areas, including labeling (regulated by the FDA) and product claims. And the FDA has determined that your claims include not only what you say on the label but what you say in any advertising material. You will also be the first one contacted if a consumer experiences any adverse reactions to your product. This means you should educate yourself about such things as stability, shelf life and product liability insurance.

There are many resources available to you, some of them free. Check out industry resources and trade associations, such as the Independent Cosmetic Manufacturers and Distributors (ICMAD). ICMAD can provide general guidance on regulations and government support and even has a group products liability policy for members. Contact ICMAD at (800) 334-2623 or check them out on the Web at www.icmad.org.

**First Things First:** Find work at beauty supply store or chic downtown cosmetics store and pay attention to what customers are asking for, not what they're actually buying. Buy a wide variety of nail polishes and lipsticks and begin mixing and matching colors that you think women want to see. Don't worry what the traditionalists say: If you think nails in garbage-can gray are cool, then follow your instincts. There's no more creative industry than cosmetics.

**Price Tag:** Cosmetics companies can be started out of your home for less than $500. You'll need a makeshift lab to mix your colors; a healthy supply of polish, eyeliner, lipstick, facial creams and the like, and some business cards and maybe a small brochure to leave at cosmetic retailers in your area. If you decide to open a store, the price for rent, utilities, staffing and so on will push that figure up into the $25,000 to $50,000 range.

**The Price Is Right:** If you want to take the nail polish route, start out at between $5 and $10 for the bottles. A lot depends on manufacturing and distribution. If you have a great setup and are getting into major stores, you can charge less and make out on the volume. If you're cramming polish into bottles in your garage, charge for the effort.

**Tools Of The Trade:** Time, really. If you can manage the time to learn the ropes, then you're on your way down the primrose path. Some cosmetics company owners started as part timers (like Ripe and Tony & Tina Vibrational Remedies), but you really won't make a lot of money until you're talking a full-time commitment.

**Basic Training:** You can go to beautician school if you want, but your money might be better spent on business school, where you'll learn how to set up a distribution system, track inventory and develop a budget. The creativity lessons you'll receive at beauty school might lead you astray from what your heart wants to accomplish. In short, trust your creative instincts and bone up on your business instincts.

**The Bottom Line:** Annual revenues for start-up cosmetic companies of $500,000 and up are not unheard of. The key is getting your products onto beauty store counters and building a word-of-mouth following, both in the industry and with customers.

**Hot Tip:** Ripe Cosmetics sells a recipe book that allows young women (their core audience) to mix and match on paper before trying it out for real. Getting kind of close to the Dutch Boy paint world, but why not?

# Scooping Up Profits With The Net: E-Commerce

**Here's The Deal:** There's no doubt about it. E-commerce is the gold rush of the late 21st century. While Internet commerce is an unpredictable industry that changes by the day, all

indications suggest it will continue to thrive: According to Forrester Research, worldwide Internet commerce revenue (both consumer and business-to-business) is expected to grow from $18.6 billion in 1997 to $1.3 trillion by 2003.

Only a small percentage of consumers who visit Web commerce sites

PHOTO© ADOBE IMAGE LIBRARY

make a purchase, with concerns about credit card security and difficulty in finding merchandise listed as the key reasons people browse but don't buy. While books, music and computer-related items are still the most popular products on the Web, other ideas can work—especially if you target a niche market. A niche market, combined with excellent customer service and a keen sense of the online community can enable you to succeed with very low start-up costs.

Top barriers to Internet commerce growth are consumers' security fears, slow transmission speeds, unreliable Web sites and lack of coordination among Web sites and distribution channels.

**First Things First:** The types of e-commerce businesses you can start on the Web vary only by your imagination. Of course, having your own business is an obvious launching point. Even if you don't, you can start a mail order business that sells goods online à la Dell Computer or Amazon.com for a lot less than leasing retail space. Another e-commerce idea is starting a Web site that's sort of like a virtual reference librarian. Professional types request research information and you supply it through articles on the subject of choice for a fee.

**Price Tag:** The usual suspects: technology (creating and maintaining a Web site) and marketing yourself to customers. In a recent study, Internet commerce providers reported spending heavily on marketing and advertising—an average of $26 an order, substantially more than the $2.50 for traditional stores. That includes money spent for distribution on large Web gateway or "portal" sites such as those offered by Yahoo! and AOL. The price for creating your own Web site varies, from as low as $200 to as high as $15,000, depending on what you're trying to accomplish and how much content, design and gizmos and gadgets you need to accomplish it. Also, depending on your level of techie expertise, you can go the do-it-yourself route (much cheaper, obviously) or hire a firm to create one for you (in which case, you're lookin' at the high end).

**Tools Of The Trade:** An absolutely fluid Web site and a good distribution system. An 800 number is also key.

**Basic Training:** Take classes in entrepreneurship as well as some Internet courses for background. If you're going the do-it-yourself route, plan on signing up for some Web site design classes, too, which you can find at your local college, library or continuing education program. Another resource to check out is CommerceNet (www.commerce.net), which offers scads of materials for the e-commerce community, including an e-newsletter.

**The Bottom Line:** Major. If you can get some traffic on your site, you can make a fortune. Some small-business owners boast of making north of $100K their first year. But ultimately, it's all about filling a market niche, like Amazon.com did. If you can't find the market and can't get the traffic, don't give up your day job.

**Hot Tip:** Study Web sites like Amazon.com to find out why their "shopping cart" strategies are so successful. With an online shopping cart program, "shoppers" can drag goods into a "drop and click" basket and continue shopping. At the end of their shopping excursion, they go to a page labeled "checkout" where their basket of goods is waiting for them. Very convenient, even for cyberspace.

# Chapter 14

My recipe for success? 33% inspiration, 33% perspiration and 33% preparation— with 1% desperation tossed in for good measure.

## Resources?
## You Need These
## Stinkin' Resources

In Chapter 4, I took Thomas Edison to task for his calculation that success was "1 percent inspiration and 99 percent perspiration." So what is my recipe for success? I'd say a successful entrepreneurial venture is 33 percent inspiration, 33 percent perspiration and 33 percent preparation—with 1 percent desperation tossed in for good measure. While the inspiration and perspiration must come from somewhere deep inside of you, much of the preparation will come from information culled in the early research phase of your entrepreneurial endeavor. That's what you'll find here—a guide to everything entrepreneurial. Take advantage of the organizations, classes, books, magazines, Web sites and companies listed below to prepare yourself properly for the task ahead. Do your research right and you're a third of the way there.

# Books On Entrepreneurship

Unfortunately, too many business books serve no better purpose than using them as $35 paper weights. You've heard the titles: *When Bad Businesses Happen to Good People*; *Profits are from Mars, Losses are From Your Business*; and *Buy This Business Book So I Can Send My Kids to College*. If you intend to base your business solely on the research you find in *The Fathead's Guide to (fill in the blank)*, do yourself a favor: Go to the bank, take out your life savings, go downtown to the biggest building you can find, climb that building, and scatter your money to the four winds, thus saving yourself a lot of time. That said, there are some business books that any entrepreneur can benefit from reading.

- *A Goal Is a Dream With a Deadline: Extraordinary Wisdom for Entrepreneurs, Managers & Other Smart People* (McGraw-Hill), by Leo B. Helzel

- *All I Really Need to Know in Business I Learned at Microsoft: Insider Strategies to Help You Succeed* (Pocket Books), by Julie Bick

- *Bloomberg by Bloomberg* (John Wiley & Sons), by Michael Bloomberg and Matthew Winkler

- *Business Plans Made Easy: It's Not as Hard as You Think!* (Entrepreneur Press), by Mark Henricks

- *Deal Power: 6 Foolproof Steps to Making Deals of Any Size* (Henry Holt), by Marc Diener

- *Disclosing New Worlds: Entrepreneurship, Democratic Action, and the Cultivation of Solidarity* (MIT Press), by Charles Spinosa
- *Engineering Your Start-up: A Guide for the High-tech Entrepreneur* (Professional Start-ups), by Michael L. Baird
- *The 4 Routes to Entrepreneurial Success* (Berrett-Koehler Publishing), by John B. Miner
- *How to Make Millions With Your Ideas: An Entrepreneur's Guide* (Plume), by Dan S. Kennedy
- *Knock-out Marketing: Powerful Strategies to Punch Up Your Sales* (Entrepreneur Press), by Jack Fererri
- *The Portable MBA in Entrepreneurship* (John Wiley & Sons), by William D. Bygrave
- *The Portable MBA in Entrepreneurship Case Studies* (John Wiley & Sons), by William D. Bygrave
- *Richard Branson, Virgin King: Inside Richard Branson's Business Empire* (Prima Publishing), by Tim Jackson
- *Small Time Operator: How to Start Your Own Small Business, Keep Your Books, Pay Your Taxes and Stay Out of Trouble!* (Bell Springs Publishing), by Bernard B. Kamoroff
- *Start Your Own Business: The Only Start-up Book You'll Ever Need* (Entrepreneur Press), by Rieva Lesonsky and the editors of *Entrepreneur* magazine
- *Success for Less: 100 Low-cost Businesses You Can Start Today* (Entrepreneur Press), by Terry and Robert Adams
- *303 Marketing Tips Guaranteed to Boost Your Business* (Entrepreneur Press), by Rieva Lesonsky and Leann Anderson
- *To Build the Life You Want, Create the Work You Love: The Spiritual Dimension of Entrepreneuring* (St. Martins Press), by Marsha Sinetar
- *The Way of the Guerrilla: Achieving Success and Balance as an Entrepreneur in the 21st Century* (Houghton Mifflin), by Jay Conrad Levinson
- *What's Luck Got to Do With It? Twelve Entrepreneurs Reveal the Secrets Behind Their Success* (John Wiley & Sons), by Gregory K. Ericksen
- *Young Millionaires: Inspiring Stories to Ignite Your Entrepre-*

*neurial Dreams* (Entrepreneur Press), by Rieva Lesonsky and Gayle Sato Stodder

# Business Plan Software

Writing your business plan is one of the most critical tasks you'll do during start-up—with the possible exception of choosing between a "Star Wars" or an "Austin Powers" screen saver for your PC. Choose one of these software tools when drawing up your business's financial blueprint:

- *BizPlanBuilder* (www.jian.com): From Jian, this business plan program is different from the others on the market because its templates can be used with the word processor and spreadsheet programs that you already have on your computer (including Microsoft Works, Microsoft Word, Word Perfect, ClarisWorks, Lotus, Microsoft Excel and Quattro Pro). This enables you to customize the fonts and layout of your business plan.

- *Business HeadStart* (www.budgetmaestro.com): From Planet Corp., Business Headstart is one of the simplest programs to learn. In addition to its novice-friendly operating format, it offers Planet Tutor, an online tutorial that walks you through the steps of entering data.

- *Business Plan Pro* (www.palo-alto.com): This program from Palo Alto Software is also easy to set up and use. Business Plan Pro comes with several sample plans, along with an outline that it will automatically customize to fit the needs of the type of business you specify. There's even a home-office option.

- *Plan Write for Business* (800-423-1228): This program from Business Resource Software is also simple to use. Its design runs a close second to Business Plan Pro, since it allows you to have multiple text, spreadsheet and graph templates open at one time for easy comparison. By viewing several parts of your plan simultaneously, you can get a good picture of how the numbers are coming together without having to print.

# Employee Resources

Maybe in your travels to far-off places, you'll get lucky and find that Java code pounder or accounting genius you need to keep your business on track. If not, don't fret. The Web also provides guidance for finding the next Waylon Smithers—as well as the next Homer Simpson. But if you know what you're looking for, chances are you'll have lots of good job candidates to choose from on the Web. Think about it. The very first thing college graduates do is to post their resumes on a Web job site.

- *Career Paradise Colossal List of Career Links* (www.service. emory.edu/CAREER/Main/Links.html): This site has links to dozens of employment-related sites, with site summaries and ratings.

- *Career Resource Center* (www.careers.org): This site boasts links to more than 7,500 job-related resources, organized for your convenience.

- *CareerCity* (www.ajb.dni.us/html): There's mostly technical job listings for the 125,000-plus postings in this massive, searchable database.

- *Monster Board* (www.monster.com): At this site, employers can post jobs and browse through a database of resumes for a fee. As the self-proclaimed "#1 career hub on the Web," this site receives more than 25,000 visits daily.

# Family-Owned Business Resources

- *Entrepreneurial Parent* (www.en-parent.com): At this site, you'll learn how to start, manage and grow your home business and balance your growing family at the same time. Sponsored by healthaxis.com, a medical health-care coverage organization, this site provides lots of case studies and online tutorials for young entrepreneur parents.

- *Family Business Roundtable Inc.* (www.fbrinc.com): This site, sponsored by Family Business Roundtable Inc. in Phoenix, offers resources for family-owned businesses. There's good data on family-owned businesses with lots of case studies, commentary and links to other business resources.

- *Family Firm Institute* (http://ffi.org): This professional organization of family business advisors and educators is geared toward helping family-owned businesses. Lots of stuff on working with Mom, Dad, Uncle Irv and so on.

# Homebased Business Resources

Homebased warriors everywhere are crowing about the advantages of working in the same building where they eat, sleep and argue with roommates, spouses and lovers—often all at the same time! But if you hate commuting, get a kick out of doing phone meetings with bigwigs wearing your favorite "Buzz Lightyear" pajamas and yearn for meaningful conversation with your mailman, a homebased business might be for you. If so, look into the following Web sites:

- *The American Home Business Association* (www.homebusiness. com): This site provides a free weekly home business newsletter and more.

- *Business@Home* (www.gohome.com): In this e-zine, you will find a wealth of information on technology, marketing opportunities and useful tools.

- *Homebased Business Connection* (www.oswego.com/home-base.html): Not only does this site provide good tips on running any one of hundreds of businesses from your home, but you can also add a link to your Web site to promote your business.

- *International HomeWorkers Association* (www.homeworkers. com): Uniting home employees from around the world, this site offers resources for jobs, consumer product discounts, networking and more.

- *Keeping Your Sanity in a Home Business* (www.pwgroup.com/ces/ceskeep.shtml): This is an online training course for aspiring entrepreneurs from Marnie Pehrson, homebased business author and consultant. She developed this course from her book (of the same name) to help home business owners survive and thrive. Each chapter contains links to supplemental online resources.

- *Small & Home Based Business Links* (www.bizoffice.com/index.html): This is a great site for linking up with a variety of resources available on the Web, such as budgeting and marketing tips, as well as links to other homebased business sites.

- *Small Office/Home Office Association International* (www.sohoa.com): This association offers members networking opportunities with other entrepreneurs, buying power and educational seminars on topics like marketing over the Internet and handling homebased workplace tax issues.

- *SOHO America* (www.soho.org): This site provides legislative support and other benefits for the homebased businessperson. SOHO is an acronym used by many small office/home office advocates.

- *The SOHO Guidebook* (www.toolkit.cch.com/scripts/soho_toc. dll?): This is a practical guide to starting, running and growing a small business. Worth checking out.

- *The U.S.A. Home Based Business Information Superhighway* (www.usahomebusiness.com): This site is designed to help homebased businesses survive the shift to a global economy.

# Lost And Found

During the due diligence phase of opening your new business, you'll invariably need to dig up a phone number, address or Web site for an organization, person or business. The Web offers a few great online search tools for locating all three. It's a bit Orwellian when you think about it, but we'll leave the ethical dilemma to the philosophers—or "60 Minutes."

## Find A Person

- *Find an E-Mail Address* (http://www.switchboard.com/bin/ cgiemail.dll?MG=&MEM=1): This section of the Switchboard Web site locates people's e-mail addresses.

- *Four11 U.S. Telephone Directory* (www.four11.com/cgi-bin/ Four11Main?fonesearch): This Internet white pages tracks down phone numbers and addresses.

- *InfoSpace* (www.infospace.com/info/people.htm): Here's another site for finding phone numbers and addresses.

- *Find a Person* (www.switchboard.com/bin/cgiqa.dll?MG=): This section of the Switchboard Web site locates phone numbers and addresses.

## Find A Business

- *555-1212.com* (www.555-1212.com/aclookup.html): This site locates phone number area codes.

- *AT&T AnyWho Toll Free Internet Directory* (www.anywho. com/tf.html): This site locates toll-free phone numbers.

- *EmailBigFoot* (www.bigfoot.com): This site locates ZIP codes.
- *FaxInfoSpace* (www.infospace.com/info/fax.htm): This site locates fax numbers.
- *Find a Business* (www.switchboard.com/bin/cgidir.dll?MG=& MEM=1): This section of the Switchboard Web site locates business phone numbers and addresses.
- *Four11 Yellow Pages* (www.four11.com/cgi-bin/Four11Main? MapSearch): This site includes a point-and-click map of the United States.
- *GTE Business Web Site Search* (http://wp.gte.net)
- *GTE Yellow Pages* (http://yp.gte.net)
- *InfoSpace* (www.infospace.com/info/800.htm): Here's another toll-free phone number locator.
- *White Pages Companies Online* (www.CompaniesOnline.com): At this site, you can get information on a company's sales, size, ownership structure, Web and e-mail address and more.
- *Zip2* (www.zip2.com): Enter your home or business address to find companies near your home and to get step-by-step directions from your doorstep to theirs.

## Find A Company Home Page

- *Bigbook Company Search* (www.bigbook.com)
- *InfoSpace* (www.infospace.com/info/bizweb.htm)
- *Yahoo! Home Pages Search* (www.yahoo.com/search/people/ people.html)

## General Search Engines

- *Excite* (www.excite.com)
- *Infoseek* (www.infoseek.com)
- *Lycos* (www.lycos.com)
- *WebCrawler* (www.webcrawler.com)
- *Yahoo!* (www.yahoo.com)

# Magazines On Entrepreneurship

Some of the best reference guides for making it as a young entrepreneur can be found right down the block at your local newsstand (if not there, at the local library or on the Internet). Check these out for size:

- *American Individual Magazine and Coffeehouse* (www.aimc. com/aimc): This e-zine for resourceful individualists offers survival guides for self-employment, SOHO and small-business skills, self-help, forums and chat rooms.

- *Business Start-ups* (www.entrepreneurmag.com): A monthly sister publication to *Entrepreneur*, *Business Start-Ups* targets entrepreneurs age 35 and under.

- *CCH Business Owner's Toolkit* (www.toolkit.cch.com): This site provides small-business news and articles, plus special information for subscribers.

- *Consumer Information Catalog* (www.pueblo.gsa.gov/smbuss. htm): Here, you get a list of government publications keyed to small businesses.

- *Entrepreneur* (www.entrepreneurmag.com): This monthly magazine focuses on news, articles and business and cultural trends for the small-business owner.

- *Entrepreneur's HomeOfficeMag.com* (www.homeofficemag.com): This is *Entrepreneur* magazine's monthly e-zine for the home-based entrepreneur.

- *Entrepreneurial Edge Online* (www.edgeonline.com): This quarterly e-zine for entrepreneurs offers links to business resources.

- *IdeaCafe: The Small Business Channel* (www.IdeaCafe.com): This e-zine serves up a fun approach to the serious business of entrepreneurship.

- *Network Journal* (www.tnj.com): This publication offers articles of interest to the African American, Caribbean American and African Business community.

# Office Equipment Resources

Good office equipment can mean the difference between recording your bottom line in red ink or black. Who can deny the agony of watching your life flashing before your eyes as you wait for a critical document to slide through your "handyman's special" fax machine at the speed of a DMV clerk handling a driver license renewal? It may be a cliché, but when it comes to office equipment, you get what you pay for. Unless, of course, you know where to look. . . .

## Consumer Resources

- *BuyersZone* (www.buyerszone.com): This Web site offers buyer's guides, lingo lessons, vendor information and links for "1,000s of products and services"—everything from color printers to information on providing 401(k) plans.

- *Consumer Information Center* (www.pueblo.gsa.gov): This site offers a catalog of free federal publications of consumer interest to help you know your rights when making office equipment purchases.

- *ConsumerWorld* (www.consumerworld.org): This collection of more than 1,500 consumer resource links covers an enormous variety of topics, including consumer rights and agencies, product reviews and credit rates.

- *GTE Consumer Guide* (http://cg.gte.net): Here, you'll find product reviews, prices, recommendations and links to other business commerce sites.

## Online Catalogs

- *Merced Office Supplies* (www.qualitysupplies.com/index.htm): Merced claims to beat Staples prices by a long shot. Their Web site also has a listing of thousands of office supplies for businesses—with delivery, too.

- *Viking Office Products* (www.vikingop.com): This listing of more than 500 office products is priced to save business owners up to 69 percent off the list price. Big-name brands are delivered overnight almost anywhere in the United States.

# Organizations For Entrepreneurs

- *Center for Entrepreneurial Leadership* (www.celcee.edu): This site provides a good education for entrepreneurs; a nice mentoring approach.

- *Chubb Group of Insurance* (www.chubb.com/businesses/smallbus.

html): You'll find good nuts-and-bolts on the financial side of owning a business, but since the site sponsor is an insurance company, expect a sales pitch while you're there.

- *EntrepreNet* (www.enterprise.org/enet): This business library with links to other business resource sites is sponsored by the Enterprise Corporation of Pittsburgh.

- *Entrepreneur America* (www.entrepreneur-america.org): This site provides financial advice for entrepreneurs from Entrepreneur America, a venture capital firm that has been providing mentoring services since early 1995.

- *Entrepreneur Club Links* (www.stanford.edu/group/gsb-ec/links.html): Sponsored by Stanford University, this site has links galore for entrepreneurs, everything from legal, patent and financing information to business school and entrepreneur club Web sites.

- *Entrepreneurial Edge Online* (www.edgeonline.com): This is a great, all-encompassing site for young entrepreneurs. You'll love the detailed case studies on successful start-ups.

- *EntreWorld* (www.EntreWorld.org/Content/SYB.cfm): This has many resources for entrepreneurs, including information on hiring, managing, financing and every other "ing" you can think of regarding running your own shop. It's sponsored by the Kauffman Center for Entrepreneurial Leadership.

- *Heroz Enterprises Inc.* (www.netmoneyin.com/book.htm): This provides franchise, marketing and incorporation information for small and homebased businesses, with a good step-by-step outline on how to open a small or homebased business.

- *Internet Business Marketing Resources/Web Resources at St. Louis University* (www.slu.edu/eweb): This site gives support to start, run and grow a business.

- *Inventure Place* (www.invent.org): Discover the inventor in you at this Web site that caters to the Thomas Edison in all of us. It's sponsored by the National Inventor's Hall of Fame.

- *Resources for Entrepreneurs & Small Business* (www.libraries.rutgers.edu/rulib/socsci/busi/smallbus.html): Rutgers University Library's Entrepreneur & Small Business site focuses on the trials and tribulations of opening and running a small business.

- *Small Business Resource Center* (www.webcom.com/seaquest/ sbrc/reports.html): Sponsored by business consulting firm Seaquest, this site gives free reports and helpful hints for entrepreneurs, with lots of great how-to stuff on starting and running different businesses.

# Organizations For Young Entrepreneurs

While there's no shortage of organizations geared toward the American entrepreneur, the list narrows when looking for an organization that caters to the needs of the twentysomething or thirtysomething entrepreneur. Here's a short list of the best groups:

- *Students in Free Enterprise (SIFE):* SIFE volunteers are students from colleges and universities nationwide. Their goal: to teach others—from kids to adults—about free enterprise. Through teaching others, they, in turn, develop a firsthand understanding of economics, management, marketing, government and education. Hence SIFE's philosophy: "Tell me and I will forget; show me and I might remember; involve me and I will understand." Through their community outreach programs, SIFE volunteers teach entrepreneurship classes and workshops in a variety of areas—from sales, advertising and money management to business plan writing and computer and Internet training. Ask your local college or university for more information, or visit SIFE on the Web at www.sife.com.

- *Young Entrepreneurs Organization (YEO):* This organization is a volunteer group of business professionals, all of whom are under 40 years of age and are a founder, co-founder or controlling shareholder of a company with annual sales of $1 million or more. The YEO mission is to support, educate and encourage young entrepreneurs to succeed in building companies and themselves. For more information, contact YEO at 1321 Duke St., #300, Alexandria, VA 22314, or call (703) 519-6700 or fax (703) 519-1864.

- *The Young Entrepreneur's Network (YEN):* This network is an online community that, in its own words, "supports the needs of thousands of young entrepreneurs from around the world as they attempt to build and thrive in their own businesses." Members can talk to other young entrepreneurs via Web discussion forums, get discounts on airline and travel reservations, speak with expert advisors online and a whole lot more. Membership is free—all YEN asks is that you fill out a brief profile to add to their database. Contact them at www.youngandsuccessful.com.

# Shipping And Tracking Packages

Whole civilizations have collapsed because important packages were sent regular mail. You won't read it in any history book, but Pompeii would have survived the ravages of Mount Vesuvius if a handy can of "Volcano-Be-Gone" had been sent for next-day delivery from the manufacturer back in Athens. Don't let that happen to you—keep the following e-mail addresses on file.

## Letters And Packages

- *Airborne Express* (www.airborne-express.com): This site has a complete overview of services but no interactive features besides shipment tracking.

- *Federal Express* (www.fedex.com): Get rates instantly through an online form, find the nearest drop-off location and purchase and print shipping labels.

- *RPS* (www.shiprps.com): At this site, you can determine rates by searching through a text file or Excel spreadsheet, and a service map estimates how long delivery will take. You can also track packages both online and by e-mail.

- *U.S. Postal Service* (www.usps.gov): Look up ZIP codes, track your Express Mail packages, use the "postage calculator" to determine the most cost-effective way to send letters and packages, even place an order to have shipping supplies sent to your door.

- *United Parcel Service* (www.ups.com): Determine shipping costs via an automated work sheet, locate drop-off sites, schedule a pickup or read up about any of UPS' non-Internet-based services.

## Freight And International

- *DHL Worldwide Express* (www.dhl.com): With this fairly basic site, this international shipping company presents its information in a straightforward, easily accessible manner. Contents include contact information for DHL locations in 217 countries.

- *Emery Worldwide:* (www.emeryworld.com): Get thorough descriptions of all services offered. The "QuickZip!" feature tells you what services (air, ground and sea) are available for a destination ZIP code.

- *Parcel Plus* (www.parcelplus.com): This international shipping company offers an online "Quick Quote" service through which you can request both U.S. domestic and import/export bids. There's also a ZIP-code-based store locator.

# Subcontracting Resources

Subcontracting is where companies that receive a contract for services and/or goods farm out to other suppliers some of the responsibilities to provide those goods or services. Subcontracting offers start-ups a great way to gain new business and get a foot in the door of high-profile clients. These Web sites can help you get going:

- *CBDNet* (http://cbdnet.access.gpo.gov/index): This is the Web site of the government newspaper Commerce Business Daily, which lists government procurement opportunities and other subcontracting leads.

- *National Association of Purchasing Management* (www.napm.org): If you attend this association's meetings, you can develop important relationships with the procurement representatives of large corporations.

- *Pro-Net* (pro-net.sba.gov): Getting listed in this free, SBA-sponsored procurement database is a must for any small business seeking subcontracting opportunities. Federal buyers and large corporations use it to find the right firm by scanning the online network of more than 170,000 small businesses.

- *Thomas Register of American Manufacturers* (www.thomasregister.com): If you're not already in here, get listed. Big corporations and federal government agencies consult this resource for suppliers that operate nationally.

# Trade Groups And Government Organizations

There's no shortage of business and government organizations for young entrepreneurs to check out. All you need is a computer, a modem, access to the Web and a tolerance for data that would make the Marquis de Sade wince:

- *International Trade Administration* (www.ita.doc.gov): Get trade statistics, find export assistance centers in your area and more.

- *The Federal Web Locator* (www.law.vill.edu/Fed-Agency/ fedwebloc.html): This is a one-stop shopping point for federal government information on the Web.

- *IRS Digital Daily* (www.irs.ustreas.gov): This is a surprisingly attractive and useful site, where you can download tax forms and publications as well as tax information for businesses.

- *Minority Business Development Centers* (www.mbda.gov): Focusing on minority-owned businesses, these centers offer similar services to Small Business Development Centers (see below).

- *Patents, trademarks and copyrights resource site* (www. patentpending.com): This site, put together by the Law Offices of Gilliam, Duncan & Harms, offers plenty of free information relating to intellectual property rights.

- *SBA Online* (www.sbaonline.sba.gov): Every loan program the SBA offers is posted online—from guaranteed loans and Microloans to loans for women and minorities. In addition to loan programs, the SBA offers scads of financial, technical and management assistance programs to help entrepreneurs start, run and grow their businesses.

- *Service Corps of Retired Executives* (www.score.org): A branch of the SBA, SCORE offers free and low-cost counseling and workshops to small-business owners. Browse through their list of counselors, their areas of expertise and drop them an e-mail.

- *Small Business Development Centers* (access all state Web sites at www.smallbiz.suny.edu/sbdcnet.htm): Located in every state, these centers are staffed by seasoned business counselors who can assist entrepreneurs with a variety of business issues—from developing a business plan and finding financing to market research and export opportunities. All counseling services are free or low-cost. You can also call your local SBA office for more information, or check out *Start Your Own Business* from Entrepreneur Press, which provides a listing of every SBDC in the United States.

- *U.S. Bureau of the Census* (www.census.gov): This site provides demographic data and multiple ways to search through it.

- *U.S. Department of Commerce* (www.doc.gov): From this page, users can access the subagencies of the Commerce Department, such as the Office of Consumer Affairs and the Patent and Trademark Office.

- *U.S. Department of Labor* (www.dol.gov): Find out the latest on the minimum wage issue or access "America's Job Bank," where employers can post jobs.

- *U.S. Small Business Advisor* (www.business.gov): Discover resources made available by the federal government for businesses, including finding funds and investors, tax information and how to navigate the bureaucratic red tape that can ensnare newbie entrepreneurs before opening a business.

# Travel Resources

- *Biztravel.com* (www.bizreservations.com): Plan your entire trip, including flight, hotel and car reservations. This site tracks most frequent-flier miles programs.

- *Epicurious Travel* (http://travel.epicurious.com): This online travel magazine features weekly airline bargains/specials, destination information, reviews, travel advice and so on.

- *Instant Air* (www.instantAir.com): This has an excellent hotel search feature; air and hotel reservations are also available.

- *Internet Travel Network* (www.itn.com): Book flights with secure online ticket purchasing. Its "fare mail" service notifies you of specials on selected trips via e-mail.

- *Mapquest* (www.mapquest.com): Looking for an address, town or ZIP code? Get and print maps worldwide with this funky Web site.

- *Microsoft Currency Converter* (http://expedia.msn.com/pub/curcnvrt.dll?qscr=alcc): This site provides information on current monetary exchange rates.

- *Microsoft Expedia TravelAgent* (http://expedia.msn.com/pub/eta.dll): This has a great flight search system; hotel and car reservations are also available.

- *Preview Travel* (www.previewtravel.com): This site provides extensive tips and advice columns for any travel scenario.

# ATM Locators

- *ACS MoneyMaker* (www.acsmoneymaker.com/atmloc/atmloc. html): If you're traveling with a laptop computer or have access to the Web in a foreign city, this ATM finder database will lead you to the nearest ATM in a pinch.

- *Mastercard Money Machines* (www.mastercard.com/atm/): With more than 430,000 ATMs worldwide, including at the world's top international airports, MasterCard/Cirrus makes sure you are never far from one of their ATMs.

- *VISA ATM Locator,* (www.visa.com/cgi-bin/vee/pd/atm/main. html): Ditto for VISA's helpful ATM site finder.

# Index

Current titles from Entrepreneur Press:

*Business Plans Made Easy:*
*It's Not as Hard as You Think*

*Knock-Out Marketing:*
*Powerful Strategies to Punch Up Your Sales*

*Start Your Own Business:*
*The Only Start-up Book You'll Ever Need*

*Success for Less:*
*100 Low-Cost Businesses You Can Start Today*

*303 Marketing Tips*
*Guaranteed to Boost Your Business*

*Young Millionaires:*
*Inspiring Stories to Ignite Your Entrepreneurial Dreams*

*Where's The Money?*
*Sure-Fire Financial Solutions for Your Small Business*


Forthcoming titles from Entrepreneur Press:

*Get Smart:*
*365 Tips to Boost Your Entrepreneurial IQ*

*Financial Fitness in 45 Days:*
*The Complete Guide to Shaping Up Your Personal Finances*

# get in the
# KNOW

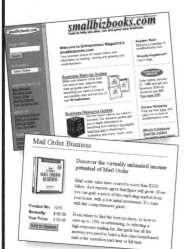

# Discover the Secrets of Today's Brightest Entrepreneurs

**Proven techniques, tips and advice from such innovative entrepreneurs as...**

**Dan Dye, 39**
**Mark Beckloff, 34**
**THREE DOG BAKERY**
Upscale Bakery for Dogs
Founded: 1990

**Dave Kapell, 36**
**MAGNETIC POETRY**
Make Your Own Poetry Kits
Founded: 1993

**Dineh Mohajer, 26**
**HARD CANDY**
Cosmetics With an Attitude
Founded: 1995

*Please visit*
***EntrepreneurMag.com***
*for more information*
*or to order.*

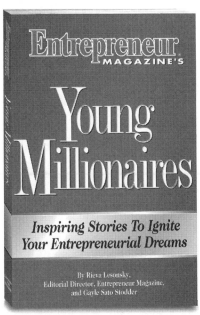

*Entrepreneur MAGAZINE'S*

# Young Millionaires

*Inspiring Stories To Ignite Your Entrepreneurial Dreams*

By Rieva Lesonsky,
Editorial Director, Entrepreneur Magazine,
and Gayle Sato Stodder

## Learn How Nearly 100 Young Entrepreneurs Started Their Own Million-Dollar Businesses... and How You Can Too!

In this entertaining collection of profiles, nearly 100 of today's brightest entrepreneurs share with you the secrets of their success.

Through the inspirational stories of their extraordinary achievements, you'll find out how they got started, how much it cost and what challenges they had to overcome. You'll also learn winning strategies, insider tips and proven techniques you can use to start your own million-dollar business.

But most important, you'll discover that even if you make a million mistakes, or are not entirely prepared, with hard work and determination you, too, can become a young millionaire!

# Help Ensure Your Success with This Easy-To-Understand Guide

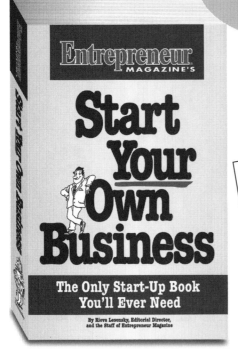

*"...all true entrepreneurs won't want to put this book down."*

**LILLIAN VERNON**
**Chairman and CEO**
**Lillian Vernon Corporation**

*You'll find our special tip boxes loaded with helpful hints on everything from working smarter to saving money.*

*The easy-to-follow, illustrated format features plenty of forms, work sheets and checklists you can actually use in your business.*

Whether you're just thinking of starting a business, have taken the first few steps, or already have your own business, this comprehensive, easy-to-understand guide can help ensure your success.

Written in a friendly, down-to-earth style, *Start Your Own Business* makes it easy to understand even the most complex business issues so you can reach your goals and enjoy the rewards of owning your own business.

### Inside you'll find:

■ Our easy-to-navigate format loaded with work sheets, tip boxes features, charts, graphs and illustrations.

■ Practical, proven, hands-on techniques so you can get started right away.

■ Expert guidance from the nation's leading small-business authority, backed by over 20 years of business experience.

■ And much more!